KNOV

Knowledge and Lotteries

John Hawthorne

Clarendon Press · Oxford

This book has been printed digitally and produced in a standard specification
in order to ensure its continuing availability

OXFORD
UNIVERSITY PRESS

Great Clarendon Street, Oxford OX2 6DP

Oxford University Press is a department of the University of Oxford.
It furthers the University's objective of excellence in research, scholarship,
and education by publishing worldwide in

Oxford New York

Auckland   Cape Town Dar es Salaam   Hong Kong   Karachi
Kuala Lumpur Madrid Melbourne Mexico City   Nairobi
New Delhi Shanghai Taipei Toronto
With offices in
Argentina Austria Brazil Chile Czech Republic France Greece
Guatemala Hungary Italy Japan South Korea Poland Portugal
Singapore Switzerland Thailand Turkey Ukraine Vietnam

Oxford is a registered trade mark of Oxford University Press
in the UK and in certain other countries

Published in the United States
by Oxford University Press Inc., New York

ISBN 978-0-19-928713-0

For Sean, my son

ACKNOWLEDGEMENTS

I have learned most of what I know about epistemology from three people. At graduate school William Alston taught me how to find my way around the subject, serving up numerous insights and useful distinctions that have stayed with me. In the mid-1990s Stewart Cohen revived my interest in epistemology and helped me get much clearer in my thinking about three related topics: contextualism, epistemic closure, and skepticism. At that time and since, we have had many discussions about knowledge that have benefited me greatly. More recently I got to know Timothy Williamson, who through his written work and conversation has helped my thinking enormously. I am extremely grateful for having had the opportunity to learn from these people.

A number of philosophers read one or more complete drafts of this book, providing me with detailed comments from which I have benefited. They include José Benardete, Troy Cross, Tamar Gendler, Gilbert Harman, Karson Kovakovic, David Manley, Ram Neta, Jim Pryor, Stuart Rachels, Jonathan Schaffer, Ted Sider, Jonathan Vogel, and Ryan Wasserman. I am also grateful for conversations with and comments from Frank Arntzenius, Keith DeRose, Cian Dorr, Adam Elga, Richard Fumerton, Alvin Goldman, Peter Klein, Ernie Lepore, David Lewis, Daniel Nolan, Mark Scala, Stephen Schiffer, Adam Sennet, Scott Soames, Ernest Sosa, Jason Stanley, Brian Weatherson, and Dean Zimmerman. I am especially grateful to Ryan Wasserman, who assisted me with the research for this monograph and with whom I have had many invaluable conversations. Peter Momtchiloff, my editor, was extremely helpful and supportive throughout this project. Laurien Berkeley was an excellent and patient copy-editor. Finally, I would like to express special thanks to Tamar Gendler. She has offered me detailed and insightful feedback—along with untiring support and friendship—at every stage of this project. This book would have been considerably less well thought out and considerably less well written without her.

CONTENTS

I INTRODUCING THE PUZZLE

1.1 A Puzzle

THIS monograph is organized around an epistemological puzzle, one that has received increasing attention in recent years.[1] Its attention is well deserved: first, it affords an excellent entry point into some of the most intriguing questions about the verb 'to know'; and second, it generates considerable embarrassment for much of the epistemological theorizing of the last fifty years. In essence, the puzzle consists of a tension between various ordinary claims to know and our apparent incapacity to know whether or not someone will lose a lottery.

Here is a blunt statement of the problem. Suppose someone of modest means announces that he knows he will not have enough money to go on an African safari this year. We are inclined to treat such a judgment as true, notwithstanding various far fetched possibilities in which that person suddenly acquires a great deal of money. We are at some level aware that people of modest means buy lottery tickets from time to time, and very occasionally win. And we are aware that there have been occasions when a person of modest means suddenly inherits a great deal of money from a relative from whom he had no reason to expect a large inheritance.

[1] For a sampling of the relevant literature, see Audi (1991), Brueckner (1985), Cohen (1988, 1991, 1998, 1999, 2000, 2001), DeRose (1992, 1995, 1996), Dretske (2000a), Feldman (1995, 1999, 2001), Hambourger (1987), Harman (1968, 1973, 1986), Hawthorne (2002a), Heller (1999a, b), Klein (1995), Lewis (1996), Nelkin (2000), Nozick (1981), Schiffer (1996), Sosa (2000), Stine (1976), Unger (1975), Vogel (1990, 1999), Yourgrau (1983).

But despite all this, many normal people of modest means will be willing, under normal circumstances, to judge that they know that they will not have enough money to go on an African safari in the near future. And under normal circumstances, their conversational partners will be willing to accept that judgment as correct. [2]

However, were that person to announce that he knew that he would not win a major prize in a lottery this year, we would be far less inclined to accept his judgment as true. We do not suppose that people know in advance of a lottery drawing whether they will win or lose.[3] But what is going on here? The proposition that the person will not have enough money to go on an African safari this year entails that he will not win a major prize in a lottery.[4] If the person knows the former, then isn't he at least in a position to know the latter by performing a simple deduction?

Are we to say that he doesn't know the relevant fact about his future vacations? Or are we to say that, after all, one can know that one will lose a lottery in advance of a drawing and without special insider information? The flaw in the following type of argument, if there is one, is not easy to identify:

> S knows that S won't have enough money to go on a safari this year.
>
> If S knows that S won't have enough money to go on a safari this year, then S is in a position to know that S will not win a major prize in a lottery this year.

---

[2] An early discussion of the puzzle is provided by Gilbert Harman: 'we might infer and come to know that we will be seeing Jones for lunch tomorrow even though our total view includes the claim that Jones does not win the lottery (e.g., because if he won he would have to be in Trenton tomorrow to receive his prize and would not be able to meet us for lunch)' (1973: 161). I discuss the surrounding text in Ch. 3.

[3] Unless they do not own a ticket.

[4] Or at least does so when combined with certain obvious facts such as that an African safari does not cost nearly as much as a major prize in a lottery. Such fussing hardly gets to the heart of the problem. One can easily rewrite the ordinary and lottery propositions respectively so that the entailment is strict; e.g.: 'S will not have enough money to afford a very expensive vacation any time soon' and 'Not: S will soon win a major prize in a lottery and thereby have enough money to afford a very expensive vacation'.

> Hence, S is in a position to know that S will not win a major prize in a lottery this year.

As a number of philosophers have noticed (in good part thanks to the work of Jonathan Vogel), the problem generalizes.[5] For example: I am inclined to think that I know that I will be living in Syracuse for part of this summer. But once the question arises, I am not inclined to think that I know whether or not I will be one of the unlucky people who, despite being apparently healthy, suffer a fatal heart attack in the next week.[6] (If only medical self-examination were so easy!) Indeed, I am just as unwilling to count myself as knowing about the heart attack as I am to count myself as knowing about the lottery.[7] The analogy continues. Just as I have excellent statistical grounds for supposing that any given lottery ticket will lose, I have excellent statistical grounds for supposing that a given apparently healthy person will not have a fatal heart attack very soon. Just as there was no special reason in advance for supposing that the winning ticket was going to win, there was no special reason in advance for expecting the worst for some heart attack victim who was apparently healthy. And just as many of our ordinary commitments entail that this or that person will lose a lottery, many of our ordinary commitments entail that this or that person will not soon suffer a fatal heart attack.

The cases that we have considered so far can be generalized further to cases not involving the future. Most obviously, one can consider cases in which some lottery drawing has already occurred but the winner has not yet been announced. But it is worth having some other cases involving the here and now explicitly in view, ones that do not involve lotteries per se.

---

[5] See, notably, Jonathan Vogel (1990), who to my knowledge was the first person to make vivid that the problem posed by lotteries is not an isolated oddity but is actually widespread.

[6] See Vogel (1990: 20).

[7] Another example: Timothy Williamson notes in passing that 'it is reasonable for me to believe that I shall not be run over by a bus tomorrow, even though I know that I do not know that I shall not be run over by a bus tomorrow' (2000: 255) (See also Slote 1979: 180.) How, then, can I know anything about my future? In his otherwise synoptic book it is odd that Williamson does not address this problem.

So, for example, I am inclined to think that I know where my car is parked right now. But once the question arises, I am not inclined to think that I know whether or not I am one of the unlucky people whose car has been stolen during the last few hours.[8] This obviously generalizes to all cases of non-observational beliefs: who the US president currently is (perhaps he died in the last five minutes), whether my refrigerator is running (perhaps there has been an electrical outage in my neighborhood), whether my football team won last night (perhaps there was a misprint in the newspaper).

Indeed, we need not even restrict ourselves to cases involving putative knowledge of unobserved objects or events; we can generate cases involving putative perceptual knowledge and lottery-style considerations.

First, a case that, while farfetched, vividly brings out the structure of the problem: A person takes a pill from a bucket of 10,000 pills. One of the pills induces blue-green color reversal—that is, it makes blue things look green and green things look blue—while the rest of the pills are inert. The pill-taker knows this. As it happens, he takes an inert pill that leaves his color perception mechanisms undisturbed. He looks at a blue patch and forms the belief that it is blue. We may well be inclined to count him as knowing that he is seeing a blue patch. And we will of course count him as knowing that the patch he is seeing *looks* blue. But we will be far less open to the suggestion that he can deduce and come to know that the pill he took was inert.[9]

Next, a case with more general application: Suppose that there is a desk in front of me. Quantum mechanics tells us that there is a wave function that describes the space of nomically possible developments of the system that is that desk. On those interpretations of quantum mechanics according to which the wave function gives probability of location, there is some non-zero probability that, within a short while, the particles belonging to the surface of the

---

[8] Also from Vogel (1990).
[9] The case described above is similar to one described in Vogel (1993: 238).

desk remain more or less unmoved but the material inside the desk unfolds in a bizarre enough way that the system no longer counts as a desk.[10] Owing to its intact surface, the system would be reckoned a desk by normal observers. Call such a system a desk façade.[11] I will be ordinarily inclined to think that I know by perception that there is a desk in front of me. But once the question arises, I will be far less inclined to think that I know by perception whether or not this is one of those unusual cases in which the desk recently developed into a desk façade. And, obviously, the example generalizes.

In each of these cases, the structure of the problem is the same. There is what we might call the *ordinary proposition*, a proposition of a sort that we ordinarily take ourselves to know. There is, on the other hand, a *lottery proposition*,[12] a proposition of the sort that, while highly likely, is a proposition that we would be intuitively disinclined to take ourselves to know. And in each case the ordinary proposition entails the lottery proposition.[13]

These considerations generate powerful pressure towards a skepticism that claims that we know little of what we ordinarily claim to know.[14] For when confronted with the data, we philosophers feel a

---

[10] This raises the specter that nearly all counterfactuals of the form 'If p had been the case, q would have been the case' are false. After all, on standard semantics for counterfactuals, such a claim is true only if q is true at *all* the closest worlds where p. Assuming the relevant quantum mechanics, it seems that for any nontrivial categorical description C, it will always be the case that a few of the closest p worlds will unfold in a way that is nomically acceptable and which matches the past of the actual world but where C doesn't obtain. Note that if one tinkers with the semantics, requiring only that *most* of the closest p worlds be q worlds in order for the counterfactual to be true, then the logic of counterfactuals will have to be rewritten, since certain intuitively acceptable inference patterns will turn out invalid. A clue for solving the problem *may* be provided by David Lewis's (1986*a*, postscript) discussion of 'quasi-miracles'. I explore these issues further in Hawthorne (forthcoming *b*).

[11] An analogous result holds for classical statistical mechanics: The region in phase-space associated with the macroscopic state of being a desk of that shape and material has a subregion of nonzero measure such that the Hamiltonian for any given point in the region will plot a path of evolution that will yield a desk façade in a short while. (Thanks to Frank Arntzenius here.)

[12] The term 'lottery proposition' is Vogel's (1990: 17).

[13] Or near enough. See n. 4.

[14] Cf. Vogel (1990).

strong inclination to stick to our judgment about the lottery proposition and retract our original judgment about the ordinary proposition. Indeed, lottery-style considerations are arguably a more dialectically effective tool for the skeptic than standard brain in a vat or deceiving demon thought experiments. While many contemporary philosophers are inclined to resist the skeptic by claiming that they can, after all, know that they are not brains in vats,[15] they are not nearly so eager to embrace the claim that they know they will lose a lottery for which they hold a lottery ticket. And once this has been conceded, it is extremely hard to justify a different attitude to the other 'lottery propositions' that figure in the above examples.

Moreover, those philosophers who see their way to embracing the claim to know the relevant lottery proposition will find themselves quickly embarrassed by conjunction introduction. Suppose I hang tough and claim that since I know I will be spending part of the summer living in Syracuse, I know I will not be one of the unlucky heart attack victims, and that since I know I will not be able to afford a safari, I know I will not win the lottery. Well, if I can know such things about myself, I can presumably know such things about my friends as well. Consider 1,000 such friends. If I know of each of them that they will lack sufficient resources to go on an African safari, then I can know of each of them that they will not win a lottery. But assuming that I can extend my knowledge by conjunction introduction, I can now know of all of them that they will lose.[16] But that is crazy: soon enough, by such methods, I will take myself to know of a large chunk of lottery ticket-holders that they will all lose and of a sizeable chunk of the population that they will all be free from fatal heart attacks. (And if there are 1,000 lottery

---

[15] Cf. Richard Feldman, who notes that 'The typical response, at least among my students and non-philosopher friends, is to find preposterous the mere assertion that one does not know one is no brain in a vat' (1999: 100).

[16] That is to say, if $f_1 \ldots f_n$ are my friends, I will know that the conjunction f_1 will lose and … f_n will lose is true. To know, say, the universally quantified claim that all of my friends of modest means will not win requires an extra bit of knowledge (one that may well be readily available), namely that the list $f_1 \ldots f_n$ exhausts the list of my friends of modest means.

ticket holders, 999 of which are my friends, I can even know the winner by deduction!) In an effort to prevent us from knowing too little, the anti-skeptic risks allowing that we know too much.

Faced with this dilemma, even those who initially resisted may find themselves inclined towards a skeptical reaction. People don't really know that they will not be able to afford extravagant things in the near future, or where they will be in a few hours' time. People don't really know that their cars are parked in the garage, or who the president currently is. People don't really know that they are not looking at desk façades, tree façades, and the like.[17] I am by no means fully convinced that the skeptical reaction is the wrong one. But, for reasons that will become clear in Chapter 3, I do suspect that it is the wrong one. And for the most part, the present monograph will be investigating non-skeptical solutions to the puzzle. The remainder of the present chapter will be devoted to appropriate ground-clearing and stage-setting. First, I shall try to say something more about why we are inclined to think that lottery propositions are unknowable. Second, I shall link those unknowability intuitions to certain other intuitions concerning our assertoric and deliberative dispositions with regard to lottery propositions. (This will help us later, in Chapter 2, to articulate some plausible ground rules for solving the puzzle.) Third, I shall discuss the topic of epistemic closure, which is vital to the force of the puzzle, and which also yields a constraint upon any acceptable solution.

1.2   The Lottery Proposition

In each of the cases described above, the puzzle depended upon what I called a 'lottery proposition'. Examples: I will not win a

---

[17] Of course, they may well try to soften the blow by allowing that one knows that one will *probably* not have a fatal heart attack and so on. Be that as it may, on the most straightforward version of this view, nearly all positive knowledge claims are false, as are the beliefs that ordinary people express by them. Skeptical views will be discussed in detail in Chapter 3.

major prize in a lottery this year; I will not be one of the unlucky people to have a sudden and unexpected fatal heart attack. In each case, the lottery proposition is true. In each case the epistemic subject under consideration has good reason for being confident that the lottery proposition is true—the lottery proposition is highly likely relative to the person's evidence. And yet I take it as a datum that there is a strong inclination to claim that the relevant lottery propositions are not known. Nor is this merely a datum about the inclinations of philosophers. After all, the motto of the New York State lottery is 'Hey, you never know'.[18]

What is it about lottery propositions that generates the inclination to say we don't know them? It cannot be their logical strength. After all, the proposition that I will not win a major prize in a lottery this year is logically weaker than the proposition that I will not have enough money to go on an African safari this year: the latter entails the former, but not vice versa. Nor is it a matter of their truth value or justificatory status: lottery propositions that we claim not to know may be both true and well justified. So what *does* explain our disinclination to reckon them known?

That there is a widespread inclination of this sort is uncontroversial. It is a far more delicate matter to identify its source. Let us begin with some preliminary observations. First, the relevant intuition does not depend vitally on there being a guaranteed winner.[19] Change the lottery scenario so that there is some chance of there being no winner at all—suppose, for example, that some tickets are always unsold and their numbers always inserted into the draw—and the inclination to say that one does not know one will lose remains unchanged. Nor does it depend crucially upon the fact that each ticket has an equal chance of winning: change the scenario so

---

[18] This epistemic feature of lotteries is the key to its widespread figurative deployment. Consider: 'Freud puts forward the suggestion that Marriage, in the stories discussed, may be symbolised by a lottery. You never know who you'll end up with and what life will result. The idea that "life is a lottery" is a subliminal metaphor that lies deep in the European mind and forms a kind of template for an outlook on the world' (from the Freud Museum website: <www.freud.org.uk>).

[19] DeRose (1996: 570).

that some tickets receive different weightings than others and the relevant intuition is unaffected.[20] Nor does it depend crucially upon the fact that the epistemic subject under consideration has merely statistical reasons for believing that he or she will lose the lottery. If someone believed that she would lose the lottery not on the basis of statistical reasons, but by simple deduction from the premise that she would not have enough money to go on an African safari in the near future, that would hardly alleviate our disinclination to ascribe knowledge of the lottery proposition to her.[21]

It should also be noted in passing that a number of popular 'analyses' of knowledge do especially badly at predicting our reactions to the lottery case. If we possessed some implicit standard of knowledge according to which knowledge is true justified belief, or true belief produced by a highly reliable belief-forming mechanism, or true belief supported by good evidence, then we would expect a positive epistemological verdict with regard to any true belief that a ticket in a (sufficiently large-scale) lottery is a loser. In effect, lottery cases all by themselves give us pretty good reason for rejecting many of the accounts of knowledge that have been offered in recent decades.[22] At the very least, one should not be hopeful that such analyses will help much by way of explaining our epistemic intuitions with regard to lottery cases. These points are especially worth taking to heart in the case of reliabilism, which is today regarded by so many philosophers as the key to answering skepticism. Unless we can find our way to discarding the relevant intuitions in lottery cases, we will not be well placed to use reliabilism as a safeguard against skeptical arguments.[23]

Let us pursue another tack. Suppose someone believes that *p*. Following recent usage, let us say that such a person *sensitively*

---

[20] Cf. Vogel (1990: 26 n. 8). Nor is the fact that lotteries pay big money particularly relevant. Diminish the prize and the intuition remains. Cf. DeRose (1996: 575–6).

[21] Contra Nelkin (2000).

[22] Notice that Gettier's (1963) targets fall prey to lottery cases as well.

[23] For more on reliabilism and closure, see Vogel (2000). For a good introduction to the varieties of reliabilism, see Goldman (1986). Goldman (1979) and Dretske (1971) have been especially influential. See also Armstrong (1973).

believes that *p* just in case, were *p* false, the person wouldn't believe that *p*.[24] Our belief in ordinary and lottery propositions often appear to admit of the following asymmetry:[25] Where *p* is an ordinary proposition, we often sensitively believe that *p*. But where *p* is a lottery proposition, we do not often sensitively believe that *p*. Concretely: When I believe that my car has not been stolen during the night, the following counterfactual is false:

(1) Were my car to have been stolen in the night, I would not believe that it had not been stolen in the night.

Yet it may be suggested that, by contrast, the following counter-factual is acceptable:

(2) Were my car not parked in the driveway, I would not believe that it was parked in the driveway.[26]

(In the fashionable language of possible worlds: the closest worlds where it is not parked in the driveway are worlds where I parked it somewhere else, not worlds where it was stolen.)

DeRose (1996) conjectures that our intuitions about knowledge and lotteries are driven by such counterfactual judgments, as is the discrepancy between our epistemological verdicts for ordinary and lottery propositions. Three points should be noted here. First, it does not really matter whether these counterfactual judgments are ultimately correct. What matters (to the current proposal) is that we reckon them correct, since that would be enough to explain our verdicts. Second, while some philosophers aspire to a sensitivity-based *analysis* of knowledge, it does not really matter for current purposes whether or not these aspirations can be vindicated. All that matters *here* is the claim that we use sensitivity as a *heuristic* for

---

[24] Nozick (1981) notoriously argued that sensitive belief is necessary for knowledge. More on that later.

[25] This point was emphasized in Vogel (1987: 212–13).

[26] Let us concede this for now, at least. The discussion of 'backtracking' later in this section makes trouble here. (Remember that 'parked' in this context is supposed to describe the state of the car upon waking, not the activity of parking it the previous day. Intuitions about the case are apt to be disrupted by adopting an irrelevant reading.)

ascertaining when a belief counts as knowledge. But third, the sensitivity test, as stated, is clearly too blunt an instrument even to serve as a heuristic. Suppose the lottery ticket has been drawn but the winner not announced yet. Suppose further that I believe that I haven't won the lottery on the grounds that I do not even own a ticket. But if I had won the lottery, I would still believe I hadn't won. For if I had won, I would have owned a ticket, but not having heard the result yet, would think it a loser. It is clear that we have no intuitive inclination in *this* case to deny that I know that I will not win the lottery, despite the verdict of the sensitivity test. And the reason seems to be that if I were about to win the lottery, my grounds for believing that I was going to lose would be very different. In the case described, my actual grounds are my perceived lack of a ticket; in the counterfactual situation, my grounds are (roughly) the unlikelihood of the ticket I own being a winning ticket.[27] Refinement is called for.

We might weaken the sensitivity requirement so as to merely require, for any piece of knowledge, that it either be sensitively believed, or else be deduced from something that is sensitively believed. But if the requirement is weakened that much, then it can no longer explain the intuitions in our initial cases. For we are secure in our judgments that one does not know the relevant lottery propositions even when they are deduced from sensitive mundane beliefs.[28] Following some suggestions by DeRose (1995: 20–2) following Nozick (1981: 179), we might sharpen the relevant notion of sensitivity (call it 'sensitivity*') along the following lines: S *sensitively** believes p iff were p false, S would not believe p using the same method that S actually uses.[29]

The proposal, then, is that we are disinclined to claim that someone knows a lottery proposition on the grounds that we do

---

[27] I am grateful to Timothy Williamson here. Consider, similarly, an example from Williamson (2000: 158): My belief that I am not now a brain in a vat who appears to be climbing a mountain is insensitive. But the epistemic credentials of this belief are not undermined in the slightest by sensitivity failure.

[28] Admittedly, such cases tend to be psychologically rather far fetched.

[29] For further proposals, see Williamson (2000, ch. 7).

not suppose that the person sensitively* believes the lottery proposition (where ordinary standards for individuating methods are in force). Meanwhile, there are plenty of ordinary beliefs that entail lottery propositions that *are* sensitive*. Hence the asymmetry in verdict.[30]

This need not be intended as a story about which verdicts are correct. At present we are merely conjecturing about the source of the relevant intuitions, whether or not those intuitions ultimately hold up. Does the above account correctly identify it? The proposal is somewhat hard to evaluate without specifying the taxonomy of methods that is supposed to be at work in our epistemic practices.[31] But even leaving that issue aside, the proposal is extremely problematic. Consider a case from Jonathan Vogel:

> Sixty golfers are entered in the Wealth and Privilege Invitational Tournament. The course has a short but difficult hole, known as the 'Heartbreaker'. Before the round begins, you think to yourself that, surely not all sixty players will get a hole-in-one on the 'Heartbreaker'.[32]

As Vogel points out, our intuitive verdicts are (*a*) one knows that not all sixty players will get a hole in one on the 'Heartbreaker' but that (*b*) if all sixty players were about to get a hole in one, one would still have believed that they were not going to, and would have believed this for exactly the same reasons as in the actual world.[33]

---

[30] Harman notes that while statistical facts cannot give one knowledge that one will lose the lottery, 'an inference in the other direction, from observed evidence to a statistical explanation of the evidence, can give one knowledge. If one tosses the die again and again, one can come to know that the probability of six on this die is closer to $\frac{1}{2}$ than $\frac{1}{6}$. What is the difference?' (1986: 71). An appeal to sensitivity will help here, as would an appeal to the considerations that I opt for below.

[31] As Williamson (2000, ch. 7) points out, if we allow methods to be externally individuated (so that, for example, being perceptually hooked up with the external world can be mentioned in the specification of a method), then it is not clear that had we been brains in vats, we would have used the very same method as our basis for thinking we are not.

[32] Vogel (1999: 165).

[33] See Vogel (1999: 165, 176 n. 24). Vogel (1990) also contains extremely helpful and relevant material.

It is easy to contrive similar cases: While a matchbox containing 200 matches may, for all we know, contain one or two duds, we intuitively reckon ourselves to know that it is not full of duds. Nevertheless, were it to be full of duds, we would think that it wasn't (and for the same reasons). While I know that there is a chance of your mispronouncing any given word to me (and even mispronounce without noticing it), I can still, intuitively, know that you will not mispronounce every word in a paragraph that I ask you to read.[34] The asymmetry between these intuitions and those for lottery propositions needs explaining.[35]

There is a more general problem. Standard treatments of counterfactuals instruct us as follows: When we ask ourselves how things would have been were such and such to have happened at *t*, we are to imagine a world where things are, as much as possible, the same as the actual world up to *t*. We shouldn't 'backtrack' and think to ourselves, 'Well, if that had happened at *t*, things would have to have been awfully different beforehand'.[36] Here is not the place to defend orthodoxy. But suppose it is right. Then when evaluating how things would have been were such and such to have happened at *t*, we hold fixed the past, including the doxastic states contained

---

[34] One could try challenging the relevant counterfactual judgments: If the matchbook were full of duds, then things would have been such that duds were much more frequent and so I would not have believed that the matchbox was not full of duds (or at least not believed for the same reasons). If all sixty players were to have gotten a hole in one on the 'Heartbreaker' they would have been much better at golf than they actually are and so I wouldn't have believed that they were not all going to get a hole in one (or at least not for the same reasons). But these ways of evaluating the relevant counterfactuals are not the intuitive ones. It would be as if one claimed 'If I had won the lottery I would not have believed I would lose, since in that case I would have held many more tickets than I actually hold'. Moreover, if one is someone who does find such counterfactuals intuitive then, as far as I can see, one will begin to take seriously such counterfactuals as the following in the car theft case: 'If the car had been stolen, I would likely have parked it in a much less safe neighborhood and so wouldn't have believed that it was not stolen'. But this would undercut the sensitivity-based diagnosis for our knowledge judgments in that case.

[35] The proponent of the sensitivity approach might insist that in the hole in one case, we do not notice a failure of sensitivity while in the lottery case we do—and that this is the reason for the asymmetry. But one would like to understand *why* we notice in the one case but not the other.

[36] Cf. Lewis (1986*a*: 32–5).

therein. Suppose at the actual world I spend a month in Santa Cruz, and believe a month earlier that I was going to do so. Consider now the counterfactual:

> (3) Were I not to have spent that month in Santa Cruz, I wouldn't have believed a month earlier that I was going to do so.

For reasons just given, the standard semantics claims that this is false. For what it's worth, this seems like the intuitively correct result for that counterfactual. Since appeal to methods is not going to help, it seems like the proponent of the sensitivity* heuristic would predict that we would have to say of all putative knowledge of the future that it is not knowledge at all.[37] But this is not our practice. So while it seems correct to say that our belief in lottery propositions is not sensitive (or sensitive*), this does not explain the relevant asymmetries in our intuitions, for there are all sorts of other cases where sensitivity (and even sensitivity*) is absent, but where we are happy to say there is knowledge. A number of writers have suggested that it is somehow the presence of probabilistic thoughts in the lottery case that is at the root of our disclaimer to know. Something in the vicinity is correct, I think, but we must handle matters with care. As noted earlier, the relevant intuitions about lottery propositions do not require that the epistemic subject deploy probabilistic reasoning himself: if his belief in a lottery proposition is deduced from a belief in an ordinary proposition, that will not increase our willingness to say that he knows the lottery proposition. We need to focus on the ascriber of the knowledge claim, not its subject. Without pretending to be able to have a full account of the relevant psychological forces driving the relevant intuitions, we can nevertheless see that in the paradigm lottery situation, something like the following often goes on: The ascriber divides possibility space into a set of subcases, each of which, from the point of view of the subject, is overwhelmingly likely to not

---

[37] A similar conclusion is reached by Vogel (1987: 206–8).

obtain, but which are such that the subject's grounds for thinking that any one of the subcases does not obtain is not appreciably different than his grounds for thinking that any other subcase does not obtain. (Vogel 1990 is especially clear on this.[38]) Using DeRose's terminology, *the relative strength of epistemic position* with regard to each subcase is not appreciably different. In general, what is often at the root of the relevant lottery intuition is a division of epistemic space into a set of subcases with respect to which one's epistemic position seems roughly similar. Once such a division is effected, a parity of reasoning argument can kick in against the suggestion that one knows that a particular subcase does not obtain, namely: If one can know that *that* subcase does not obtain, one can know of each subcase that it does not obtain. But it is absurd to suppose that one can know of each subcase that it does not obtain.

In a lottery situation the force of such reasoning does not turn crucially on whether there is a guaranteed winner: even where there is a chance that no ticket will win, the suggestion that one can know of each ticket that it will lose will seem absurd. Grant the absurdity of the latter and it is hard to maintain that one can know of any given ticket that it will lose. Nor does the force of the reasoning turn on whether the chance of any given ticket winning is exactly the same as that of any other ticket. Suppose that matters are weighted so that some tickets enjoy a slightly better chance of winning than others. Here, it is still the case that one's epistemic position with regard to each subcase is not *appreciably* different.[39] In these cases, the following kind of reasoning is at work:

[38] See Vogel (1990: 21–2).

[39] Suppose instead that in a 10,000 ticket lottery there is, say, a 10 percent chance of each of ticket ##1–5 winning, and that every other ticket has a tiny chance of winning. It is natural, *inter alia*, to effect a division into two subcases—<one of ##1–5 wins; one of ##6–10,000 wins>—with respect to which our epistemic position is intuitively the same. It is absurd to think that we can know of each of the pair that it does not contain a winner; so it is natural to think that we cannot know any such thing of either. Meanwhile, it is natural to divide the case of one of ##6–10,000 winning into 9,995 further subcases, with regard to which we have an equal epistemic position. Further reasoning of the sort in question will convince us that we cannot know of any one of those subcases that it will fail to obtain, given that we are convinced that we cannot know that the possibility of one of ##6–10,000 winning will fail to obtain.

Parity Reasoning. One conceptualizes the proposition that p as the proposition that one particular member of a set of subcases $(p_1, \ldots, p_n)$ will (or does) not obtain, where one has no appreciably stronger reason for thinking that any given member of the set will not obtain than one has for thinking that any other particular member will not obtain. Insofar as one reckons it absurd to suppose that one is able to know of each of $(p_1, \ldots, p_n)$ that it will not obtain, one then reckons oneself unable to know that p.

Why does one think it absurd to suppose one can know of each of $p_1, \ldots, p_n$ that it will not obtain? There are essentially two kinds of thoughts that can be at work here. (i) Sometimes one knows that one of $p_1, \ldots, p_n$ *will* obtain, as when there is a guaranteed winner in the lottery. (ii) Even where (i) doesn't apply, one may recognize that it is absurd to think that one can know the generalization that all of $p_1, \ldots, p_n$ do not obtain, or that $\sim (p_1 \text{ or} \ldots \text{or } p_n)$, and on that basis, reckon that one cannot know of each of $p_1, \ldots, p_n$ that it does not obtain.[40]

There is plenty more to be said, of course, by way of developing and examining the kind of parity arguments I have gestured at; I will be doing just that in due course.[41] Articulating and evaluating the relatively inchoate thoughts and arguments that guide our intuitions is part of the job of a philosopher. For now, we are merely aiming for a reasonable—albeit somewhat rough and ready—picture of at least one source of the discrepancy between how we evaluate belief in ordinary propositions on the one hand and lottery propositions on the other. (This is not yet to solve our puzzle, quite obviously. An account of the source of certain epistemic intuitions is one thing. Determining which claims to know are actually correct is quite another.)

[40] Note that (ii), though not (i), relies on what I shall later call Multi-Premise Closure.

[41] As Tamar Gendler pointed out to me, it is worth exploring the bearing of the psychological literature on 'representativeness' on the intuitions we are discussing. (See, for example, Kahneman and Tversky 1982*a*).

It is clear enough, of course, that parity reasoning of the sort described is not the only source of skeptical doubt. The following kind of reasoning, which moves from a claim of metaphysical modality—one which posits a possible experiential duplicate, who thinks falsely that *p*—to one of epistemic modality—the epistemic possibility of not-*p*—is familiar enough:

> *Duplicate Reasoning.* Things could be such that: Not-*p* and everything seems just as it actually is to me. So even if it is very likely that *p*, there is at least a small chance that not-*p*. So it *might be* that not-*p*. So I don't know that *p*.

This kind of reasoning has a different source, namely our temptation—one that runs fairly deep—to suppose that all we have to go on when forming beliefs about the world are the experiences (intrinsically characterized) with which we are presented (together with those truths to which we have a priori access). Duplicate Reasoning is not our main topic here.

Let us return to the 'Heartbreaker' scenario. Why am I inclined to answer 'Yes' without hesitation when asked, 'Do you know whether or not they will all get a hole in one?' I suspect that when our knowledge intuition is undisturbed, the salient division of epistemic space is not organized in such a way that parity reasoning can apply. Of course, even if such reasoning is not at work, one might balk at a knowledge claim on other grounds. One might say—perhaps deploying duplicate reasoning—'You don't really know they will not; there is after all a tiny but real chance that they will'. However, it is also very easy—much easier than in the case of lottery propositions—to get oneself in a frame of mind in which one is willing to say one knows that there will not be sixty holes in one. Such was the frame of mind that Vogel managed to achieve above. And on the picture I am advancing, one's willingness to do so depends on not having divided the Heartbreaker case into a set of subcases to which parity reasoning can apply. DeRose (1996) has criticized diagnoses of the lottery intuition that appeal to the probabilistic structure of our thinking in such a case. He compares the lottery intuition with a case in which we believe we know the Bulls won on the basis of reading a newspaper. He objects that:

we don't just happen to think probabilistic thoughts in the lottery case: it seems they are forced upon us. Perhaps all we think in the newspaper case is the non-statistical and non-probabilistic: The newspaper says it; so, it is so. But why wouldn't similar, non-probabilistic reasoning come off in the lottery case: it's a Super Lotto ticket (for heaven's sake!); so, it's a loser. (1996: 577)

Here DeRose—like many philosophers—seems to have lost sight of certain features of our ordinary practice. Try raising the possibility of lottery success to people who are planning out their lives. Very often, they will respond with 'You know that's not going to happen' or 'I know full well I'm not going to get that lucky'.[42] Similarly, when someone is deliberating about whether to buy a lottery ticket, ordinary people will often say 'You know you are wasting your money'. Granted we sometimes make knowledge claims using a tone indicating that we are not to be taken literally.[43] But I see no good evidence that this is always going on in these cases. On the contrary, there is a parallel between the frame of mind in which ordinary people say that they know they will lose the lottery, and the frame of mind in which Vogel announces that he knows that not all sixty golfers will get a hole in one on the Heartbreaker. The operative division of subcases is into 'I win; one of the other million or so ticket-holders wins', the former of

---

[42] Similarly, in this sort of setting one will be willing to baldly assert 'That's not going to happen'. This frame of mind is exploited by a T-shirt produced by the E-trade company, which informs us that someone will win the lottery tomorrow, but that 'It just won't be you'.

[43] Williamson remarks, 'There is a special jocular tone in which it is quite acceptable to say '[Come off it] Your ticket didn't win,' but the tone signals that the speaker intends not to make a flat-out assertion' (2000: 246). Observe ordinary practice. Try raising questions about lotteries in ordinary conversation. You will discover that not all of the uses I have in mind are accompanied by a jocular tone. I should also add that it does not seem to me that the 'Come off it' tone invariably signals something less than a flat-out assertion. If a colleague were to tell me that he could write better articles than Saul Kripke, I may well resort to that tone, but my admonishment would be none the less flat-out for all that.

which is in turn disregarded, even to the extent that one will be willing to flat-out assert of the lottery victory 'There is no chance of *that* happening' (just as in the Heartbreaker case, many people will be willing to flat-out assert 'There is no chance that they will *all* get a hole in one').[44]

We can, meanwhile, with a bit of work, conceptualize the Heartbreaker case on the model of a standard lottery case. For instance, a scientifically minded person might consider a wave function for the system consisting of the sixty golfers and the course, picturing the associated state space divided into a number of tiny strips of equal measure, one of which corresponds to the genuine nomic possibility of all sixty golfers getting a hole in one. This conceptualization of things triggers the standard parity argument: Our epistemic position with regard to one small strip in the state space is more or less the same as our epistemic position with regard to any of the other small strips. So if one can know of any given strip that it will not obtain, then one can know of any other given strip that it will not obtain. It is absurd to suppose that one is in a position to know of each strip that it will not obtain. So it is absurd to suppose that one is in a position to know of the strip in which all sixty players achieve a hole in one that it will not obtain. More simply still, we might imagine that the tournament is played every day, and has been for the last 10 million years.[45] It is hard to believe that you know that there hasn't been a day in the last 10 million years when all sixty players have gotten a hole in one. But if so, it's hard now to see how you could know that this won't happen today. After all, if you did know that, then you could, by the same reasoning, come to know that it didn't happen yesterday, or the day before, or indeed on any of the 3,652,500,000 days on which the tournament has been played.

---

[44] That is not to say that they will stick to their guns under dialectical duress; nor is it to assume that such utterances express truths. (Note, however, that our willingness to retract does not in itself show that the original claim was mere hyperbole, a figurative simplification that we knew to be false at the time of utterance. The question of how to treat such oscillation is explored in the subsequent pair of chapters.)

[45] I am grateful to Brian Weatherson here.

Of course, in the lottery case, the kind of structuring of epistemic space that triggers such parity arguments is quite natural, whereas it feels somewhat contrived in the case of the Heartbreaker (and in the case of the 'ordinary' propositions with which we began our discussion). It is true that with some work, a conception of epistemic space can be effected that triggers the relevant kind of parity argument—but effecting such a conception does take some work. This can hardly strike us a great mystery: while basic mastery of the idea of a lottery encodes some such division, the same is not so for golf tournaments.[46]

One final illustration. It is relatively easy to get ourselves in the frame of mind where we reckon ourselves to know that we will not win the New York State lottery each of the next thirty years (even if we expect to buy a ticket each year). Just ask people. They will happily claim to know that *that* will not happen. Now of course, with a little cognitive effort, that attitude can be disrupted. Suppose, using normal statistical calculations, the chance of winning the New York Lottery each of the next thirty years was 1 in n (I make the simplifying assumption that it is certain that one will buy a ticket each year). We might point out to someone that if he had a ticket in one great big lottery with n tickets, he would not reckon himself able to know he would lose in *that* case. Intuitions would then switch.[47] The pattern of intuitions, and their aptness for disruption, can readily be understood within the current framework.

---

[46] Another case worth considering is the weighted coin. If the coin is weighted so that it comes up heads 9/10 of the time, then intuitions that one does not know the outcome of the toss will be secure: the chance of tails is just too high to be disregarded. But if it is weighted so that it comes up heads 99,999 times out of 100,000—and one knows this—then the intuition of not knowing will still be more durable than in the Heartbreaker case. The thought experiment of a golf tournament repeated 10 million times, described above, is not especially natural. Where one's basic knowledge of a case is statistical, matters are different. (Cf. Vogel 1990.)

[47] We might even imagine that the procedure for determining the winner of the big lottery was a series of mini lotteries, each associated with a particular subsequence of the final winning number, such that the chance of winning a mini lottery was the same as that of winning the New York State lottery in a given year.

1.3   Assertion, Probability, Practical Reasoning

So far I have been dwelling on our epistemic intuitions regarding lottery propositions. It is time to begin articulating some constraints upon a solution to the puzzle that they raise. Doing so should help us to better appreciate why this puzzle matters in the first place. (After all, there are lots of puzzles we could spend our time trying to solve, but not all of them are worth the effort.[48]) We shall need to pay especially careful attention to three phenomena that are closely tied to knowledge: assertion, epistemic modality, and practical reasoning.[49]

(i) As a number of writers have noted, the disinclination to self-ascribe knowledge of lottery propositions tends to be accompanied by a disinclination to flat-out assert them.[50] Despite having good reason to think a lottery ticket will lose, it is typically out of place to declare outright 'He won't win the lottery' in advance of the drawing and without special insider information. Our reluctance to assert this cannot be explained by the suggestion that it violates the conversational maxim: Do not say what people already have good reason to believe (a subcase of Grice's Maxim of Quantity).[51] For in a case where I know that someone does not have a ticket and you think that he does, I can certainly flat-out assert that he will not win the lottery. But if a maxim of informativeness were what disinclined me from assertion in the original case, it ought to disincline me in this case as well. Perhaps, then, a more refined maxim is at work: To assert p, I must think of myself as having good reasons that are substantially different from those that you already

---

[48]   Speaking for myself, I find the puzzles so obviously interesting that it is scarcely worth asking myself whether the inquiry is worth the effort. I understand that some readers will need more convincing than that.

[49]   This section owes a very obvious debt to Williamson (2000).

[50]   See Unger (1975, ch. 6), DeRose (1996: 568), and Williamson (2000, ch. 11).

[51]   See Grice (1989a: 26).

have for thinking that p.[52] But this will not explain the data either. If you know that Bill lacks a ticket and I know that too, but I also come to know that the lottery will have no winner at all this time, it would be strange for me to assert that Bill will not win the lottery. But the revised maxim of informativeness would predict that such an assertion would be acceptable. Moreover, as Williamson points outs, 'parallel Gricean reasoning' would rule out 'Your ticket is almost certain to lose'. But the latter assertion, while 'banal and unkind', is not as intuitively unacceptable as its starker cousin.[53] Indeed, there are settings where the latter assertion may even serve as a useful reminder to someone who is becoming excessively optimistic, but where the flat-out assertion 'Your ticket will lose' would still be out of place.

Correlatively, in those settings where people *are* happy to self-ascribe knowledge of lottery failure, they are correspondingly willing to assert '*That's* not going to happen' when the possibility of lottery success is raised. So too with 'ordinary propositions', where our general willingness to assert them (the pragmatics of conversation permitting) seems very much tied to our willingness to self-ascribe knowledge concerning them. There is a natural explanation of the tie between flat-out assertion and knowledge attribution. It is the one given by Unger (1975), namely, that in

---

[52] Williamson (2000: 247) worries that the maxim of informativeness would entitle me to assert that you will lose in a case where you think you have a 1 in *n* chance of winning but I know there are many more tickets and so the odds are much lower than 1 in *n*. As he points out, it does not feel like this difference gives one a license to assert. One might try to argue that the reasons possessed by the assertor are not sufficiently different in kind here from the imagined interlocutor to warrant flat-out assertion, and hence the datum is sufficiently explained by the revised maxim. A test case: Bill has a ticket in the Soccer Pools, which will only win if six particular games end in a tie. I discover that a team involved in one of the games has lost their two star players in a car accident, making it much less likely that that game will end in a tie. You are unaware of this. I have evidence that is different in kind than yours for 'Bill won't win', and which makes it substantially less likely that he will win. Can I flat-out assert 'Bill won't win'? (Thanks to Brian Weatherson here.)

[53] See Williamson (2000: 247).

asserting that *p*, one represents oneself as knowing that *p*.[54] This is not to say that when one asserts that *p*, one asserts that one knows *p*. It is common to distinguish what is asserted by an utterance from the information conveyed by it.[55] Plausibly, when someone asserts that *p*, she conveys that she knows that *p* though she does not assert that she knows that *p*. But what is the mechanism by virtue of which such information is conveyed? One plausible story is the one offered by Unger (1975) and Williamson (2000): The practice of assertion is constituted by the rule/requirement that one assert something only if one knows it.[56] Thus if someone asserts *p*, it is proper to criticize that person if she does not know that *p*. The suggestion can be illustrated by the following analogy: When someone utters 'The meeting is adjourned', that person represents herself as having the authority to adjourn the meeting. How? Because it is a constitutive rule of that illocutionary act that one who makes it should possess the relevant authority. While the person does not assert that she possesses such authority, she conveys this by her illocutionary act and can be criticized if the authority is absent. On the (plausible) story we are entertaining, a similar mechanism connects asserting *p* with knowing *p*.[57] (Of course, that is not to say that knowing *p* suffices for appropriate assertion.[58] An assertion that *p*, even if one knows that *p*, might be out of place for any number of reasons: where it is irrelevant or because its

---

[54] See Unger (1975, ch. VI). It is of course a further question whether this norm is more basic than any other norm (such as the requirement of relevance) that governs assertion.

[55] See, for example, the discussion in Soames (2002, ch. 3).

[56] I shall not try to tackle the thorny question as to the nature of the 'ought' that is in play here.

[57] Stewart Cohen told me of an incident where he asked a friend to advise him whether he had enough room to back his car out of a tight spot. The friend claimed that there was indeed enough room. A collision immediately ensued. The friend announced 'That was just my opinion.' The absurdity of the speech is very well explained by the current framework.

[58] Though insofar as we can distinguish the 'epistemic correctness' of an assertion for other aspects of propriety, it may be arguable that knowledge suffices for epistemic correctness.

implicatures mislead, or simply because one is in a conversation where p is up for debate.[59])

(We might also note that there are complementary features that typically belong to the activity of questioning. Just as knowledge is the norm of assertion, ignorance is the norm of questioning. At least in the normal case, we shouldn't ask a question if we already know the answer. Now of course this isn't true for certain kinds of questions. When a teacher asks a student a test question, she does not represent herself as ignorant of the answer. But in the paradigmatic case of questioning, a questioner represents herself as lacking knowledge and, indeed, could be properly criticized for asking a question to which she already knew the answer. The concept of knowledge thus provides the framework in which both the giving and requesting of information takes place.)

(ii) There is also a striking tie between our willingness to assert 'It might be that p' and 'There is a chance that p' on the one hand, and our willingness to assert 'I do not know that not-p' and 'I do not know whether or not p' on the other. It sounds extremely odd to assert 'I know that p but there is a chance that not-p' or 'I know that p but there is a chance that q' (where q is known to be incompatible that p).[60] So too for 'It might be'.[61,62] One approach is the pragmatic

---

[59] Thus smooth conversation requires some mutual sense of who is to be given authority over what. Note that we sometimes attempt to restructure a conversation from one where p is up for debate to one where we are in 'instructional mode' with respect to our listeners. Tiring of debate, I may say, using an intonation contour that indicates that I am switching to instructional mode: 'Look, this is how it is. P.Q.R....'. Sometimes interlocutors will be impressed enough to acquiesce in this 'power play'; more often not. The main point for our purposes is that we are often in no position to flat-out assert that p because we are in a situation where, while we know p, we do not have the relevant conversational authority.

[60] As Tamar Gendler and Brian Weatherson have pointed out to me, there are exceptions to this generalization: 'I know they are going to lose but I'm going to carry on watching just in case'; 'I know it's not going to rain, but still, I'm going to take an umbrella just in case'. Such utterances do have an air of retraction about them, however.

[61] Not so, of course, for locutions that express metaphysical modality rather than epistemic modality: there is nothing odd about 'I know that p, but things could have been such that not-p'.

[62] Such considerations lead Lewis to assert that 'If you are a contented fallibilist, I implore you to be honest, be naïve, hear it afresh. 'He knows, yet he has not eliminated

one, which claims that the impropriety is conversational—it is a matter of flouting the norms of conversation. Perhaps the reason why 'I know that *p*, but there is a chance that not-*p*' is unassertable is that it is already obvious to audiences (for nearly any *p*) that there is always a chance that not-*p* and it is therefore not worth saying. However, this does not happily accommodate the fact that we can respond to such an assertion, not by complaining that too much has been said, but by noting that the claim is self-defeating: 'Well, if there is a chance that not-*p*, then you don't know that *p*, do you?' Relatedly, the approach would predict that the speech 'I know that *p*. There's no chance that not-*p*' would be unassertable for a different reason—by containing an obvious falsehood. But such speeches are commonplace.[63]

There is a much more natural explanation of the unassertability of 'I know that *p* but there is a chance that not-*p*', namely we have a conception of epistemic possibility operative in such claims which is constitutively linked to facts about what the subject knows. This is the conception that David Hume had in mind when he reckoned mere probability to be contrary to knowledge: 'But knowledge and probability are of such contrary and disagreeing natures, that they cannot well run insensibly into each other, and that because they will not divide, but must be either entirely present, or entirely absent' (*Treatise*, I. iv. 1; 1968: 181)[64]

all possibilities of error,' Even if you've numbed your ears, doesn't this overt, explicit fallibilism *still* sound wrong?' (1996: 550). It is a little strange however, that Lewis does not directly address the more straightforward '*p* and it may be that not-*p*' and '*p* and there is a chance that not-*p*'.

[63] There are further epicycles. Perhaps while 'There is a chance that *p*' is literally banal, an assertion of that claim conveys the contentful suggestion that the chance is large enough to be taken seriously. This in turn can offer a distinctive explanation of why 'There is a chance that not-*p* but I know that *p*' is unassertable. I leave further development of the pragmatic approach to others.

[64] DeRose notes that even when I flat-out assert that the Bulls won, I may have such underlying thoughts as 'The paper says the Bulls won; the probability that the paper's right is very high; so they probably won; it's overwhelmingly likely' (1996: 577). Doesn't this conflict with Hume's picture (assuming that knowledge is the norm of assertion)? While the issue merits further investigation, there are reasons to think that it does not run counter to Hume. Notice, for instance, that it is crucial to the case that one keeps

In the relevant epistemic sense of possibility:

(1) It is possible that p for S at t (There is a chance that p for S at t) iff p is consistent with what S knows at t.[65]

And in the epistemic sense of necessity:

(2) It is necessary that p for S at t (There is no chance that not-p for S at t) iff not-p is inconsistent with what S knows at t.

This conception provides us with very natural analyses of various locutions of epistemic modality. For example:[66]

(3) An utterance of 'It might be that p' by S at t is true iff it is possible that p for S at t.

---

quiet about those underlying thoughts; if one were to reason out loud that way and then assert 'The Bulls won', the assertion would seem rather out of place. Notice, moreover, that there is no frank admission that there is a chance that the Bulls didn't win in the underlying thoughts (though of course that is implied). Insert that frank admission into the underlying thoughts and they will seem like a stranger background. Note also that there are parasitic cases where I assert p flat-out because I gauge that others will be happy to accept that I know even though I think that I do not. Note, finally, that sometimes some such underlying thoughts are a preamble to 'Forget it. There is no chance the Bulls didn't win', where one shifts to a state of mind in which the possibility of the Bulls not winning is, at least temporarily, disregarded altogether. We see this, for example, in Norman Malcolm: 'There is overwhelming evidence that printed words do not behave in that way. It is just as conclusive as the evidence that houses do not turn into flowers. That is to say, absolutely conclusive evidence' (1963: 38).

[65] It is worth noting that it is this conception of epistemic possibility that is at work in Meyer's writings on epistemic logic, where it is assumed that a world w_2 is epistemically accessible to a subject at w_1 only if the set of propositions true at w_2 is consistent with what the subject knows at w_1 (see, for example, Meyer 2001). See also Hintikka's (1962) foundational *Knowledge and Belief*. Note also that, for some purposes, we may prefer to say that it is possible that p for S at t just in case p is not *obviously* incompatible with what S knows at t (where some albeit vague notion of manifest incompatibility is at work). This explains why we might wish to allow the truth of 'Goldbach's conjecture might be true and it might be false' in my mouth, even if what I know entails a verdict in one direction. (Thanks to Tamar Gendler and Ted Sider here.)

[66] Relatedly: An utterance of 'a might F' by S at t is true iff it is possible for S at t that a F's some time after t. (And the same holds for the epistemic use—as opposed to the deontic and concessive uses—of 'a may F'.)

(4) An utterance of 'It must be that *p*' by S at *t* is true iff it is necessary that *p* for S at *t*.[67]

This oversimplifies things a little. If you are in a maze and I know X is the way out but I know that you have not ruled out Y as the way out, I can say 'X might be the way out and Y might be the way out'. Here it is *your* epistemic perspective that governs my utterance, not mine.[68] There is thus some context-dependence concerning *whose* knowledge is germane to a statement of epistemic chance. Relatedly, when I am asked why I took an umbrella with me this morning, and I answer 'It might have rained', my assertion is intuitively made from the vantage point of my earlier self (in contrast to a situation where I sleep through the day and use the same sentence to give voice to my current meteorological ignorance). I do not think that the oversimplification matters much to the current discussion. What matters is the basic tie between the concept of knowledge and epistemic possibility. Regardless of whose epistemic perspective is semantically relevant, it is the body of knowledge enjoyed at that epistemic perspective that determines the correctness of epistemic 'might's and 'must's.[69]

---

[67] Some (though not I) think that sentences containing epistemic modals have no truth conditions, only assertability conditions. In that case, one might think of these 'analyses' as merely pointing to the assertability conditions for such sentences.

[68] Interestingly, it is much harder to extract a reading whereby the relevant epistemic perspective is associated with some contemporary person external to the conversation. A related peculiarity is that, as far as I can tell, ordinary people evaluate present-tense claims of epistemic modality as true or false by testing the claim against their own perspective. So, for example, suppose Angela doesn't know whether Bill is alive or dead. Angela says 'Bill might be dead'. Cornelius knows Bill is alive. There is a tendency for Cornelius to say 'Angela is wrong'. Yet, given Angela's perspective, wasn't it correct to say what she did? After all, when I say 'It might be that *p* and it might be that not-*p*', knowing that Cornelius knows whether *p*, I do not naturally think that Cornelius knows that I said something false. There is a real puzzle here, I think, but this is not the place to pursue it further.

[69] A conversation with Timothy Williamson was helpful here, who also pointed out that 'It must be that *p*' suggests that one's evidence for *p* is indirect. That is another way that the text oversimplifies. For an extremely useful discussion of further subtleties, see DeRose (1991).

Perhaps it might be suggested the truth conditions of epistemic modals turn on the psychological states of being sure and unsure, and more generally with degrees of confidence. For example:

(5) An utterance of 'It might be that p' by S at t is true iff S is not sure that not-p at t.

(6) An utterance of 'Probably p' by S at t is true iff S is highly confident that p at t.

This gives less satisfying results. If someone is sure that p when it is the case that not-p, an utterance of 'It must be that p' is intuitively incorrect. Perhaps some alternative third account ultimately does better than either the knowledge-based one or the psychological one just alluded to. For now we need only note the strong prima facie plausibility of the knowledge-based account.[70]

It goes without saying that the epistemic conception of possibility discussed above is not the only conception of possibility that we have need for. Nor should we assume that the only notion of chance is given by the above analyses. We may in particular wish to embrace a notion of objective chance.[71] (How such a notion connects with the epistemic notion is a topic that I shall speak to in due course.)[72]

---

[70] For more on epistemic possibility, see DeRose (1991), Sainsbury (1997), and Teller (1967, 1972, 1975).

[71] For the Lewisian, the notion of objective chance is one according to which, if determinism is true, then for every proposition p about the future, there is either no chance that p or else no chance that not-p. I shall not pursue the question of whether there is a notion of chance that is objective rather than epistemic, but which does not bear the aforementioned relationship to determinism. (See Lewis 1994; Hall 1994).

[72] The reader might also wonder how the epistemic conception of chance adumbrated above connects with the notion of chance at work in Bayesian literature. Bayesians come in subjective and objective strains—where the former take themselves to be offering a theory of how to update degrees of confidence without pretending to make sense of any objective notion of what confidence levels one ought to begin with. For the subjective Bayesian, one's credences can be evaluated as rational or irrational only in relation to one's previous body of credences. The objective Bayesians, on the other hand, take their subject matter to be an unrelativized notion of rational credence, which turns on the credence levels that it is objectively rational to have. Rational credence, so understood, will connect with our central—and ordinary—notion of

(iii) I turn finally to the intuitive link between knowledge and practical reasoning. That one does not know a lottery proposition prohibits one (at least in a large range of settings) from asserting it. It also seems to prohibit one from using it as a premise in one's deliberations about how to act. I shall have plenty more to say about this in later chapters. For now, a simple example will suffice. Suppose someone is offered a penny for a lottery ticket and reasons as follows:

> The ticket is a loser.
> So if I keep the ticket I will get nothing.[73]
> But if I sell the ticket I will get a penny.
> So I'd better sell the ticket.

Two bits of data: First, it seems clear enough that such reasoning is unacceptable.[74] Second, it is clear that if one asks ordinary folk why such reasoning is unacceptable, they will respond by pointing out

---

epistemic probability only to that extent that something like the following equation holds: It is rational to be confident of p to degree n iff the epistemic probability of p is n. Note that such an equation will not likely be palatable to a nonskeptic who thinks that knowledge entails epistemic probability of 1, assuming that rational confidence of degree 1 in p brings with it a rational disposition to bet at any odds on p. (I wouldn't even bet on the law of noncontradiction at any odds, and I think myself rational on that score.) The discussion of 'Practical Environment' in Chapter 4 is relevant here.

[73] In the current work I ignore certain delicate issues about the place of indicative conditionals in practical reasoning. Pretend for a moment that there is a smoking gene that induces both smoking and lung cancer, but that smoking is itself causally unrelated to lung cancer. I know this and am deciding whether to smoke. The indicative conditionals 'If I smoke I will likely get lung cancer' and 'If I do not smoke I will likely not get lung cancer' are intuitively correct. Yet those who side with causal as opposed to evidential decision theory (see, for example, Lewis 1986b) will not reckon those indicative conditionals as a legitimate basis upon which to refuse to smoke. I trust that the points in the text do not hang on these subtleties.

[74] This is so, even if I was given the ticket for free. So 'sunk cost' considerations are not the whole story. Nor do I assume that dollars are linear with utilities. Relaxing that assumption hardly helps here. I also avoid cases where some will be inclined to think it reasonable to invoke a 'sure thing principle'—which allows an immediate gain to trump a chancy option with expected higher utility. (Thanks to Tamar Gendler here.)

that the first premise was not known to be true.[75] By contrast, if the person had just heard the winning number, seen it was not his, and then sold his ticket for a penny to someone who was unaware that the number had been announced, then the reasoning would not ordinarily be subject to analogous criticism.[76] On the face of it, then, we operate with a conception of deliberation according to which, if the question whether p is practically relevant, it is acceptable to use the premise that p in one's deliberations if one knows it and (at least in very many cases) unacceptable to use the premise that p in one's practical reasoning if one doesn't know it. At a rough first pass: one ought only to use that which one knows as a premise in one's deliberations.[77] (It goes without saying that this conception allows one to use premises of the form 'Probably p' in one's practical reasoning. But the norm still applies—if one does not know that probably p, one should not use that as a premise in one's practical reasoning.) The impropriety of the above practical syllogism is aptly explained by its violation of that norm.

I have gestured at three dimensions along which there is a prima facie connection between knowledge and our broader cognitive activities. In brief: The question whether someone knows p seems directly relevant to (i) whether that person ought to assert p, (ii) whether there is a chance for that person that not-p, and (iii)

---

[75] Of course, some *philosophers* will offer different reasons. Some, for example, will insist that the facts of knowledge are irrelevant to expected utility calculations, and that the facts of expected utility are the standard by which rationality of action is to be judged. I shall return to this issue later. Here it is beside the point.

[76] Of course we might still criticize the agent for restricting his cares to his own monetary situation, but that is a different matter.

[77] There are complications that call for *ceteris paribus* style qualifications. In a situation where I have no clue what is going on, I may take certain things for granted in order to prevent paralysis, especially when I need to act quickly. Further, if I am in a situation where the difference between 'Probably p' and 'p' is irrelevant to the case at hand, I may use 'p' as a basis on which to act even though I only know that probably p. (Thanks to Ram Neta here.) That said, I do not think that once qualified, the norm will be devoid of content. However one fiddles with the norm, let us not forget the data: ordinary people *do reckon the above reasoning bad* (many more examples will be provided in the chapters that follow) and *will advert to a lack of knowledge* in providing an account of what is bad about it.

whether that person ought to use *p* as a premise in practical deliberation. As we try to evaluate the various solutions to our main puzzle, we should see to what extent they respect these connections. This is not to say that we should mandate from the outset that any solution respect the ideas advanced in this section. We cannot easily say in advance which view will have the best package of costs and benefits. Moreover, as we explore further, we may reckon those constraints less plausible than they first appeared. But for now, at least, it certainly seems that the importance of the concept of knowledge consists, in large part, in such connections as those just outlined; in turn, it seems likely that any view that severs such connections will be highly disruptive to our intuitive sense of the epistemic landscape.

1.4 Epistemic Closure

The lottery puzzles, as I and others have presented them, derive their force from the idea that, roughly speaking, knowledge transfers across known entailments, and hence that some sort of closure principle holds for knowledge. The standard formulation of epistemic closure runs as follows:

> *Closure.* Necessarily, if S knows that *p* and S knows that *p* entails *q*, then S knows that *q*.[78,79]

[78] See, for example, Cohen (1988), Dretske (2000*a*), Feldman (1999), Nozick (1981), and Stine (1976). I shall not be discussing the stronger thesis that if one knows *p* and *p* entails *q*, one knows *q*. Closure principles that involve conditions of this sort are defended, respectively, by Lewis (1996) and Klein (1995). Such a proposal is only plausible on a conception of thought according to which, if *p* is modally equivalent to *q*, the thought that *p just is* the thought that *q*. Combine this with the thesis that knowledge distributes over conjunction, and the stronger closure principle follows. Such a conception of thought, vital to Lewis's picture of things, is altogether anathema to our ordinary ways of thinking, and also to mine. For a general survey of the ways in which closure principles can be stated, see Hales (1995) and Unger (1975, ch. 1).

[79] DeRose entertains the principle that in order to know *p*, 'one must know that not-*q*, for any *q* (but here restrictions must be added), such that if *q* were true, S would not

Some popular views treat singular terms within the scope of propositional attitude verbs as transparent. These views, if correct, make the standard closure principle utterly unacceptable.[80] But even leaving that aside, the principle is not especially intuitive as it stands.[81] If at *t*, I know that *p* and know that *p* entails *q*, I may still have to *do* something—namely perform a deductive inference—in order to come to know that *q*.[82] Until I perform that inference, I do not know that *q*. At any rate, that seems to be the natural view of the matter. Williamson's statement of the closure idea is thus preferable: 'knowing *p₁,..., pₙ,* competently deducing *q*, and thereby coming to believe *q* is in general a way of coming to know *q*' (2000: 117).[83] A special case of this closure principle concerns deduction from a single premise: Knowing *p*, competently deducing *q*,

---

know that *p*' (1995: 31–2 n. 33). This is inspired by Barry Stroud, who canvassed the principle that 'if someone knows something, p, he must know the falsity of all those things incompatible with his knowing that p (or perhaps all those things he knows to be incompatible with his knowing that p)' (1984: 29–30). Assuming the transparency of double negation, Stroud's version implies the KK principle—that if one knows *p* one knows that one knows *p*—which to my mind is evidence enough of its unacceptability. DeRose's gloss is harder to evaluate, since it is hard to guess what his 'restrictions' are supposed to amount to.

⁸⁰ See, for example, Soames (2002). On his view, if I know that Hesperus is F, I *ipso facto* know that Phosphorus is F. Suppose I know that Hesperus is loved by me and Phosphorus is loved by you, but I do not realize that 'Hesperus is Phosphorus' expresses a truth. I know that □ ((Hesperus is loved by me and Hesperus is loved by you) ⊃ some single thing is loved by both of us). And I know that Hesperus is loved by me and Hesperus is loved by you (since I know that Hesperus is loved by me and Phosphorus is loved by you, which, on the transparency view, is just the same thing as knowing that Hesperus is loved by me and Hesperus is loved by you). But in this situation, I by no means know—nor am even in a position to easily come to know—that some single thing is loved by both of us. On this view, then, it is not at all true in general that if one knows *p* and knows *p* ⊃ *q*, then one is in a position to come to know *q*.

⁸¹ To be fair, most of those who articulate the principle acknowledge the need for further refinement.

⁸² Note, moreover, that if one supposes that knowledge is compatible with less than absolute confidence, then there may be situations where one has sufficient confidence (in combination with other suitable credentials) to know that *p* and to know that *p* entails *q* but where one is unable to summon sufficient confidence to know that *q* by deduction, for standard subjective Bayesian reasons. (Thanks to Stephen Schiffer here.)

⁸³ What of the case where one has other beliefs that imply not-*q*? (Gilbert Harman raised this matter in correspondence.) I doubt that materials for a counterexample are

and thereby coming to believe q is in general a way of coming to know q.

As Williamson remarks, such principles articulate what is an extremely intuitive idea, namely that 'deduction is a way of extending one's knowledge' (2000: 117).[84] (Consider, for example, the paradigmatic status of mathematical knowledge that proceeds by way of deductive proof.) However, they may well stand in need of refinement along two dimensions.

First, imagine a case where, at t_1, S knows $p_1, \ldots, p_n$ and starts upon a long deduction on the basis of which he comes to believe q at t_3. At t_2, sometime between t_1 and t_3, S's knowledge of some or all of $p_1, \ldots, p_n$ gets destroyed by misleading counterevidence. We do not intuitively suppose that in such a case the person knows that q at t_3. This suggests the following improvement: Knowing $p_1, \ldots, p_n$, competently deducing q, and thereby coming to believe q, retaining one's knowledge of $p_1, \ldots, p_n$ throughout, is in general a way of coming to know q. Since the force of 'in general' is a bit unclear, we should for the sake of maximal clarity prefer to consider the slightly less guarded:

> *Multi-Premise Closure* (MPC). Necessarily, if S knows $p_1, \ldots, p_n$, competently deduces q, and thereby comes to believe q, while retaining knowledge of $p_1, \ldots, p_n$ throughout, then S knows q.[85]

---

available here. If those other beliefs destroy knowledge of the premises, then the reasoning will not be from known premises, in which case the principle will not be relevant. If they do not, then I do not see why the presence of those beliefs should preclude knowledge of the conclusion.

[84] Cf. Russell's definition of 'derivative knowledge' as 'what is validly deduced from known premises' (Russell 1912: 133). Hales (1995) discusses a related closure principle (his K6), which he treats as 'trivially true', even 'formally trivial, given certain assumptions about the semantics of "know"'. These claims of triviality strike me as wrongheaded. In any case, what matters most here is the question of truth, not that of triviality.

[85] Perhaps knowledge requires a level of conviction beyond that secured by the truth of a belief ascription. (For example, there are some who think that knowing requires 'being sure'.) Readers who think this should modify the principle (along with the single-premise version) accordingly.

The single-premise version reads as follows:

> *Single-Premise Closure* (SPC). Necessarily, if S knows *p*, compe-
> tently deduces *q*, and thereby comes to believe *q*, while
> retaining knowledge of *p* throughout, then S knows *q*.[86]

There is a second dimension along which one might fuss. What if
one's deduction is competent but one does not know that it is
competent? Does this merely impede one's capacity to know that
one knows the conclusion, or does it instead impede knowledge of
the conclusion itself? After all, don't we have to check our proofs
before we can be said to know their conclusions? As Hume reminds
us: 'In all demonstrative sciences the rules are certain and infallible;
but when we apply them, our fallible and uncertain faculties are
very apt to depart from them, and fall into error.... There is no
Algebraist or Mathematician so expert in his science, as to place
entire confidence in any truth immediately upon his discovery of it'
(*Treatise*, IV. I; 1968: 180). And there are other worries in the neighborhood. What if we do in fact operate with the correct logic but we
have some evidence, perhaps misleading, that militates in favor of
some deviant account of logically valid inference? What if we
validly infer *q* from *p* but there is some risk, one that does not in
fact obtain, that the sentential expression of *q* expresses no proposition at all?[87] There are delicate issues here which lie beyond the

---

[86] Note that these principles are consistent with the thesis that for some knowable
proposition *p*, it is impossible that one come to know some entailed proposition *q* by
deduction on account of the fact that in order to know *p* one must know *q* already.
(Simplest case: one deduces *p* from itself.) For example, it might be maintained that to
know that one has a hand, one has to already know that one is not dreaming and so can
never know that one is not dreaming by competent deduction from one's manual
knowledge (see Wright 1991). Such theses are consistent with the closure thesis. (I
might add that I find most alleged examples of this phenomenon unconvincing.)

These principles, as stated, are silent with respect to those cases where one believes *q*
already but, as a result of deduction, comes to base one's belief that *q* on known premises.
In those cases too it is intuitive to suppose the deduction will deliver knowledge, but I
shall not worry here about liberalizing the principles to handle such cases.

[87] Suppose that sentences containing empty proper names do not express propositions. Suppose 'Atlantis' refers but I do not know whether it refers. I make the
inferential transition from 'I exist' to 'I exist or Atlantis exists'. There is an evident

scope of the current work. For current purposes, let us allow 'competent deduction' to be a reasonably flexible notion. If deduction extends knowledge so long as one thoroughly checks one's proofs, let 'competent deduction' include proof-checking. If deduction extends knowledge so long as one is not taking deviant logics seriously, let 'competent deduction' include the relevant kind of single-mindedness. And so on. I assume that if the only worries about closure principles are the kinds of worries just voiced, then something in the vicinity of the above closure principles is correct.

Let me be clear about two further issues.

First, as I shall be conceiving of it, a competent deduction need not consist of a formally valid argument. One can trace out the a priori consequences of a claim without one's reasoning being formally valid. Example: I deduce 'Something is colored' from 'Something is red'. Those who (ill-advisedly) insist upon treating such an inference as enthymematic are invited to make appropriate adjustments to the text as they see fit. Little that I have to say turns on this matter.[88]

Second, we should note that our closure principles are perfectly compatible with the possibility that certain inferences from known premises are self-defeating. Suppose that knowing p requires that some condition C obtain. And suppose that deducing some proposition q from p is incompatible with condition C remaining in

---

risk that the latter sentence is contentless and hence does not express a fit object of belief. Suppose in fact that the latter sentence is contentful and thus, using those sentential vehicles, I have deduced a disjunctive proposition from a Cartesian premise. Should we say that owing to the risk of reference failure, I do not now know that I exist or Atlantis exists? There is certainly some pressure to say this, but I shall not pursue the matter here.

[88] Granted, the enthymeme approach will treat certain cases that I discuss under SPC as involving multiple premises. Those who accept SPC but reject MPC may thus feel that a good deal is at stake here. But those who accept SPC will also, presumably, be happy with the following special case of MPC: Necessarily, if one knows p and, in conjunction with a set of premises that are known with certainty a priori, competently deduces q, thereby coming to believe q, retaining one's knowledge that p and of that set of premises throughout, then one comes to know q. The standard kind of worry concerning MPC—that small risks add up to big risks—has far less force with regard to this special case.

place (or, worse still, with condition C's ever having been in place). Then we shall say that the inference from p to q is self-defeating. Here is a case (albeit somewhat silly) of self-defeating inference.[89] Suppose a very trustworthy oracle tells you that you will never perform any deductive inferences ever again and you come to know this. You also know that if you will never perform any deductive inferences again, you will never do what you enjoy best ever again. You are hardly in a position to deduce that you will never do what you enjoy best ever again.[90] But this is no counterexample to the closure principles just provided.[91] Perhaps we shall come across more interesting examples of self-defeating inferences. Instructive though they might be, they will not provide reason to give up on closure.

Our closure principles are perfectly general principles concerning how knowledge can be gained by deductive inference from prior knowledge. It goes without saying that any general principle of this sort will require caveats, the details of which are often difficult to get perfectly precise. But none of this should distract us from a conviction that such principles appear to articulate something very important about how the concept of knowledge operates. It is striking, then, that some philosophers have gone so far as to deny that anything in the vicinity of even SPC is correct. Might this provide the key to solving our puzzles?

1.5 Denying Single-Premise Closure[92]

Let us look at the African safari case through the lens of SPC. Suppose S knows that S will not acquire enough money to go on an

---

[89] This case is discussed in Hawthorne (2000a).
[90] See also Unger (1975: 15).
[91] They are more troublesome for the standard closure principle presented at the outset.
[92] The contents of this section overlap significantly with Hawthorne (forthcoming a).

African safari before the end of next year (for short, *p*). Let us agree that the latter proposition entails that S will not acquire more than enough money to go on an African safari by winning a major prize in a lottery before the end of next year (for short, *q*). SPC now tells us that one of the following is true:

(1) S already knows that *q*.

(2) S is able to know that *q* by performing a competent deduction from *p* to *q*, believing *q* thereby, and retaining his knowledge that *p* throughout.

(3) S is unable to competently deduce *q* from *p*.

(4) While able to competently deduce *q* from *p*, S is unable to form a belief that *q* on the basis of a competent deduction from *p* to *q*.

(5) While able to perform a competent deduction from *p* to *q* and to form a belief that *q* thereby, S is unable to perform a competent deduction from *p* to *q*, and to form a belief that *q* thereby, while retaining his knowledge that *p* throughout.

If S is a normal human subject, (3) will strike us as crazy. If we accede to our intuitions about lottery propositions, we will resist (1) and (2) At first blush, (4) and (5) appear utterly unpromising. Nor are many of us very ready to concede to the skeptic that we were wrong in assuming that many ordinary subjects know such things as that they will not have enough money to go on an African safari in the near future. But if we are not to concede to the skeptic, where are we to resist? Since (1)–(5) seem prima facie unpromising targets, it is not surprising that some philosophers have chosen to give up closure, both in its single-premise and its multi-premise versions.[93]

The kind of strategy that I have in mind has been advocated by Robert Nozick (1981) and Fred Dretske (2000*a*) as an all-purpose trick for dealing with skepticism. Thus, Dretske famously asserts that one can know upon visiting a zoo that some animal in a cage is a

---

[93] Though their formulations differ somewhat from those presented in the text above, it is clear that they would dispute both Single- and Multi-Premise Closure.

zebra and yet be in no position to know that the animal in that cage is not a cleverly disguised mule. Similarly, Nozick claims that I can know that I have hands but that I am in no position to know that I am not a handless brain in a vat. Such a tack can be readily extended to the cases with which I began.

I have some sympathy here with Richard Feldman's remark: 'To my mind, the idea that no version of the closure principle is true— that we can fail to know things that we knowingly deduce from other facts we know—is among the least plausible ideas to gain currency in epistemology in recent years' (1999: 95).[94]

The absurdity of denying Single-Premise Closure can be overstated. The case is not quite like that of a philosopher who writes a paper denying the transitivity of the *taller than* relation. That said, I am inclined to side with Feldman. The intuitive consequences of denying Single-Premise Closure seem to be extremely high. Let me say why.

To begin, it is worth being clear that when we notice a lottery proposition and find ourselves convinced that a subject is unable to know it, we thereby tend to put ourselves into a frame of mind where we do not think that the person knows an ordinary proposition that entails it. It is very difficult to put oneself in a frame of mind where one affirms that one does not know the lottery proposition but that one does know some ordinary proposition that entails it. We thus appear, at least, to proceed as if something in the vicinity of the closure idea were correct. We should admit at the outset, then, that there is something rather revisionary about the Dretske–Nozick proposal. Admittedly, that need not itself be a decisive objection: I shall be suggesting that any cogent view about the extension of the verb 'knows' will have to adopt a revisionary attitude regarding some aspect of ordinary practice. But in this particular case, the conflict with intuition appears particularly deep and wide-ranging, as discussion below will bring out.

---

[94] See also Cohen (1999: 64), quoting Fumerton (1987).

First, a denial of closure interacts disastrously with the thesis that knowledge is the norm of assertion. One who attempts to conform to this norm but simultaneously attempts to adhere to the Dretske–Nozick strategy will end up behaving rather like a familiar subject of ridicule—Lewis Carroll's (1895) Tortoise. For if you place such a character in front of a zoo cage containing a zebra and ask him, 'Do you agree that the thing in the cage is a zebra?', he will say 'Yes', and if you ask him, 'Do you also agree that if the thing in the cage is a zebra, then the thing in the cage is not a cleverly disguised mule?', he will also say 'Yes'. But if you then ask him, 'So you agree that the thing in the cage is not a cleverly disguised mule?', he will now say, 'Oh no. I'm not agreeing to that'. (By his lights, he does not know the conclusion and thus, given the controlling norm, will not assert it.) Now sometimes when we have a consequence of our beliefs pointed out to us, we do not embrace the consequence. Rather, given the unpalatability of the consequence, we give up one of the original beliefs. But that is not what is going on here either. The premises of a modus ponens argument are stably adhered to, and yet the conclusion stably repudiated.[95]

Second, one would have thought that we would at least want to embrace Addition Closure:[96]

> *Addition Closure* (AC). Necessarily, if S knows p and competently deduces (p or q) from p, thereby coming to believe (p or q), while retaining knowledge of p throughout, then S knows (p or q).

It is also very hard to deny that if you know a priori that p and q are equivalent and you know p, then you are in a position to know q.[97] Call this the *Equivalence Principle*. (Note that the counterfactual

---

[95] Note that just like the Tortoise, Nozick and Dretske would agree with the relevant instance of modus ponens put into premise form: If it is the case that there is a zebra there and if it is the case that if there is a zebra there, there is no painted mule there, then there is no painted mule there.

[96] I am assuming that Addition Closure will seem compelling even to those who do not embrace more general closure principles.

[97] Assuming appropriate deductive competence and opportunity.

considerations that Dretske and Nozick adduce to divorce the epistemic status of some p from its a priori consequences do not similarly divorce p from its a priori equivalents. For example, it is easy to find cases where my belief that p is sensitive even though my belief in some entailed q is not. But it is much harder to find cases where my belief in p is sensitive, but not my belief in an a priori equivalent q.[98]) If we combine the Equivalence Principle with Addition Closure, we will secure the results that Dretske and Nozick are trying to avoid. For example, Dretske and Nozick grant that I know:

(6) I have a hand.

With AC I can then deduce:

(7) Either I have a hand or I am not a brain in a vat.

This is a priori equivalent to:

(8) It is not the case that I lack hands and am a brain in a vat.

Similarly, Dretske and Nozick grant that I can know (in the relevant setting):

---

[98] Perhaps there is a bit of room for denying this on the basis of the fact that we do have some tendency to evaluate a priori equivalent claims differently when they are embedded in counterfactual settings. 'There is a diamond in front of me' is a priori equivalent to 'There is a real diamond in front of me'. But 'If there were not a diamond in front of me, then p' has intuitively different truth conditions than 'If there were not a *real* diamond in front of me, then p' on account of the fact that in the latter but not the former case one looks to worlds where there is a fake diamond in front of the speaker. Nevertheless, the Equivalence Principle is intuitively very powerful: so much the worse for counterfactual tests, so construed. I note in passing that the general issue of how focus makes a difference to the truth conditions of counterfactuals (and the bearing of this phenomenon on the prospect of counterfactual analyses of this or that) has not been properly explored by philosophers. My own view is that shifting to a focus-sensitive conception of counterfactuals would hardly help with the project of using them to analyze knowledge. Note also that where p and q are a priori equivalent but nevertheless believed for utterly different reasons, then perhaps one may be sensitive and the other not. This is hardly the normal case, however, and certainly does not show that one who knows p and deduces an a priori equivalent q might still fail to know q. (I am grateful to discussions with Tamar Gendler here.)

(9) That is a zebra.

Given AC I can deduce:

(10) That is a zebra or that is a thing that is not a cleverly disguised mule.[99]

And (10) is a priori equivalent to:

(11) That is not a cleverly disguised mule.

Since Dretske and Nozick deny that I can know claims like (8) and (11), they must reject AC. But can we really live with the denial of this principle? I doubt it.

The following principle also seems extremely intuitive:

> *Distribution.* If one knows that *p* and *q*, one knows *p* and one knows *q*.[100]

Suppose I know

(9) That is a zebra.

By Equivalence, I can know

(12) That is a zebra and that is not a cleverly disguised mule.

By Distribution, I can know

(11) That is not a cleverly disguised mule.

But Dretske and Nozick deny this.

In relinquishing SPC, we are thus forced to relinquish certain other principles—Addition Closure and Distribution (or instead, Equivalence)—that are very compelling. A denial of SPC thus ramifies into costs that are extremely high.

---

[99] With Dretske, I am pretending that 'That is not a painted mule' is a priori deducible from 'That is a zebra'. In truth, of course, it is at best a necessary a posteriori truth that zebras are not mules. Such details are neither here nor there, of course.

[100] A slightly weaker version—that if one knows *p* and *q*, then one is in a position to know *p* and to know *q*—would serve my current purposes just as well.

Third, Nozick and Dretske's rejection of closure is inspired by the idea that only sensitive beliefs are known, which in its crudest version is the view one knows *p* only if, were *p* false, one would not believe *p*. What they trade on is the point, noted earlier, that competent deduction can yield insensitive conclusions from sensitive premises.

As Dretske and Nozick both realize, the crude account quickly runs into trouble. For a belief to be known, it is not necessary that it be sensitive. Suppose I observe a real dog that obscures an excellent facsimile of a duck. I believe a dog is in front of me. That belief is sensitive. I deduce that there is an animal in front of me. That isn't sensitive: if there weren't an animal in front of me, I would see the fake duck and believe there was an animal there. But we can't live with the idea that I know that there is a dog there but I do not know that there is an animal there.[101] Nor can we very well live with the idea that the presence of the duck facsimile destroys knowledge of the dog's presence. So it seems that I know there is an animal there despite the fact of the belief's being insensitive.

When considering such examples, closure-challenging philosophers do not resign themselves to living with the consequences; rather, they propose 'fixes' to their accounts of the necessary conditions on knowledge.[102] Let us begin with a somewhat vague, but nevertheless workable, concept of a 'heavyweight' proposition:[103] Let *p* be a 'heavyweight proposition' just in case we all have some strong inclination to say that *p* is neither the sort of thing that one can know by the exercise of reason alone nor by use of one's perceptual faculties (even aided by reason). Rough and ready

---

[101]   Recall from earlier that one option is to weaken the sensitivity condition so as to require only that knowledge be based on a sensitive belief (without having to be sensitive itself)—but that will make sensitivity considerations impotent as a way of denying closure. (In any case, the weakening does not produce a plausible principle. See Williamson 2000: 160.)

[102]   In Nozick's (1981) case, the 'fix' to these anticipated worries famously took the form of an appeal to methods: one knows *p*, only if, were *p* false, one wouldn't have believed *p* by the same method. It is not my purpose to immerse myself in the details of Nozick's account here, though many of the remarks that follow are pertinent.

[103]   I borrow this terminology from Dretske (forthcoming).

though it is, this category is a familiar one: it includes precisely the sorts of propositions to which Dretske and Nozick make appeal—that we are not looking at white things illuminated by red light (when in fact something looks red), that we are not brains in vats, that we are not looking at a cleverly disguised mule (instead of a zebra), and so on. With regard to such heavyweight propositions, my immediate and strong inclination is to say that I do not know them. But no such corresponding inclination governs my response to their lightweight counterparts: that the wall before me is red, that I am typing on a computer right now, that there is a zebra in the cage before me. Of course, I might derivatively generate some inclination to say that I do not know the latter via reflection on the former. But in the case of the former, doubts are natural and immediate, whereas in the case of the latter, doubts tend to be derivative. Regardless of our views on the nature of knowledge, we should all at least agree that the relevant contrast is a salient fact about human psychology and that it is one of the bases of epistemic puzzlement.

Closure-denying philosophers aim to provide an account of knowledge that permits the inference of lightweight but not heavy-weight propositions from what is known. If I point out to such a theorist that by her lights, one can know that I have hands but not that I am not a brain in a vat, she will welcome the result; if I point out that by her lights there are situations where I can know that there is a cat in front of me but not that there is an animal in front of me, she will not welcome the result. Faced with such pairings, she will scurry back to her epistemological laboratory to contrive an account that delivers the welcome result while avoiding the embarrassing one. Time and again, closure-deniers fail to pull this off.

By way of illustration, consider Dretske's 'fix'.[104] Suppose I believe *p* on the basis of reasons *r*. Dretske tells us that if one

---

[104] My discussion in the text focuses on Dretske's 'Conclusive Reasons' proposal. One might also directly consider his 'Relevant Alternatives' suggestion (see Dretske 2000*a*). According to this view, when one knows *p*, there are relevant alternatives *q*, *r*, *s*,... incompatible with *p* that one has ruled out. My epistemic achievement in knowing

knows p on the basis of reasons r, then one would not have reasons r unless p.[105] Knowing that p requires 'conclusive reasons', and one's reasons are conclusive just in case, were p false, one wouldn't have them.

For this to do the trick, it had better not turn out that plenty of heavyweight propositions have conclusive reasons, or that plenty of mundane consequences of known propositions lack conclusive reasons. Unfortunately for Dretske, this is exactly the situation that prevails. In this connection, we can exploit some earlier themes. Consider first the conjunction

I have a headache and $\sim$ I am a brain in a vat.

My reasons for believing this include my headache. Were the conjunction false I wouldn't have had the reasons that I do for believing the conjunction (the 'nearest worlds' where it is false are ones where I lack a headache). I thus have conclusive reasons for believing the conjunction. Yet this proposition raises just the same epistemic alarm bells as the proposition that I am not a brain in a vat; it is manifestly heavyweight.

---

p is to rule out those relevant alternatives. Relevant alternatives are then indexed to contents, such that the situation in which there is a painted mule in the cage is a relevant alternative to the proposition that there is no painted mule in the cage, but not to the proposition that there is a zebra in the cage. Unless supplemented by the Conclusive Reasons story, this account founders on an unexplained use of 'ruling out'. Isn't to rule out p to be in a position to know that not-p? If so, then this story is impotent as a weapon against Single-Premise Closure, since the opponent will not concede that I cannot 'rule out' the possibility that there is a painted mule in the cage. One suggestion sometimes voiced by closure-deniers is that outrageous possibilities, ones that no one would normally consider, do not count as relevant alternatives. From this we are invited to conclude that one cannot know the denial of such possibilities. But this idea seems to be hard to make good on. I look at someone and see that he is under six feet tall. The possibility that he is over twenty-five feet tall is one that I would not even consider. But it would be embarrassing (to say the least) to contend that I am not in a position to know that the person is under twenty-five feet tall simply on account of the fact that the possibility that he is over twenty-five feet tall is too outrageous even to be relevant.

[105] See Dretske (1971, forthcoming). Similar points are pertinent to Nozick's (1961) appeal to methods.

Consider next knowledge of the future. I think on Monday that I am going to meet you on Wednesday on the basis of familiar sorts of reasons. I meet you on Wednesday. It is natural to say, in many such cases, that my belief on Monday was a piece of knowledge. Consider now the counterfactual: If you hadn't met me on Wednesday, I would not have had those reasons on Monday for thinking that you would meet me on Wednesday. I do not find that counterfactual very compelling. Mundane knowledge of the future thus appears to be excluded by Dretske's account.

Another case to consider: I eat some salmon for dinner. I am no glutton. I eat a modest quantity and form the belief that I have eaten less than 1 pound of salmon. I infer that I have eaten less than 14 pounds of salmon. In fact my perceptual system is very reliable indeed. In those nearby possible worlds where I feast on salmon and eat a pound, or a little more, I do not believe that I have eaten less than a pound. Dretske, no skeptic, will happily concede that I know that I have eaten less than a pound of salmon. Suppose (and for all I know this is correct) that while it is utterly unlikely that any human being would eat over 14 pounds of salmon in a single sitting, doing this would induce (among other things) severe hallucinations. Indeed, it might even induce the hallucination that one had eaten a rather small quantity of salmon.[106] Suppose, then, that if I had eaten over 14 pounds of salmon, I may have had the eaten-less-than-1-pound-ish visual experiences that I have at the actual world. Thus while it is true that I would not have had my reasons *r* for believing that I have eaten less than a pound of salmon unless I had, it is not true that I would not have had my reasons *r* for believing that I have eaten less than 14 pounds of salmon unless I had. Dretske's apparatus (in conjunction with the verdict that I know, in the given case, that I have eaten less than a pound of salmon) delivers the embarrassing result that I know that I have eaten less than a pound of salmon but not that I have eaten less than 14 pounds

---

[106] One could illustrate the same point with pints of beer, which may be more easily grasped (so long as it is agreed that the world where the subject drinks enough beer to hallucinate that he's drunk a moderate amount is a distant one!).

of salmon (even though I believe the latter and have deduced it from the former).

The cumulative lesson is clear enough. Dretske's machinery is intended to align itself with our instinctive verdicts about what we can and cannot know by perception. But, in fact, it draws the can–cannot line in a very different place. And as readers will easily see for themselves, other philosophers who deny SPC have fared no better.

Of course, one might retreat to an account that gets more intuitively satisfying results by brute force, along the lines of:

> If one knows p and deduces q from p then one knows q, unless q is a heavyweight proposition.

But we should all agree that such an account would be *very* unsatisfying.

We have seen that the costs of denying SPC are significant indeed. I shall thus be assuming henceforth that such a principle is correct. Having taken stock of other treatments of our puzzle, some readers will no doubt wish to reconsider SPC, even given the intuitive shortfalls of such a strategy. My own sense is that a denial of SPC ought to continue to seem too high a price; but readers are very welcome to explore the matter further for themselves.

1.6 Multi-Premise Closure

We have seen that there are good reasons to think that a denial of SPC is out of the question. But what of Multi-Premise Closure (MPC)? MPC appears extremely intuitive: the idea that one can add to what one knows by deduction from what one knows has a powerful grip on us regardless of whether the deduction proceeds from one premise or many. Moreover the 'Tortoise' objection above, exploiting the link between knowledge and assertability, pertains just as readily to multi-premise cases.

Henry Kyburg (1970) famously attacks MPC by considering lotteries. He points out that we cannot conjoin reasonable true beliefs about who will lose a lottery to secure other reasonable true beliefs. In a 1,000 ticket lottery in which #1,000 will win, I can reasonably think #1 will not win and that #2 will not win and so on, but I cannot reasonably think #1–999 will not win. If knowledge were identical to reasonable true belief, this would quickly secure the denial of MPC. But of course, the identification of knowledge with reasonable true belief, or with reasonable high subjective probability assignment to a true proposition, is problematic. After all, it is reasonable to think one will lose the lottery and it is reasonable to assign high subjective probability to the proposition that one will lose the lottery, but, intuitively, one does not know that one will lose the lottery. So using Kyburg's case as a ground for denying MPC for knowledge is not completely straightforward.[107]

Another way to press Kyburg's worry—admittedly a somewhat seductive one—runs contrary to the conception of epistemic probability articulated above. Here is the thought: Deductive inference from multiple premises aggregates risks. The risk accruing to one's belief in each premise may be small enough to be consistent with the belief having the status of knowledge. But the risks may add up, so that the deduced belief may be in too great a danger of being false to count as knowledge. Granted, deductive inference from a single premise does not seem like a candidate for risky inference. If p entails q then q must be logically weaker or equivalent to p.[108] But the same is not so for inference from multiple premises. The problem with this version of the Kyburg argument arises from the

---

[107] Of course, a philosopher who holds that one can know propositions to the effect that some individual will lose the lottery (when it is true) could happily pursue Kyburg's line without relying on any identification of knowledge with reasonable true belief. It would be enough that reasonable true belief is necessary for knowledge. Combine that necessary condition with the (putative) knowledge of each loser x that x is a loser and Multi-Premise Closure is in trouble, since it is manifestly unreasonable to believe some long conjunction of loser ascriptions. I shall return to these themes in Chapters 3 and 4. (Thanks to Jim Pryor here.)

[108] I leave aside issues connected to proof-checking.

relevant notion of risk.[109] If there being a risk that not-*p* amounts to there being a chance that not-*p*, then knowing *p* is not compatible with there being any risk at all that not-*p*.[110] Of course, the alleged connection between chance and knowledge may be severed, but that must first be defended before the worry can be pressed successfully. Let us not judge in advance whether the alleged connection is indeed illusory.

A final way to pursue the matter proceeds by analogy with the Preface paradox.[111] Here is a case:

> *The Philosophy Conference.* In familiar ways, I come to know that Tamar will be attending the American Philosophical Association Meetings in Washington. On similar grounds (*mutatis mutandis*) I come to know that Ted will be attending those meetings. On similar grounds, I come to know that Dean will be attending those meetings. On similar grounds I come to know that Brian will be attending those meetings. I go on and acquire this sort of knowledge for about 150 individuals. (All 150 individuals turn up at the APA.)[112]

It may be argued that it is just obvious that I was in no position to know in advance that all 150 of those individuals would show up at the APA. At the same time—skeptical worries aside—it is hardly natural to say that the premises were not known. Since I knew of each individual that he or she was going to show up, and was

[109] Here I follow Williamson (2000: 123–30).

[110] Another way to pursue the worry is by glossing risk in terms of some notion of objective chance. For more on this, see Chapter 4.

[111] Makinson (1965).

[112] Another suggestive thought experiment, which raises similar issues: Take some feature F and distance *d* for which a glimpse of F from distance *d* will not suffice for knowledge, but where a sufficiently long look at F will secure knowledge of its presence. Consider first a case A where the look is just short enough to preclude knowledge that F is present. Consider, by comparison, a case B where a person looks just a little bit longer than in case A at each of twenty subjects and then comes to believe that they are all F. It may seem odd to suppose that the epistemic credentials of the generalization in B exceed those of the single case judgment in A. But Multi-Premise Closure delivers that result.

perfectly capable of performing the relevant deduction while maintaining the relevant bits of knowledge, one is invited to conclude that MPC should be abandoned.

The argument is far from decisive.[113] Suppose that I form the belief, for each x on the list, that x will be at the APA and then deduce and come to believe the long conjunction involving all 150 of them. In this situation, it would be exceedingly strange for an onlooker to say 'Yes' to each question of the form 'Does John know S will be at the APA?', where 'S' corresponds to a name on the list, but then balk at 'John knows that all the people listed will be at the APA' (unless he wished to retract certain of his initial claims). So it seems as if the setting in which one ascribes knowledge of the individual propositions to me is a setting in which (given that I have deduced and come to believe the conjunction) one is willing to ascribe knowledge to me of the conjunction.[114]

Notice, in this connection, that the settings where we most vividly wish to deny that one can know the conjunction—by thinking of family emergencies, or thinking about the statistical track record of similar conjunctions—are settings where we are also somewhat unwilling to say that the conjuncts are known.

All this militates in favor of the truth of MPC. The following considerations are also relevant:

(i) There may be cases where one knows each of a sequence of propositions but has misleading evidence that inclines one against believing some proposition entailed by the sequence, without destroying knowledge of the members of the sequence. Thus suppose I know of each person x on a very long list that the person will be at the APA. Someone comes in and announces 'I'm not going to tell you who, but one of the people on the list has just died'. The person

[113] I am grateful to Ryan Wasserman here.

[114] Of course, if my belief in the conjunction was rather tentative, so that, for example, I will only ever assert 'I believe that they will come' with a tentative intonation contour, then one might withhold knowledge on that score. This merely indicates that our closure principles should be formulated in terms of an attitude that carries more conviction than tentative belief of this sort.

is in fact lying, though I have no reason to suspect this. In this situation, it is arguable that I still know of, say, Tamar, that Tamar will be at the APA. That said, it would still be perfectly understandable if I was not inclined to believe the conjunction. But *that fact* hardly makes trouble for MPC.

(ii) Even granting that knowledge is necessary for proper assertion, it is not sufficient. Of particular relevance here is the fact that if someone knows p but believes that he or she does not know that p, then it is at best unclear whether that person is entitled to flat-out assert that p. Now suppose a person knows each of a long sequence of propositions and has deduced and thereby comes to believe the conjunction. Suppose, further, that while she believes the conjunction, she believes that she does not know the conjunction (perhaps on the grounds of Preface-style considerations: 'There's an excellent chance that I've made a mistake somewhere'). Her own belief that knowledge is absent explains well enough the dubious status of the assertion 'The conjunction is true' in her mouth, without automatically impugning MPC.[115]

Let us not try to resolve matters further just yet. For now, let us acknowledge that the intuitive pressures in favor of MPC are quite significant indeed.

[115] I return to Preface-style worries in Chapter 4.

2 CONTEXTUALISM AND THE PUZZLE

2.1 Introducing Contextualism

FOLLOWING Peter Unger, we can distinguish approaches to the semantics of 'know' that are *invariantist* from approaches that are *contextualist*. Appeal to the latter has seemed to many to offer a promising solution to the puzzle that confronts us. But careful examination reveals that prospects for this sort of account are far less rosy than its advocates have acknowledged. At the same time, invariantist approaches are also unsatisfying in certain ways. I will devote this chapter to examining the advantages and disadvantages of contextualism; the subsequent chapter will do the same for invariantism.

Semantic Value

In distinguishing invariantist from contextualist approaches, I shall avail myself of the notion of semantic value. Let me thus make some remarks about that notion, as I am employing it. There are at least three basic strands to the notion of semantic value as it is used in contemporary philosophical semantics. First, a distinction is standardly drawn between what is semantically expressed by a sentence ('the proposition expressed by a sentence') and what is communicated to an audience by a token of that sentence on a particular occasion of use, where it is understood that the latter may considerably outstrip the former in informational content.[1] A paradigm case

---

[1] And where the sentence is being used nonliterally, the semantic value may not even be included in what is communicated to an audience.

is provided by Grice's examples of conversational implicature. If I say 'There is a gas station around that corner', I may communicate to someone that the gas station in question is open, even though the latter was not implied by the semantic content of my utterance. Often the distinction is cashed out in terms of 'what is said' by a sentence, as opposed to 'what is communicated or implied', but that way of glossing the distinction is dangerous unless 'say' is being used as a term of art: the ordinary use of 'what is said' in English is extremely liberal.[2] Second, it is also standardly assumed that the semantic value of a sentence at least determines a set of truth conditions—roughly a function from possible worlds to truth values.[3] For sentences with indexicals and demonstratives in them, we cannot speak of the semantic value of a sentence *simpliciter*: a sentence has a semantic value only relative to a context in which the designata of indexical expressions are fixed.[4] Third, it is standardly assumed that the semantic value of a sentence is a function of the semantic values of its constituent expressions (and how those expressions are arranged), where the semantic contribution of subsentential constituents can be articulated by some kind of compositional meaning theory. Here is not the place to explore these three central strands of orthodoxy. The notion of semantic value ought, I hope, to be intuitive enough for it to play a serviceable role in the discussions that follow. (The reader will certainly notice certain key junctures where theoretical issues concerning the very notion of semantic value may prove pertinent.)

---

[2] It is not hard to imagine situations in which one is happy to state 'He is saying that *p*', where '*p*' merely expresses what is conversationally implied. See Soames (2002: 72–86); Lepore and Cappelen (1997).

[3] It is more controversial whether the semantic value of a sentence is *exhausted* by the associated truth conditions.

[4] See Soames (2002, ch. 4). Some adopt a conception of 'semantic value' according to which it is invariant across contexts in which the referents of indexical expressions vary. This requires a theoretical gloss on 'semantic value' that drops the posited connection between semantic value and truth conditions. It is a subtle matter to determine which of these issues are terminological and which are substantive. I cannot explore the matter here.

According to invariantist approaches, the verb 'know'—at least as it appears in 'know-that' constructions (and embedded-question constructions)[5]—has a single, invariant, semantic value, so that the contribution of 'know' to the truth conditions of an utterance remains constant from utterance token to utterance token. We can usefully distinguish two kinds of invariantists: The *skeptical invariantist* claims that the semantic value of the word 'knows' is such that all (or nearly all) positive knowledge ascriptions of the form 'S knows that *p*' are false. The *moderate invariantist* claims that the semantic value of the verb 'know' is such that very many of the positive knowledge ascriptions that we make in daily life are true.[6]

The contextualist, meanwhile, denies that there is any such thing as the semantic value *simpliciter* of a sentence containing the verb 'know'—say, 'Donald Davidson knows that he has feet'. Any such sentence will have different semantic values relative to different contexts of utterance, where this is at least in part due to contextual parameters connected to the verb 'know' itself.[7]

Bare-Bones Contextualism

Contextualism about knowledge is often introduced and developed by analogy with various comparative adjectives. I shall do the same. It is widely agreed in semantics that the truth conditions of an utterance containing a comparative adjective—'short', 'tall', 'flat', 'bumpy', and so on—depends on the reference class associated with the comparative adjective by the sentence user.[8] A basketball coach

---

[5] As I am understanding him, the invariantist can allow that 'know' has a different meaning when it takes a noun phrase as direct object, as in 'John knows Paris' and 'Bill knows Helen'.

[6] Some may find the labels 'skeptic' and 'moderate' biased. Skeptical invariantists will no doubt prefer the label 'dogmatic invariantism' for the species of invariantism they oppose.

[7] And not merely, for example, due to such facts as that 'Donald Davidson' is used on different occasions to name different people and that the present-tense marker will hook onto different times according to the time at which the sentence is uttered.

[8] See Kamp (1975) and Klein (1980, 1991) for detailed discussion. Note that, even having fixed a reference class, there may be context-dependence generated by the need

may look at an individual who is 6 foot 3 inches tall and utter 'He is not very tall'. Someone else may look at the same individual at the same time and utter 'He is very tall'. Both utterances can come out true given the different standards for tallness being deployed by the respective speakers. Even relative to a particular assignment to 'he' and a fixed time of evaluation, there will be no semantic value that can be associated *simpliciter* with 'He is very tall', since its truth conditions can vary from utterance to utterance. Speaking with maximal abstractness, it seems that there is some contextual parameter associated with the comparative adjective 'tall' so that the semantic value—and in turn the extension—of the adjective on a particular occasion of use depends upon a standard that is supplied by the context of use.[9]

Let us outline the bare bones of a contextualist semantics for 'flat' and then extend that style of theory to the verb 'know'.[10,11]

---

for a standard of application—some kind of threshold on a scale—relative to that reference class. (To be tall do you have to be taller than 85 percent of the reference class? 80 percent?)

[9] The relevant comparison class is not always given by some explicit predicate—no such predicate is available in 'He is very tall'; and even where there is an explicit predicate it does not always provide appropriate guidance to the standard in force (see Kamp 1975).

[10] Peter Unger (1975, ch. 2) distinguishes absolute terms from relative terms. An absolute term (e.g. 'flat') admits such modifiers as 'perfectly' and 'absolutely' (in contrast with the relative term 'bumpy'). Further (and this is the canonical test for Unger), absolute terms are ones where the inference from 'X is Fer/more F than Y' to 'Y is not F' is acceptable. Note that terms such as 'insane' pass the first test, but not the second, perhaps because there are distracting ambiguities besetting the modifier 'perfectly', which admits of a use that means simply that the subject is up to the minimal standards of the adjective, as in 'perfectly decent meal'. It is also not clear that the use of 'completely/absolutely/perfectly insane/bonkers/nuts/off his rocker' is the same use of 'perfectly' and 'absolutely' that one finds in 'perfectly flat' and 'absolutely circular'. Perhaps, suitably regimented, the two tests march in step. Thanks to Tamar Gendler here. Some contextualists—David Lewis, for instance—use absolute terms as their guiding analogy; others—Stewart Cohen, for instance—do not rely on an explicit comparison with absolute terms. (As Stewart Cohen has pointed out to me, this difference in approach is related to the question of whether contextualism is to be understood on the model of restricted quantification.)

[11] What follows borrows, obviously, from the 'relevant alternatives' approach to knowledge. See, notably, Goldman (1976) and Stine (1976).

The things that we call 'flat' turn out on more or less close scrutiny to have various small bumps and elements of curvature. But unless we are happy to allow that all claims of the form '*a* is flat' are false,[12] we shall allow that such imperfections are sometimes compatible with the truth of some such claims. So let us say that '*a* is flat' is true on an occasion of use just in case the referent of '*a*' has no bumps or curvature *that are relevant* on that occasion.[13,14] What counts as relevant depends on the interests and intentions of the user. Two people may look at the same field, one with the plan of landing a plane on it, another with the plan of playing hockey on it. Assuming that what is flat for an airstrip is different from what is flat for a hockey field, they may both utter 'That is flat' and yet one speaks truly while the other speaks falsely. In short, the interests and intentions of each speaker determine different standards for flatness so that a bump that counts as relevant to one flatness ascription may be irrelevant to another.[15]

This style of theory can easily be extended to the word 'know'. Here is a natural way to do it. Whether a true belief that *p* counts as

---

[12] Cf. Unger (1975, ch. 2).

[13] In the ordinary sense of the term, 'bump' is itself context-dependent. For the purpose of this toy semantic theory, it is crucial that 'bump' is being used as liberally as possible.

[14] Lewis (1983) does things slightly differently, though the picture is essentially the same. There he says that '*a* is flat' is true iff *a* has no bumps of any kind, though it is understood that the quantifier that appears in the truth condition is often restricted so as to exclude irrelevant bumps. That style of analysis will not work, note, for the purposes of providing a general semantics for sentence of the form '*a* is flat'. We cannot say '*a* is flat' is true in a context *c* iff it has no bumps of any kind, since the context in which we use 'bump' may not be that associated with context *c*.

[15] The story can of course be extended to comparative and superlative uses of the adjective in question. Roughly: '*a* is flatter than *b*' is true on an occasion of use just in case the referent of '*a*' has fewer relevant bumps than the referent of '*b*' (an oversimplification, obviously, since size and number of bumps both matter here); '*a* is the flattest of the Fs' is true on an occasion of use just in case the referent of '*a*' belongs to the extension of 'F' and every other member of that extension has more relevant bumps than the referent of '*a*'. Lewis (1983: 245–6) in effect points out that this style of treatment by the contextualist prevents him from being saddled with truths of the form '*a* is flat but *b* is flatter'. See also Lewis (1996: 553–4). (For what it's worth, a number of people have remarked to me that there are settings where sentences such as 'That is flat but this is flatter' do not sound too bad.)

knowledge depends, it would seem, on how easily that believer could have been mistaken about p and about similar subject matter.[16,17] But how easily is easily enough? Which possible mistakes that a person could have made about p and about similar subject matter defeat a knowledge ascription? In general, the easier it is for a subject to make a particular mistake, the more semantic pressure there is to count that mistake relevant to the knowledge claim. But what determines the threshold?[18] Let our toy semantic theory say that an ascription of the form 'S knows that p' is true on some occasion iff there is no possible world in which S makes a

---

[16] Sosa (2000) discusses a version of contextualism that focuses on this notion of *epistemic safety*. The idea that knowledge and safety are intimately connected can also be found in Williamson (2000) and Sainsbury (1997). Here is Williamson: 'If one knows, one could not easily have been wrong in a similar case' (2000: 147).

[17] Some points of clarification. (i) By 'a mistake' I just mean a false belief. A case of veridical hallucination, for example, is not a mistake, but we reckon knowledge absent in such a case because, intuitively, a mistake could easily have been made. (ii) Some cases can be constructed (see Hawthorne 2002*b*) where there is no risk of a mistake, but there is a risk of a truthvalueless claim (owing to paradox). To handle such cases, we need to extend the notion of a mistake to include failed attempts at a true belief. (iii) For the purpose of epistemic evaluation, the epistemically relevant notions of danger aren't to be cashed out in terms of any straightforward metric on objective risk, or any general-purpose notion of metaphysical closeness at play in discussions of counterfactuals. Suppose a demon protects X in such a way that whenever X is in danger of forming a false belief, the demon intervenes and stops the belief from being formed. X's belief-forming process up to that point might exactly resemble that of Y, who does form a false belief. Here we are tempted to claim that X does not know when, but for the demon, he would have formed a false belief in nearby worlds and, correlatively, to speak of a 'danger' of error, even though there is also a very good sense in which the objective risk of X falling into error was vanishingly low. (iv) The reference to 'similar subject matter' is important. For example, an unreliable method may generate a belief in a necessary truth but still, the fact that it is prone to generate mistakes is reason enough to deny the belief in the necessary truth the status of knowledge. Similarly if, in fake barn country, I say 'That is a barn', the singular proposition believed may be true at all worlds where it is believed—assuming barns are essentially barns—but the liability to be mistaken about similar subject matter is reason enough to hesitate to ascribe knowledge. (v) Insofar as we withhold knowledge in Gettier cases, it seems likely that 'ease of mistake' reasoning is at work, since there is a very natural sense, in such cases, in which the true believer forms a belief in a way that could very easily have delivered error. (I am grateful here for discussions with Jim Pryor and Ted Sider.)

[18] Analogy: In general, the less money someone has, the more semantic pressure there is to count that person as poor; still, we need a story about how the line between poor and nonpoor people is determined.

mistake that is relevant on that occasion.[19,20] And let the standards of relevance vary from ascriber to ascriber. Supposing the theory true, two ascribers may look at a single subject and both utter 'He knows that *p*' (using semantically equivalent that-clauses), and yet the ascriptions have different truth values, owing to the fact that a certain possible mistake is relevant vis-à-vis one ascription and not the other.

Let us be clear: Which mistakes are and are not possible is not ascriber-dependent.[21] Which mistakes I am and am not capable of making are a matter of how I am constituted and how I am related to the world. Our toy theory merely insists that there is a contextual parameter of relevance such that which mistakes count as relevant to a knowledge ascription depends, at least in part, on the ascriber and not the subject of the ascription (unless ascriber and subject happen to be the same, as with self-ascriptions).[22] As a corollary, some ascribers may have higher standards associated with the verb 'know' than others.[23] The easier it is for a mistake to count as

---

[19] It is arguable that, contrary to recent epistemological tradition, one can allow that knowledge might be based on false beliefs, so long as this does not make for relevant mistakes—as when a child knows there will be toys under the Christmas tree on the basis of the false belief that Santa Claus is coming or when I know that someone is short on the basis of a perceptually based belief that the person is under four feet tall (when the person is in fact four foot one). Relevant here is Williams (1978).

[20] The theory would presumably have to be extended to allow that the knowledge predicate, as used on an occasion, can be semantically evaluated in connection with propositions and/or subjects that are not designated by any utterance on that occasion. (Does 'know', on such and such an occasion of use, express a relation that holds between *x* and proposition *p*, where *p* and/or *x* might not be spoken about on that occasion?) This will be important to the evaluation of certain quantificational sentences that *are* uttered, such as 'He knows something I don't'. As a corollary, sentences deploying 'know' will be evaluable relative to contexts at which they are *not* uttered.

[21] Here, as in many other places, I take liberties with use and mention for ease of exposition. Those inclined to fuss should consult Lewis's (1996) closing remarks.

[22] One might also wish to allow that an ascriber's local interlocutors have special semantic relevance to the semantic value of 'know' in the mouth of the ascriber. I shall not go into that here.

[23] I do suspect, however, that the notion of 'standards' is sometimes taken too seriously in these discussions. To say that you have higher standards than I for 'know' is just to say that there are subject–time–proposition triples that fall under my extension of 'know' but not under yours—and not vice versa. We needn't reify *standards*

relevant, the harder it will be for a knowledge ascription to come out true. 'He knows that p' will, in the mouth of some ascribers, mark a higher epistemic achievement than in the mouth of others. (Of course, there may not always be an easy comparison of higher-to-lower standards—ascribers may crisscross with regard to the sorts of mistakes they count as relevant.) And so, if two ascribers have differing standards, then a claim of the form 'He knows that p' (said of the same person at the same time) may be false in the mouth of one ascriber, true in the mouth of the other. Similarly, a generalization of the form 'Everyone who is F knows (doesn't know) that p' may be true in the mouth of one ascriber, false in the mouth of the other, even though the domain of quantification of 'everyone', time of ascription, and semantic value of 'F' is constant across the contexts of the ascribers. (In this regard, it is helpful to think of the extension of 'know' on some particular occasion of use as a set of subject—proposition—time triples. According to the contextualist, then, the extension of some tokening of 'know' may include some particular triple that does not belong to the extension of some other tokening.[24])

The ascriber-dependence of relevance that is postulated by the standard contextualist merits special emphasis. Suppose that by the standards of the ascriber some mistake is relevant to S's true belief that p, but that such a mistake is not relevant by S's own standards. One could imagine a theory which claimed that 'know' had a flexibility analogous to the English word 'nearby'.[25] If I say

into some kind of index around which to build a semantics for 'know'. We should also be careful not to take for granted that 'one's standards' for knowledge are a priori available, as if we had ready access to how one's dispositions—in combination with the world—determine an extension of 'know' in one's own mouth.

[24] There are radical forms of contextualism that I shall not consider here. One radical view denies that tokens of the predicate 'know' have an extension, denying that the truth of a particular token utterance is compositionally determined in the way that standard semantics assumes. Another claims that the truth of a particular token utterance—and relatedly the extension of a particular predicate token—is itself context-dependent. (Mark Richard and John Macfarlane have work in progress that develops this idea.)

[25] Thanks to Ernest Sosa here.

'Ernie went to a nearby restaurant', I may mean that he went to a restaurant that is nearby to where I am speaking or that he went to a restaurant that is nearby to where he lives or that he went to a restaurant nearby to some other location that is salient in the conversation. Such a theory would claim that when I say S knows that *p*, I sometimes mean S knows by my standards, sometimes S knows by S's standards, and so on. This would certainly be a theory according to which 'know' is context-dependent. But it is not the kind of theory embraced by contemporary contextualists. According to the theory we just imagined, there is a certain contextual parameter that always needs to be fixed, namely: Whose standards are to count? Contemporary contextualism does not posit any such parameter. It is always the ascriber's standards that call the semantic shots, so to speak. Prima facie, this is a good thing. We can 'hear' the various readings available for sentences involving the word 'nearby'. But we don't have *any* analogous sense of flexibility when it comes to the verb 'know'.

This feature of contextualism provides its defender with an easy response to one common, but mistaken, objection to the view: namely, that if S has lower standards for knowledge than T does, then S ends up knowing more than T due simply to the difference in their standards, not to a discrepancy in their epistemic skills. To think that contextualism has this consequence is to forget the ascriber-dependence of relevance: what I should count you as knowing depends upon my standards, not yours. The proper way to think about the matter is as follows. Suppose that, so to speak, you know that *p* by your standards but not by mine. Then I should claim that you simply don't know that *p*. What remains true is that, if you were to utter 'I know that *p*', that utterance would express a truth in your mouth.

I have been at pains to present the outlines of a bare-bones framework within which a contextualist epistemology might fruitfully be articulated, as opposed to presenting particular contextualist theories (such as those of Cohen 1988, DeRose 1995, and Lewis

1996), each of which contains idiosyncrasies that would distract us from our central themes.[26] I have been especially careful to avoid framing a contextualist epistemology using the notion of 'ruling out', standard to 'relevant alternatives' epistemology, whereby the

---

[26] Cohen's approach is to think of context as setting a threshold concerning how well supported by the evidence a proposition has to be—how likely it is on the evidence—in order to count as being known. Such an approach requires that Williamson's (2000, ch. 9) equation of evidence with what is known is incorrect. It also seems to require a conception of epistemic probability that does not respect that idea that if one knows that *p*, the chance of *p* is 1. (For the main idea to get off the ground, some refinement will also be needed to respect the fact that in Gettier cases, one's failure to know is not due to a failure to meet a likelihood threshold.) Nor does the account provide an easy way of dealing with lottery puzzles. Cohen wants to allow, for example, that there is some chance that I won't be living in Syracuse this summer. Now mightn't the chance of my not living in Syracuse this summer be greater than the chance of winning the lottery? How then can he account for the existence of contexts where I can say 'I know I will be in Syracuse but not whether I will win the lottery'? DeRose, meanwhile, uses a contextualized (and refined) version of Nozick's tracking approach. Many—including myself—will be skeptical of using the latter as a springboard (see the relevant remarks in Chapter 1 and also Cohen 1999: 70–4). Lewis, finally, is working within a framework in which hyperintensionalism—the (natural) view that distinct attitude contents may have the same transworld truth conditions—is eschewed: If *p* and *q* are true in exactly the same set of possible worlds, then on his account one knows that *p* if and only if one knows that *q*. He offers the following definition: 'S knows that *P* iff S's evidence eliminates every possibility in which not-*P*—Psst!—except for those possibilities that we are properly ignoring' (1996: 425). Here's the idea: A speaker makes a knowledge ascription to a subject, deploying a claim of the form 'S knows that *p*'. Call the possibilities that the speaker is not properly ignoring the 'relevant possibilities'. The ascription is true just in case there is no relevant possibility where the subject's evidence is just as it actually is, but where *p* is not true. Note that Lewis's definition directly yields the thesis that if *p* entails *q* and one knows that *p*, then one knows *q* (for if, in a given case, there are no relevant not-*p* possibilities and *p* entails *q*, then there are no relevant not-*q* possibilities). For the hyperintensionalists among us—that is, most of us—this thesis will be altogether unacceptable. Moreover, Lewis's account also directly secures the thesis that we automatically know any fact that supervenes on our evidence (where for Lewis 'evidence' means the intrinsic facts pertaining to one's experience and memory). This is very odd: If I have a visual array with 137 phenomenally red dots, it would not seem that I automatically know that. More generally, we ought not to think that we can know any intrinsic fact about our experience for free. Another style of approach that has much in common with contextualism is Jonathan Schaffer's *contrastivism* (see Schaffer, unpub.; forthcoming), which takes the basic logical form of knowledge ascriptions to be 'S knows *p* rather than *q*'. While the idea is provocative and engaging, I shall not undertake a detailed evaluation of Schaffer's contrastivism in this work. For further suggestions concerning the proper form of a contextualist analysis for 'knows', see Neta (2002).

truth of a knowledge ascription requires that one rule out the relevant counterpossibilities. The natural understanding of 'ruling out the possibility that p' is (to my mind) 'knowing that p does not obtain'; on that understanding, when one knows that p, then, assuming closure and appropriate deductive competence, one is in a position to rule out any counterpossibility, relevant or otherwise.[27] Meanwhile, I do not know of any surrogate notion of 'ruling out' that is likely to prove satisfactory.

The Mechanisms of Relevance

To put flesh on the bones of the theory presented so far, we must say more about the mechanisms by virtue of which mistakes get to count as relevant or irrelevant. Ideally, one would wish for some kind of epistemic recipe book that specified exactly how features of context would suffice to make a certain possible mistake relevant to a particular knowledge ascription. Nothing like that recipe book is currently in our possession, nor are we close to possessing one. Perhaps the concept of knowledge is sufficiently primitive that some analytic ambitions will inevitably be foiled, including any attempt to analyze the pertinent notion of relevance. Perhaps, in disputed areas, there will be a plethora of borderline cases.[28] More generally, perhaps the mechanisms by virtue of which context-dependent predicates get their extension is neither readily accessible to a priori reflection nor fully amenable to empirical investigation.[29] But whether or not such a recipe book is ultimately obtainable, one would still hope for *some* kind of picture of how context contributes to extension. In the case of 'tall', for example, while we may have no very complete account available of how

---

[27] Or at least any counterpossibility q such that it is a priori that $p \supset$ not-q. (Some counterpossibilities will grounded in necessary a posteriori truths.)

[28] Which on an epistemicist view of vagueness will amount to the existence of hidden boundaries, determined by inscrutable semantic mechanisms (see Williamson 1994).

[29] Cf. Chomsky (1993) on the prospects of semantics as an empirical science.

context serves to set a boundary between extension and anti-extension, we can imagine well enough some reasonably satisfying account of how context determines a comparison class and in turn an extension for a tokening of that predicate. One would hope for something similar in the case of 'know'.

So what sorts of factors will the contextualist invoke as contributing to the relevance or irrelevance of certain kinds of mistakes?

Let us begin with a salience constraint, which, since Stewart Cohen's groundbreaking work on contextualism, has been a recurrent theme in the contextualist literature: If, on some occasion, an ascriber is worried about—that is, takes seriously—the possibility that the subject has made a certain kind of mistake, then that creates a presumption that some possibilities involving that kind of mistake are relevant.[30] (Note that we are not assuming here that salience is *required* for relevance. A possible mistake may, for example, be relevant because the ascriber should be worrying about it even if he isn't; cf. Lewis 1996).

A rough analogue of this salience constraint can be found in David Lewis's Rule of Attention: 'No matter how far-fetched a certain possibility may be, no matter how properly we might have ignored it in some other context, if in this context we are not in fact ignoring it but attending to it, then for us now it is a relevant alternative' (1996: 559).[31]

---

[30] What might defeat the presumption? Well, if the worry is grounded in mistaken beliefs about the actual world, for example, this may well defeat it. Suppose S believes he has not won the lottery. I might fixate on the possibility of him holding a winning ticket and thus winning. But unbeknownst to me, S might believe he has not won on the grounds that he believes, quite correctly, that he does not have a ticket. If a mistake is salient on account of a certain alleged resemblance between that world and the actual world, then that mistake is relevant only if the alleged resemblance in fact obtains. For more, see Lewis's (1996: 555–6, 559–60) combined use of the Rule of Resemblance and the Rule of Attention.

[31] A salience-based approach to contextualism makes its first developed appearance in Cohen (1988). As he remarks in a later paper, 'In contexts where we consider whether I know I do not see a cleverly-disguised mule, the chance of error is salient. ... And when the chance of error is salient in a context, the standards tend to rise' (Cohen 1999: 66). I note in passing that Cohen's notion of salience is not straightforwardly psychologistic: 'something can be salient without actually being attended to—think of the

He goes on to draw the grim conclusion that as soon as we engage in epistemological reflection, we land ourselves in a context where few, if any, true knowledge ascriptions are possible: 'Do some epistemology. Let your fantasies rip. Find uneliminated possibilities of error everywhere. Now that you are attending to them … you have landed in a context with an enormously rich domain of potential counter-examples to ascriptions of knowledge' (1996: 559). (Let us not dwell on the notion of 'eliminated' and 'uneliminated' possibilities of error—that turns on the very kind of idiosyncrasy that we ought not to focus on just now.)

Lewis speaks as if merely entertaining a possibility forces it into relevance. That can't quite be right. If I ask you whether or not you have hands, I get you to entertain the proposition that you lack hands—but that does not, by Lewis's lights, make the possibility that you lack hands relevant.[32] Lewis's own way with this kind of worry is to say that what he means by a possibility is something maximally specific relative to our cognitive powers of discrimination: 'A possibility will be specific enough that it cannot be split into subcases in such a way that anything we have said about possibilities, or anything we are going to say before we are done, applies to some subcases and not to others' (1996: 552).

But this is no good. It discounts 'I lack hands' from being a possibility in the relevant sense. But it also discounts 'I am a brain in a vat'. That too has subcases—I am a brain in a vat with a headache. I am a brain in a vat that has phenomenally green sensations. I am a brain in a vat envatted in an aquamarine liquid. And so on. But the plain old brain in a vat hypothesis is Lewis's

cartoon character, Mr Magoo' (Cohen 1998: 305). In correspondence, Cohen suggests that perhaps salience—in his preferred sense—should be defined relative to a normal observer (though I anticipate difficulties here). DeRose's (1995: 36) 'Rule of Sensitivity' is also naturally seen as a special case of a salience rule.

[32] After all, for Lewis, that set of worlds is not one that is uneliminated by my current evidence, since (as he conceives of evidence) there are worlds where my evidence is as it is but where I lack hands.

paradigm of a possibility that, once attended to, makes trouble for knowledge ascriptions.[33]

I think the real trouble here is in the notion of attention. Entertaining or attending to a state of affairs is one thing. Taking seriously the idea that things may be actually that way is quite another. I go to the movies and see *The Matrix*, a modern brain in a vat tale about how humans are really organisms sustained in pods that generate hallucinations. I can watch the movie without taking seriously the idea that I am a pod person (even if I notice that it is true in the story that I am a pod person).[34] We don't want to say that the people watching the movie are automatically in a context where they cannot truly say 'I know I'm in a movie theatre'. By making salience too cheap, Lewis makes the relevance of skeptical possibilities too easy.[35]

There is a residual issue. What exactly is it to take a possibility seriously in the sense of 'seriously' relevant to the contextualist's purposes?[36] After all, there is a sense in which I can take someone perfectly seriously when he asks me whether or not I have hands without this in any way undermining the ascription 'I know I have hands'. (Perhaps the inquirer is someone phoning around to obtain statistical information.) The worry turns out not to be a shallow one. But I shall postpone discussion of it until Chapter 4, assuming for now a rough and ready handle on the guiding idea.

---

[33] Nor will the problem be alleviated (as one reader suggested) by treating 'I am a brain in a vat' as shorthand for 'I am a brain in a vat with all my current evidence', since that does not explain why, for Lewis, attending to the proposition that 'I lack hands' does not destroy knowledge. Both have subcases. Both are not ruled out by my evidence.

[34] I am grateful to Alyssa Ney here.

[35] This in turn makes it harder to avoid being committed to paradoxical assertions of the form '*p* and I do not know that *p*' when expositing contextualist epistemology—for in that setting one is attending to skeptical possibilities and thus, by the Rule of Attention, would by one's own lights be unable to know most of the claims that one asserts. For more on this topic, see Williamson (2001). One reader suggested that this worry is insubstantial, since attending to skeptical possibilities would not destroy knowledge of nonempirical claims made in one's philosophical study. Remember, though, that when formulating a theory about the semantic value of 'know', the contextualist relies crucially on *empirical claims* about how the word 'know' is used.

[36] Thanks to Ted Sider here.

The salience rule—or something like it—is the most common tool of contextualists. In particular, it offers a diagnosis of the enduring appeal of skepticism. In skeptical contexts, certain far-fetched possibilities of error are salient: this in turn defeats pretty much any knowledge ascription that is made in that setting. But, of course, salience principles, even in their most attractive form, cannot tell the whole story. Possible mistakes may undermine knowledge even if they are not taken seriously by the ascriber. If, unbeknownst to me, a wealthy long-lost relative is planning to bequeath me a large amount of money in the very near future, though, by happenstance, it will turn out that the money is never bequeathed, then my self-ascription that I know I will not have enough money to go on an African safari is intuitively incorrect.[37] But this cannot be explained by invoking a salience rule, since the undermining possibility of error is not salient to the ascriber. If I self-ascribe knowledge that a sheep is in front of me and, unbeknownst to me, I am looking at a sheep-shaped rock behind which there is a genuine sheep, then my judgment is intuitively incorrect (since things could easily have been such that I made the same judgment in the absence of the hidden sheep). But, again, this has nothing to do with salience to the ascriber.[38]

What else, apart from salience-related phenomena, makes for ascriber-dependence in knowledge attributions? This topic has been relatively underexplored, even by contextualists. Cohen writes that 'The standards are determined by some complicated function of speaker intentions, listener expectations, presuppositions of the conversation, salience relations, etc.' (1999: 61). Heller suggests on behalf of the contextualist that 'The evaluator's context—her interests and concerns, what is salient to her, her interaction with her conversational partners—determine the weight assigned to various respects of similarity and determine what degree of similarity is required' (1999*b*: 120). A suggestive idea of Lewis's is that high stakes may make a difference: 'When error

---

[37] Thanks to Joseph Raz here.
[38] Cohen (1998) provides a nice discussion of these issues.

would be especially disastrous, few possibilities may be properly ignored' (1996: 556).[39,40] All of this stands in need of fuller development, but we shall not attempt to undertake that project here.[41,42]

Obviously, not all factors relevant to the truth conditions of knowledge ascriptions make for ascriber-dependence. Assuming that knowing that p entails p and that knowing that p entails believing that p,[43] the truth of a knowledge ascription requires

[39] In Lewis's hands, the high stakes idea appears as an epicycle on the 'Rule of Belief,' according to which 'A possibility may not be properly ignored if the subject gives it, or ought to give it, a degree of belief that is sufficiently high…' (1996: 555). Stakes then come in when determining how high is high enough. Lewis is somewhat unclear on two matters: (*a*) When he speaks of error being especially disastrous, is it error by the ascriber, or error by the subject, or both? (Note that if only the latter is relevant, then we do not have a dimension of ascriber-dependence after all. For more on this matter, see Chapter 4.) (*b*) Does high stakes with respect to the subject have a constitutive relevance to what the subject ought to believe?

[40] This idea is entertained and rejected by Dretske (2000*b*: 60–1).

[41] Note that some think that whenever there is vagueness, there is context-dependence: Borderline cases are cases where speakers can, in effect, stipulate one way or another. See Graff (2000); Kamp (1981); Soames (1999, ch. 7). If this is right, then one source of ascriber-dependence for 'know' would be a source that is common to all vague predicates. Note that if this were the *only* source of ascriber-dependence for 'know' then we should be particularly wary of claims that contextualism is the key to solving some or all of the central problems of epistemology.

[42] In correspondence Gilbert Harman suggested a style of contextualism that downplays salience-related phenomena, emphasizing instead the differing ends of inquiry. The basic idea is that one knows for certain purposes, and not for others. Harman's example: For purposes of planning his teaching, he knows that he will be teaching at Princeton in the spring. For insurance purposes, he doesn't know that but treats it as only highly probable. One can then perhaps view ordinary knowledge ascriptions as requiring a purpose index for evaluation. Given that different ascribers may have different ends of inquiry in mind, this will obviously make for ascriber-dependence of semantic value. He also points out that such purpose-relative notions need not be primarily conceived of as the basis for some semantics of ordinary natural language deployments of 'know'. Some epistemologists may share Chomsky's (2000) attitude to the relation between common sense and the project of understanding human nature: 'common sense notions are not of much use, and…pickings remain thin' (p. 165), especially since those concepts are tailor-made for 'special human interests and goals', not the explanatory interests of naturalistic inquiry. In this spirit, one might offer the purpose-relative conception as a sharpening of or replacement for the common sense notion of knowledge, one better suited to a science of human nature. I shall not endeavor to evaluate the prospects for this kind of revisionism here.

[43] *Pace* Lewis (1996: 556), following Radford (1966), who accepts the possibility of knowledge without belief.

belief by the subject and truth of what is believed. Moreover, there are presumably *general* standards in force for what counts as something that could very easily have happened, which, in combination with the facts about the subject's situation, determine whether that subject could very easily have made a mistake.[44] Further, there may be relatively canonical ways of individuating methods, which will be relevant to questions concerning whether a subject might well have made a mistake using the very same method.[45] And so on. Also perhaps constitutively relevant are facts about what we treat as paradigms for knowledge. Perhaps there is (albeit defeasible) semantic pressure to count cases of veridical perception, testimony, and memory as bases for knowledge on account of their status as paradigms.[46] Also relevant perhaps are community-wide dispositions to change their verdicts on particular knowledge ascriptions in response to additional information, sometimes in a way that no further information would induce a further change of verdict.[47] And so on. How this confluence of factors determines an extension

[44] Sainsbury (1997) discusses how the notion of easiness of mistakes is important in general to considerations of reliability, as when we evaluate the reliability of a watch.

[45] I acknowledge that some readers will be less confident that there are 'relatively canonical ways of individuating methods' which serve us in this way.

[46] This idea is a little different from Lewis's 'Rule of Reliability' (1996: 558–9) which enjoins us to (defeasibly) treat the veridical product of any reliable method as a case of knowledge. That rule, unless suitably constrained, runs up against the problem that there will always be some way of individuating the process that generates a belief such that the belief can be regarded as the deliverance of a reliable process—a difficulty known as 'the Generality Problem'. See Goldman (1979, 1986) and Feldman (1985).

[47] Also relevant may be facts about where the joints in nature lie—some objective ranking of naturalness as opposed to gruesomeness of properties. This is what Lewis calls 'eligibility', a feature that he thinks has to play a crucial role in any satisfying metaphysics of reference. See Lewis (1999). (The key idea is that it is, so to speak, a fundamental law of semantics—one that, far from being our invention, is what allows us to think determinate thoughts in the first place—that, *ceteris paribus*, our terms refer to more rather than less eligible properties. The role such a principle has to play here will depend on one's views concerning the degree of naturalness of epistemic properties: if, for example, one thinks that every reference candidate for 'know' has only very low eligibility—none has a special naturalness halo—then eligibility considerations are not going to play a central role in this context. This is not the place to explore the issue further, though my own view is that naturalness considerations shed relatively little light on the semantics of 'know'.)

for the verb 'know' on some occasion of use is certainly worth exploring further, though the issue is no doubt to some extent cognitively elusive. Whether or not we are contextualists, we should admit that we have at best a dim appreciation of how any such confluence determines the extension in question. So it is no objection to the contextualist if she cannot give the full story here. What makes for a distinctively contextualist perspective is the thesis that some of the contributing semantic pressures make for ascriber-dependence, so that the extension of 'know' varies from occasion of use to occasion of use, depending on features of the ascriber.

2.2   The Scope of Contextualism

As I have presented contextualism in epistemology, it is a semantic thesis according to which the extension of 'know' sometimes varies across ascribers. That thesis, in itself, tells us little about how contextualism will be deployed in resolving apparent conflicts in knowledge ascriptions. In this connection, one might wonder just how charitable the contextualist will be regarding ordinary judgments about knowledge. Consider the following pair of cases that illustrate just how liberal we often are in ascribing knowledge:[48]

Case 1.[49] I give six children six books and ask them each to pick one of the books at random. All but one contains misinformation about the capital of Austria. I ask the children to look up what the capital of Austria is and commit the answer to memory. One child learns 'Belgrade', another 'Lisbon', another 'Vienna', and so on. I ask an onlooker who has witnessed the whole sequence of events (or

---

[48] Indeed, such facts about usage make me despair of the traditional epistemological project of extracting an analysis of knowledge from reflecting on use.

[49] This is an improved version (thanks to Tamar Gendler) of a case in Hawthorne (2000*b*).

someone to whom the sequence of events is described) 'Which one of the schoolchildren knows what the capital of Austria is?' or 'How many of the children know what the capital of Austria is?'[50] It is my experience that those presented with this kind of case will answer, not by saying 'None of them', but by selecting the child whose book read 'Vienna'—even though that child was only given the correct answer by luck. [51] (Note in this connection that if I make a five dollar bet on a certain child knowing that Vienna is the capital of Austria, you will pay up as soon as you are convinced that the child believes the capital to be Vienna. You will not inquire further about how the child came by that information—whether by dumb luck or from an informant that normally lies—even if you have reason to suspect such an unreliable source.)

Case 2. Someone sees a stopped clock that happens to read the correct time, sets his (working) watch by it and takes a nap. He knows a party starts at 7.30 p.m. That person wakes up and sees that his watch reads 7 p.m. An onlooker sees all this go on. I ask the onlooker 'Does he know that the party starts in half an hour?' In most cases, the onlooker will be inclined to say 'Yes'.

Now there *is* a distinctively contextualist diagnosis of what is going on in both cases. When an onlooker is asked to make a knowledge judgment in these contexts, she is not very worried about the possibility that the person to whom knowledge is ascribed has made a mistake because she is very sure that he hasn't; and it is clear, moreover, that the questioner is also not very interested in how easily the knowledge candidate might have erred.[52] Thus, in

---

[50] I note in passing that a few informants claimed to have slightly different intuitions as between 'Which one of the schoolchildren knows what the capital of Austria is?' and 'Which one of the schoolchildren knows that Vienna is the capital of Austria?'

[51] See also Chomsky's (1980) discussion of 'the Spanish pill' and related cases (pp. 92 ff.).

[52] Notice that the verb 'believes', unlike the verb 'knows', does not take embedded questions. Thus it would be cumbersome to replace the question 'Which of the children knows what the capital of Austria is?' with a question using the verb 'believes'. In certain cases this may be part of the explanation why, when the questioner chooses to use 'know' in her question, she may have no real interest in the strength of the subject's epistemic position. Linguists tell me that the fact that the concept of *belief* does not take

effect, the standards associated with the verb 'know' in such a context are extremely low.[53]

While the contextualist may be charitably inclined, she is not compelled to be. Even supposing that the semantic value of the verb 'know' is context-dependent, it does not follow that one is required to take all ordinary knowledge ascriptions as definitive. Here is an analogy:[54] We can all agree that the verb 'tall' is context-dependent. Yet suppose it turned out that you and I are in fact much more inclined to call a person of a particular height 'tall' if he is very thin than if he is not. We would not put this down to context-dependence: whatever the context, if two people have the same height, then either both are tall, or neither is. Rather, we would put this down to a sort of cognitive noise that generates a measure of incompetence in our ascriptions of 'tall'. So, even granting contextualism, it is very much an open question which phenomena of knowledge ascription reveal competent use of a context-dependent predicate, and which are manifestations of incompetence.[55]

As we move towards examining the relevance of contextualism to our original problem, I should make clear that I very much think it a serious mistake to assume that all puzzles connected to closure

embedded questions is stable across languages. This cannot simply be traced to the nonfactivity of that concept, since various other nonfactive attitude verbs ('decide', for example) do take embedded questions. This matter is certainly worthy of fuller exploration.

[53] There are some uses of 'know' that are not even factive. Here is an example from Stewart Cohen: 'The underdog is the guy that everyone knows is going to lose'. Meanwhile, other uses clearly don't require belief: I say of the quiz contestant that he knows the answer when he knows what answer people want to hear but does not believe it himself. Some uses involve inanimate objects as subjects: The car knows when it is nearly out of gas. Which of these uses are handled by an appeal to a unifying context-dependent semantics? For example, are we to say in light of the first case that, contra Lewis, the 'Rule of Actuality' (from Lewis 1996) is sometimes suspended, or instead treat that use of the term as deviant, outside the scope of the core semantics for 'know'? I do not propose to adjudicate such issues on behalf of the contextualist here.

[54] I am grateful to Timothy Williamson here.

[55] Also, assuming that there are cases where false assertions are pragmatically justified, certain ascriptions can be explained away as pragmatically justified falsehoods—so long as a case can be made that the ascriber does not in fact believe the content of those ascriptions.

have their source in the context-dependence of the verb 'know'. To illustrate, let me present three puzzles for which there are rather compelling solutions that do not appeal to ascriber-dependence.

Closure and Junk Knowledge[56]

Suppose there are two newspapers, *The Times* and *The Guardian*, which I trust equally well for the purposes of obtaining soccer information. With good reason: both are extremely reliable in their reporting of soccer results. I look in *The Times* and find a Manchester United victory reported. I trust the report. The report is in fact correct. Under such circumstances, people are inclined to say I know both that *The Times* said that Manchester United won and also that Manchester United won. Let us suppose I also know that *The Guardian* will have reported a result for the Manchester United game. I deduce that either *The Times* and *The Guardian* correctly reported a Manchester United victory or else *The Guardian* made a mistake about the Manchester United result.[57] Suppose, in fact, that, unbeknownst to me, *The Guardian* did make such a mistake. People are not inclined to say I know the above disjunction.

Similar example: People are inclined to say I know I will live a while. Suppose I point to someone who is by all accounts a similarly healthy person but who in fact, by chance, will die in ten minutes. I say: 'Either we will both live a while or else he but not I will die soon'. Even though this disjunction is deducible from 'I will live a while', people are not inclined to say that I know it.

In order to evaluate what is going on here, let us begin by noticing that when information is usefully encoded by a disjunction, one's knowledge of that disjunction is not grounded simply in knowledge of one of the disjuncts. If you tell me that you will go either to Paris or to Rome this summer, my knowledge of that

---

[56] I am grateful for discussions with Jim Pryor here.
[57] There are tricky issues concerning the semantics of 'or' in natural language. The main points that follow do not turn on those issues.

disjunction is not grounded in my knowledge of one or the other of the alternatives. Correlatively, I am primed to do disjunctive syllogism were I to acquire the belief that one of the disjuncts is false. So if I later learn that you have decided not to go to Paris, I will conclude that you will be going to Rome.

Known disjunctions that violate this pattern are special cases of a deviant class. Following Roy Sorensen (1988), let us use the term 'junk disjunctive knowledge' to refer to cases where knowledge of a disjunction is such that, for one of the disjuncts, if one were to come to believe that it is false, that would destroy knowledge of the disjunction.[58,59] But when one is in possession of junk disjunctive knowledge, one is not, for each disjunct, disposed to do disjunctive syllogism upon acquiring a belief in the negation of that disjunct (or at least one ought not to be). On the contrary, one of the disjuncts is such that if one acquires a belief in its negation, one will (or at least ought to) simply throw out the disjunction.[60]

All this suggests an attractive account of our puzzlement. When one balks at the idea that I know that either *The Times* and *The Guardian* correctly reported a Manchester United victory or else *The Guardian* made a mistake, one imagines that I am so situated that, were I to read *The Guardian* and notice it said that Manchester United had lost (or drawn), I would be able to use my disjunctive knowledge to infer that it was *The Guardian* that had made a mistake. It would indeed be absurd to suppose that I am so situated, but it does not follow that I do not know the disjunction. We are apt to confuse useful disjunctive knowledge with junk disjunctive

---

[58] As the Manchester United example illustrates, not all cases of this phenomenon are cases where knowledge of the disjunction is grounded in knowledge of one of the disjuncts.

[59] Hence Addition Closure, discussed in Chapter 1, is not threatened by the Manchester United example.

[60] I admit that there are complications here, related to those besetting nearly any attempt to analyze something in terms of counterfactuals. (Think of finkish dispositions.) I assume that the category of junk knowledge is nevertheless intuitive enough for my current purposes.

knowledge. Having recognized that disjunctive knowledge is not useful, we are prone to think that it is not knowledge at all.

Sorensen notes—following Harman (1973)—that a similar diagnosis can be provided for a puzzle associated with Saul Kripke.[61,62] Suppose that Single-Premise Closure is correct. Then, if I know that p, I can know that all future evidence against p will be misleading. From this we get the paradoxical result that knowledge breeds dogmatism. The puzzle trades on the illicit but natural assumption that knowing that all future evidence against p will be misleading will instill one with a dogmatic disposition to ignore future evidence. This ignores the fact that, were future evidence to appear, it would destroy knowledge of the universal generalization rather than trigger a disposition to apply it to particular cases.[63])

We now have a diagnosis: The original confidence that the disjunction was not known was grounded in a fairly natural kind of confusion. But none of this required appeal to the context-dependence of 'know'. It is thus far from clear that contextualist semantics is the key to understanding what is going on in this particular case.[64]

Easy Knowledge and Closure[65]

Here is a second puzzle. I wake up one morning. I am handed a ball. It might seem clear that I do not *know* before looking that:

(1) If the ball looks red then the ball is red.

---

[61] The puzzle has a clear affinity with one raised by Paul Grice: 'If it is proper for me to say "I know that there is cheese on the table," I shall have to claim (if I am asked) to know that future observations on the part of myself and of others will not render the proposition there is cheese on the table doubtful. But we are reluctant under pressure to make such claims to knowledge of propositions about the future' (1989*b*: 153).

[62] I also note in passing that the remarks in this section make trouble for Audi's (1988: 77–8) argument against closure.

[63] Similar considerations may be brought to bear against Unger (1975: 33).

[64] I am thus unsympathetic to Lewis's way with Kripke's puzzle. See Lewis (1996: 565–7).

[65] See Cohen (1988, 1999, 2002).

Contextualism and the Puzzle

Equivalently:

> (2) It is not the case that: (the ball looks red and the ball is not red).[66,67]

To suppose that I knew such a thing upon waking and being handed a ball, without looking at the ball, would be to concede too much by way of contingent a priori knowledge.[68] Or so it would seem. Suppose that I observe the ball, which is in fact a red thing that (not surprisingly) looks red. It is natural to suppose that I now come to know that the ball is red and also that it looks red. One can now deduce (2).[69] But it seems intuitively very strange that one can know (2) upon seeing a thing that looks red when one does not know (2) beforehand.[70] One's epistemic space before looking at the ball has something like the following structure: The probability of the ball's looking red is N. The conditional probability of something's not being red on its looking red is M. N will be pretty small (since there are all sorts of possible colors for the ball) and M will also be pretty small (since it is unlikely that it will look red and not be red). Let us suppose for example that N is .1 and M is .1. The

---

[66] Of course, since (1) is an indicative conditional, this may be too quick. If so, focus on (2) at the outset.

[67] Here is a testimony version of the puzzle: I wake up one morning. Prior to my reading the morning paper it might seem pretty clear that I do not know whether or not the newspaper correctly reported the Manchester United score. Suppose I read in *The Times* that Manchester United won, thereby coming to know that Manchester United won. I also, presumably, know that *The Times* said that Manchester United won. I now deduce: I now deduce that it is not the case that: *The Times* says Manchester United won and Manchester United didn't win. Analogous remarks apply.

[68] Or at least relatively a priori knowledge: The knowledge need not be purely a priori, since I will likely have had prior experience of red things and of the testimony of others regarding red things. It thus might be useful to consider a version of the case where this episode takes place early in a being's life. The puzzle will still proceed in the same way once one concedes that such a being can know that something is red upon perceptual exposure to it.

[69] As stated, the puzzle relies on Multi-Premise Closure, but since no one will quibble with my knowledge of the conjunction 'The ball looks red and the ball is red' in a case where I know each of those conjuncts, the difference between Multi-Premise Closure and Single-Premise Closure is immaterial in this case.

[70] The intuitive strangeness is brought out very well by Cohen (2002).

epistemic probability of (2) will be 1 minus the product of N and M—in this case, .99. What happens upon my looking at the red thing? On one natural model I ought to update the epistemic probability associated with the proposition that the ball is red by conditionalization—where the new piece of evidence is that the ball looks red, and the relevant conditional probability is the old conditional probability that the ball is red on its looking red. Thus, after looking, the epistemic probability of the ball's being red is .9. Assuming the epistemic probability of the ball's looking red is now 1, the epistemic probability of (2) after looking is .9. In other words, it has gone down.[71] On such a model, it is extremely hard to see how one can know (2) after looking but not before looking, since looking at the ball provided one with evidence against (2).

Taking seriously the idea that knowledge provides epistemic probability 1, one might opt for a different model: Before looking the epistemic probability of (2) is .99 but after looking it is 1 (in the case where one looks at a red-looking ball that is in fact red). This brings about a curious violation of van Fraassen's Reflection constraint on rationality,[72] the idea that one's expected epistemic probability should match one's current epistemic probability. By hypothesis, the epistemic probability for (2) before looking was .99. One expects that if the ball doesn't look red, one will know that it does not look red[73]—so that conditional on the ball's not looking red, one's expected epistemic probability for (2) will be 1. One expects that if the ball looks red and it is red, then one will know it is red. So conditional on its looking red, it is .9 that one's

---

[71] Of course, the epistemic probability of the ball's being red has gone up. If p entails q, it is still quite possible for the epistemic probability of p to go up while the epistemic probability of q goes down.

[72] I am extremely grateful for discussions with Timothy Williamson here. I am relying on van Fraassen's (1997) discussion of Reflection.

[73] For simplicity's sake I abstract throughout from certain complications—e.g. (i) that it is a borderline case of looking red and so looks red but not knowably so, or (ii) that shades of looking red have differential evidential relevance, or (iii) that even though the ball looks red with no clues to the contrary, one does not know it to be red because of the presence of balls in the areas that look red but are not red. The central issues would be the same even if those complications were to be accommodated.

epistemic probability for (2) will be 1 (given that M is .1). And one expects that if it looks red and is not red, then one will still have plenty of evidence that it is red (even though one will not know that it is red). So one's expected epistemic probability for (2) is greater than .99. Generalizing: One's current epistemic probability, C, for (2) is 1 minus the product N and M, yet one's expected evidential probability for (2) is the sum of C with the evidential probability that one would expect to have for (2) after looking, conditional on the ball's looking red and not being red—call that E. Since it is quite clear that under those circumstances, one would be in no position to know that the ball isn't red, it is clear enough that E is greater than zero. So one's expected epistemic probability is greater than one's current epistemic probability. Reflection fails.[74]

Under scrutiny, then, it is not clear at all how to think of the epistemic dynamics of this humdrum case. One view might be the skeptical one: Since one cannot know (2) in advance and one's epistemic situation with regard to (2) does not improve, one cannot know (2) after looking. Assuming closure, this entails that one cannot know that a thing is red by looking at it. A second view embraces contingent a priori knowledge.[75] A third view tells us that the lesson to be learned is that there is widespread failure of Reflection and, indeed, that Reflection is not a correct normative guide to our epistemic lives.[76] It is not my present task to adjudicate.[77] The point I wish to press is that it is not clear that context-

---

[74] It is not surprising that Reflection should fail when one anticipates brainwashing or some other kind of cognitive tampering. But it is far more surprising that it should fail in a run of the mill case of perceptual knowledge.

[75] See Hawthorne (2002*b*).

[76] For a further alternative, see Cohen's (2002) discussion of 'bootstrapping'.

[77] Nor should we assume that all cases will be treated the same. I find the following example suggestive. Suppose a creature lives in a world where nonred things that appear red are more likely to occur in dry environments than in humid environments. The creature's conditional credence in a given thing's being red on it looking red is .7. Now the creature has no real conception of humidity, but is so constituted that, when he sees an apparently red flower in a humid environment, the humidity causally induces a confidence boost, so that in fact he becomes .9 confident that the thing is red. (Of course, this aspect of his constitution is adaptive—we should admire it from a biological point of view. I also see no good reason to critique it from an epistemic point

ualist semantics provides a solution to the puzzle that this case raises. If one takes the first option, its inapplicability is manifest. If one takes something like the second option, one *might* try to combine it with a dose of contextualism. Perhaps when we consider our epistemic position with regard to (2) in advance of looking, our epistemic standards are somehow higher—this being a special case, perhaps, of our having higher standards for knowledge in aprioristic settings. Or (more likely), when we explicitly consider (2), that tends to raise certain possibilities of error to salience in such a way that our standards go up. However, one who embraces the second option might instead think that such contextualist add-ons were a distraction: The truth of the matter, one might insist, is that we—where the 'we' includes at least contemporary philosophers—radically underestimate the capacity of human beings for contingent a priori knowledge. One who took this view might think that, having learnt to live without lofty requirements for empirical knowledge, we have forgotten to make analogous adjustments in the a priori realm. On that view, the invocation of contextualism is a misguided attempt to try to get ourselves off the hook. Meanwhile, if one takes the third option, then the key to resolution will be to see our way to discarding Reflection: contextualist semantics will be neither here nor there. In sum, while I do not wish to insist that contextualism is irrelevant to this puzzle, we ought not to be sanguine that it will offer the insight required to see our way through it.

Question-Sensitivity

When someone is asked whether *p*, our intuitions as to whether that person knows that *p* will be highly sensitive to the contrastive

of view. Note that even if one is a fan of conditionalization, the creature need not be indicted on this score so long as one treats his .9 credence that he sees a red thing as part of his body of new evidence.) Suppose, prior to looking, the creature has credence .5 concerning whether the flower was going to be red. The credence that he assigns to the conditional 'The flower looks red ⊃ The flower is red' will increase upon looking. Much of our own epistemic life may (*mutatis mutandis*) be like that, given our own failure to appreciate adaptive cues that guide our perceptual systems.

structure of the question itself.[78] Suppose I show someone a photograph of an African elephant and I ask 'Is it a photo of an African elephant or a photo of an African ostrich?' Unless they are completely unfamiliar with all animal species, I will credit them with knowing that it is a photo of an African elephant when they select the first disjunct. If I ask instead: 'Is it a photo of an African elephant or a photo of an Indian elephant?' then I will credit them with knowledge when they choose the first disjunct only if they have a certain degree of pachydermal expertise. Finally, if I ask 'Is it a photo of an African elephant or a photo of an Indian elephant touched up to look like a photo of an African elephant?' then even they know a great deal about animals and choose the first disjunct, I not will credit them with knowing that it is a photo of an African elephant.

Many would reckon our intuitions about these cases to provide serious motivation for a contextualist account of 'knows'. But a more conservative and highly plausible diagnosis is apt to be overlooked. What can easily be missed is the fact that the very asking of a question may provide one with new evidence regarding the subject matter at hand. Two points in this connection: First, if someone asks us whether p or q, then, *ceteris paribus*, we can presume that he or she knows that one of p or q is the case.[79] Something would be amiss in my asking someone whether p or q is the case if in fact neither obtains. Thus, in asking whether p or q, I represent myself as knowing the disjunction of p or q. In the normal case, then, a question whether p or q serves to transmit knowledge of that disjunction to an interlocutor who did not already possess it.[80]

---

[78] I am grateful for conversations with Jonathan Schaffer here, though I do not expect that he would agree with all of my conclusions.

[79] Of course there are some cases where a mixture of context and intonation-contour indicates that the questioner does not represent himself as knowing the disjunction. Sometimes 'Is it F or G?' may have the force of 'Is it F or G or something else that I haven't thought of?' Our epistemic intuitions about such a case will be different from those elicited by the more normal case. (Thanks to Ernest Sosa here.)

[80] Similarly for unstressed material in questions, where background information is presupposed by the question. Thus if I asked whether Bill stole money from *Barclays* Bank (where the italicized word is stressed), I convey the information that Bill stole

Suppose then that I cannot distinguish African from Indian elephants. Still, if someone asks me 'Is it an African elephant or an African ostrich?', I can come to know, thanks to the very asking of the question plus my observation of the photo and background knowledge of animals, that the photograph depicts an African elephant.[81] Second, the maxims of good conversation tell us not to ask whether *p* unless there it is reason to worry that not-*p*—at least in the sort of context where one asks a question in order to acquire information rather than, say, merely to test one's interlocutor's knowledge.[82] So, for example, I would be an uncooperative conversational participant if I asked whether someone had been guilty of infidelity in a case where it was evident to me that the person had not. In the very asking of the question I would provide my interlocutor with reason to think that I was reasonably worried—especially in the case where the questioner was more familiar with the subject that the person questioned. Such is the situation with the

money from some bank. If the interlocutor did not already know this, the asking of the question serves as a channel for knowing it. (Relevant here is work by Herberger and others in linguistics on the role of focus in questions.) Of course, in the typical instance of what I have called 'the normal case', knowledge is not transmitted by the asking of the question because the presupposed material is common ground to the interlocutors.

[81] The point could, if one wished, be couched in the framework offered by Robert Stalnaker (1999), though I myself am somewhat suspicious of the project of using sets of metaphysically possible worlds to model epistemic states of information. As Stalnaker conceives of things, a conversation enjoys at any given time a 'context set', where a world belongs to the context set iff it is not mutually known to be nonactual by participants in the conversation. The effect of an unchallenged assertion that *p* is to shrink the context set to *p*-worlds. Similarly, then, the effect of an unchallenged question whether *p* or *q* is to shrink the context set to *p*-or-*q* worlds.

[82] Note that we naturally think of the 'Elephant or ostrich?' question as a test question and hence not as one that is asked in a situation where the questioner is representing herself as not knowing the answer. If one emphasized that the latter situation prevailed, one might be more intuitively pulled (depending on the details of the case) towards a reaction that treated the very asking of the question as a source of skeptical doubt. (Here's a case which involves neither a test question nor provocation to skeptical doubt: you are looking at a stack of photos from my African safari (which I took after I won the lottery), and I am sitting across the room from you. At a certain point in your perusal of the photos I hear you laugh out loud at a funny image, and, knowing which pair of photographs would provoke a laugh, I ask 'Is that the African elephant or the African ostrich?') Thanks to Tamar Gendler here.

photograph. In the case envisaged, the questioner is evidently acquainted with the photograph. A cooperative speaker would not in that situation ask about the possibility of a touch-up unless there was reason to worry. Thus in hearing the question, the hearer acquires evidence to the effect that there is a real danger that the photograph has been touched up. Supposing that the photograph has not been touched up, the person questioned gets misleading evidence that it has. But this is enough to destroy knowledge. No wonder then that we withhold knowledge attributions in such a case: even supposing the person previously knew that the photograph was of an African elephant, asking the question provides misleading evidence that destroys the knowledge. As with the previous two cases, there is reason to think that this initially puzzling epistemic phenomenon can be elegantly explained without invoking the semantic mechanisms proposed by the contextualist.

2.3   Contextualism and Lotteries

Whatever its applicability to the puzzles just discussed, it may be felt that contextualism offers an altogether compelling solution to those puzzles that comprise our main focus. In broad outlines, it is easy enough to see how the solution works. Suppose A says of a person of modest means 'He knows that he won't have enough money to go on an African safari'. In this context A, the ascriber, may well succeed in expressing a truth. That is, the relation—call it 'K₁'—that is expressed by the verb 'know' in this context may well be one that holds between the subject of the ascription B and the proposition that B will not have enough money to go on an African safari. And this may be true even if the subject B has a lottery ticket in his pocket. Bearing in mind the salience constraint, we can say that at least part of the explanation as to why the relation picked out has that feature is that A is not, in that context, taking seriously the possibility that B will win the lottery. (A more complete story would seek to provide some sketch of how it is that A is perfectly within his rights in not taking that possibility seriously—in short, of what keeps that possibility from being relevant in that context.) Suppose that on the occasion of the ascription, B also happens to believe that he will not win the lottery. The contextualist will be happy to allow that K_1 also holds between B and the proposition that he, B, will not win the lottery.[83] What now if A goes on to consider the question 'Does B know whether or not B will win the lottery?' In this setting the possibility of B's winning the lottery becomes psychologically salient and A will likely begin taking that possibility seriously. We now have a context shift. In this new context the verb 'know' will express a new relation—call it 'K_2'— such that B does not K_2 that B will not win the lottery and does not K_2 that B will not have enough money to go on an African safari.[84] What might appear to be a failure of closure gets explained away as a context shift.

The solution easily generalizes. Suppose A says of B 'B knows that B will be in work on Monday'. Suppose A is not taking seriously—and nor ought she—the possibility that B will have a fatal heart attack and so on. In her mouth, the verb 'know' may express a relation that holds between B and the proposition that B will be in work on Monday and also (by closure, and assuming that the relevant deduction has been performed[85]) between B and the proposition that B will not have a fatal heart attack. (And this is so even if B is taking seriously the possibility of a fatal heart attack, since the salience constraint applies to the ascriber. This point bears emphasis: If the *subject* is attending to the lottery proposition, and

---

[83] That is not to say that such a conclusion is forced upon the contextualist in every such case. Perhaps the subject hasn't formed a belief about this matter. Perhaps he does believe it but on bizarre and unacceptable grounds ...

[84] As Stewart Cohen has pointed out to me, instead of saying that 'know' expresses different relations from context to context, one might instead try saying that 'know' expresses the same three-place relation between a person, a proposition, and a standard, and that what varies across contexts is the value of the standard index.

[85] Or assuming that the proposition is believed on a basis that offers no special indictment of it. I do not assume that the deduction adverted to in the text is the standard route to belief in lottery propositions.

taking it seriously, this need not indict the knowledge ascription, at least according to standard contextualist accounts.[86]) If A, the ascriber, goes on to take seriously the possibility of B's having fatal heart attack, she will have put herself in a context where the verb 'know', if deployed by her, would express a different relation, one that does not hold between B and the proposition that B will be in work on Monday, nor between B and the proposition that B will not have a heart attack before Monday.

The appeal of the solution is clear enough. The contextualist allows that ordinary knowledge ascriptions often come out true. And he allows that ordinary claims to the effect that lottery propositions are not known can come out true as well. And he explains away the apparent threat to closure provided by the original puzzles. The resolution of conflicting intuitions is, at least prima facie, extremely compelling.

Some details need to be added for the picture to be rounded out. Note in particular that the contextualist approach suggests that the original statement of epistemic closure was insufficiently general. Recall the principle of epistemic closure for knowledge:

> *Multi-Premise Closure* (MPC). Necessarily, if S knows $p_1, \ldots, p_n$, competently deduces q, and thereby comes to believe q, while retaining knowledge of $p_1, \ldots, p_n$ throughout, then S knows q.

The single-premise version read as follows:

> *Single-Premise Closure* (SPC). Necessarily, if S knows p, competently deduces q, and thereby comes to believe q, while retaining knowledge of p throughout, then S knows q.

By the contextualist's lights, the context in which she is situated determines which propositions are expressed by asserting these

---

[86] Of course, one could contrive a version of contextualism which allowed, among other things, that attending by the subject did indict the knowledge ascription. But this in turn will make it less clear that contextualism (even if true) is the key to our puzzles. More on this in Chapter 4.

principles. Supposing the relation K_1 is expressed by 'know' in that context, the contextualist, in putting forward MPC, asserts that:

> Necessarily, if S K_1s $p_1, \ldots, p_n$ competently deduces q, and thereby comes to believe q, while retaining K_1 of $p_1, \ldots, p_n$ throughout, then S K_1s q.

Suppose someone else is in a different context, expressing another relation—K_2—by 'know'. In asserting his version of MPC (or SPC), the contextualist doesn't manage to offer any constraint on *that* person's use of 'know'. With this in mind, the contextualist might wish to endorse a metalinguistic version of the closure principles, one with more generality than mere object language acceptance of them, namely:

> *Metalinguistic Multi-Premise Closure* (MMPC). For any context, any sentence of the form 'Necessarily, if S knows $p_1, \ldots, p_n$, competently deduces q, and thereby comes to believe q, while retaining knowledge of $p_1, \ldots, p_n$ throughout, then S knows q' is true in that context

and

> *Metalinguistic Single-Premise Closure* (MSPC). For any context, any sentence of the form 'Necessarily, if S knows p, competently deduces q, and thereby comes to believe q, while retaining knowledge of p throughout, then S knows q' is true in that context.[87]

Note that the solution offered to our puzzle requires the contextualist to endorse at least MSPC. Let us suppose that he is happy to do so. Let us assume further that insofar as the contextualist finds the MPC intuition compelling, he will endorse MMPC as well.

---

[87] Note that I assume that the contextualist will allow that a sentence can be true at a context even if it is not asserted at a context. At a context, 'know' will have a particular semantic value, which will in turn generate a semantic value for sentences that are unasserted at that context. (This is crucial, since a sentence may serve as the vehicle of belief at a time, even if it is not asserted.)

Certain other details remain unresolved. For example: are there contexts in which the question of lottery tickets is explicitly raised but where it is still appropriate not to take seriously the possibility of winning the lottery? As we have seen, there do seem to be circumstances in which people flat-out assert that they will not win the lottery: I'm busy trying to figure out how to save my business. You say 'You may win the lottery'. I say 'You know that's not going to happen. There are over 10 million tickets sold and only one big winner'.[88] Perhaps the contextualist will allow that insofar as one succeeds in not taking the possibility of lottery victory seriously, one can in certain contexts ascribe knowledge that lottery loss will occur (to oneself or others), even once lotteries are explicitly raised. It seems to me, indeed, that the contextualist should allow this: If someone can raise the possibility of my having enough money to go on an African safari and yet I can disregard it—and acceptably so—why should it not be possible for me to do the same when someone raises the possibility of my winning the lottery?[89] Why should it be inevitable that I take the falsity of the lottery proposition seriously once the question is raised? Perhaps it is a psychological fact about us that we are more inclined to take certain possibilities seriously once raised, but there is no inevitability here.

Cohen (1988) was to my knowledge the first to propose a contextualist solution to the puzzles with which we began. Similar proposals have since been made by DeRose (1995), Lewis (1996), and other contemporary contextualists. Fine print aside, the solution offered is the one articulated above. But is it the right one? In what follows, I shall present a series of problems for the contextualist. They are not intended to conclusively show that a contextualist approach is doomed. But they ought to at least provide us with

[88] I might say in passing that Lewis, in conversation, did wish to allow for contexts in which I am entitled to flat-out assert that I will lose the lottery and, correlatively, where I correctly self-ascribe knowledge of a lottery loss. I am not clear how the machinery of 'Elusive Knowledge' would accommodate this.

[89] It is not as if there is, objectively, a greater chance of the lottery proposition being false than the ordinary proposition being false. DeRose, of course, will point to facts about tracking as the crucial disanalogy. I have already explained why I find this unpromising.

sufficient motivation to look carefully at alternative treatments before settling upon a contextualist treatment of our focal puzzles.

2.4 Assertion and Practical Reasoning[90]

In Chapter 1 we noticed some intuitive connections between knowledge, assertion, and practical reasoning. We saw that, at least for many contexts, it is not acceptable to outright assert that one will lose a lottery, and that this seems best explained by the fact that to assert such a thing would be to represent oneself as knowing it. A similar diagnosis is appropriate for the other lottery propositions in our original cases. For example, it seems (at least in many contexts) inappropriate to flat-out assert that one will not be one of the apparently healthy people to suffer a fatal heart attack this year, and the reason seems to be the same. Turning to practical reasoning, we saw that, intuitively, the fact that one does not know a lottery proposition seems to be what prohibits one from using it as a premise in one's deliberations about how to act. A paradigm case: One is offered one cent for a lottery ticket that cost a dollar, in a 10,000 ticket lottery with a $5,000 prize, and reasons as follows

> The ticket is a loser.
> So if I keep the ticket I will get nothing.
> But if I sell the ticket I will get a penny.
> So I should sell the ticket.[91]

Similarly, consider someone who offers to sell you a ticket in the same lottery for a cent, and you decline on the basis of your 'knowledge' that the ticket will lose.[92]

---

[90] In writing this section, I am particularly grateful to Timothy Williamson for helpful conversations.

[91] Of course, I am making the simplifying assumption that one's only options are to keep the ticket or sell it for a cent. (If one can sell the ticket to someone else for a dime, that will make difference.)

[92] Suppose the quantum-mechanical chance of the desk evolving into a desk façade in the next two seconds is a trillion to one. Then I think we have analogous intuitions if

It is natural, then, to think that there is some deep association between facts about knowledge and facts concerning the propriety of assertion and practical reasoning. What I want to draw attention to here is that, owing to the purported ascriber-dependence of 'know', contextualism seems to disconnect facts about knowledge from these normative facts. And this is because the relevant normative facts do *not* seem to be ascriber-dependent. Here is a case to consider, described from the vantage point of contextualist semantics. I am in a context where I can truly say 'You know you will not have enough money to go on an African safari this year'. As a matter of fact (unbeknownst to me) you have from this deduced and thereby come to believe that you will not win the lottery.[93] Having formed such a belief, you assert:

(1) I will not win the lottery.

I do not hear you. In my context the following ascription is correct:

(2) You know you will have not enough money to go on an African safari this year.

Assuming SPC, (3) is also true relative to my context:

(3) Anything that you have competently deduced from knowing that you will not have enough money to go on an African safari this year and thereby come to believe is something you know as well.[94]

But it may well be that it was outright inappropriate for you to have asserted what you did five minutes ago (namely, (1)).[95] More carefully, it seems clear enough that:

---

we are offered a contract such that, once accepted, one person in the universe gets a penny if the desk doesn't turn into a façade and ten trillion people lose their house if it does.

[93] I do not pretend that this is a normal path to such a belief.

[94] I have dropped the retention clause for ease of exposition.

[95] The argument doesn't require that (1) is *always* unassertable when made in advance of the drawing and without insider information.

(4) You ought not to have asserted what you asserted five minutes ago

is true in my mouth (whether or not I know it is true).

Now we normally suppose that the sentence 'There are things people know but ought not to assert' can only be true for such pragmatic reasons as that asserting the sentence would hurt someone's feelings, or that it would be uninformative to assert what other people know already.[96] Embellishments like the following seem strange:

(5) There are things people know but ought not to assert because their epistemic position is not strong enough with respect to those things.

But (1) was unassertable for epistemic, not pragmatic, reasons. Thus contextualism delivers the disturbing result that (5) is true.

Even more obviously, suppose my standards for 'know' are *higher* than S's, so that S stands in the relation that he expresses by 'know' to some *p* that he asserts, but that he does not stand in the relation that *I* express by 'know' to *p*. Assuming this contextualist semantic profile, it is rather tempting to think that S had every right to assert *p*. Similarly for many other subject–proposition pairs. Thus, we have the result that the following sentence is true in my mouth:

(6) People often flat-out assert things that they do not know to be true but are not thereby subject to criticism.

Yet it sounds very odd.[97] The link between knowledge and assertability has been severed.

For analogous reasons, if a contextualist stance is adopted, then the relation that someone expresses by 'know' may hold between a subject and various claims that she deploys in practical reasoning in

---

[96] There is also the possibility, raised at the end of Chapter 1, that a belief that one does not know blocks entitlement to assert. I set that to one side here, since it is not very relevant to the cases with which we are concerned.

[97] The reader will note some analogy here between the contextualist and a version of error skepticism discussed in Chapter 3.

paradigmatically unacceptable ways. Suppose I am not paying attention to lotteries. Even if you use the lottery proposition as a premise in reasoning that results in a one cent sale, it seems that the sentence 'You are reasoning from known premises' is nonetheless true in my mouth. Of course if I, the ascriber, pay attention to the reasoning and begin to worry about lotteries, then things might change. But until that happens, your reasoning will count as reasoning from known premises. Meanwhile, suppose that I have high standards, high enough so that 'You do not know that you are going on vacation' is true in my mouth. Still, it would seem that you may be in a practical environment where it is perfectly appropriate (by anyone's standards) to use the proposition that you are going on vacation as a premise in your practical reasoning. Thus the following would seem to be true in my mouth:

(7) You should rely on propositions that you don't know to be true in your practical reasoning.

This result is surprising, to say the least. (We shall pursue the topic of practical reasoning in considerably more detail in Chapter 4.)

As far as the contextualist is concerned, the notion that know-ledge serves as the standard of acceptability for assertions and practical syllogisms will stand in need of important refinement. Let us consider the case of assertion from a contextualist perspec-tive. If I have low standards and you have high standards, is it the property expressed by 'knowledge' in your mouth or the property expressed by 'knowledge' in my mouth that is the norm for your assertions? Plausibly, it is the former: If your assertions don't pass the standards for 'knowledge' in your mouth, then you shouldn't be making them. Correlatively, you should count as proper assertions of mine that can truly be labeled 'knowledge' by me even though they do not pass your high standards. Given this, the contextualist cannot quite claim that knowledge is the norm of assertion. (To do so would be to confuse knowledge with the property expressed by the verb 'know' by this or that subject.) Rather, the norm of assertion varies as the content of the verb 'knows' varies from assertor to assertor: S should assert that *p* only if S stands in the relation expressed by 'knows' in *his* mouth to *p*. Similarly for practical reasoning: on a given occasion, it may be that S should use a premise she does not know in her reasoning because the premise still passes the standards for 'knowledge' in her mouth.

The point remains, however, that there are a variety of sentences that seem intuitively incorrect (see above) but that, by the lights of contextualist semantics, come out true. That is surely a cost of the view. Moreover, is it really plausible that our conviction that knowledge provides normative constraints on assertion and practical reasoning rests on a sort of use–mention confusion? Notice that our contextualist grants that there are determinate facts about when an assertion is proper. But she then goes on to divorce the question of whether a subject has knowledge from these normative facts. Isn't any such conceptual divorce strained?[98] There is an interconnected cluster of worries here: Why should it be that 'know' is semantically highly sensitive to what is salient to the ascriber and to the interests of the ascriber, but that various related normative notions like 'what is assertable' or 'what one ought to believe'—are not context-sensitive in that way? Why should 'know' be semantically sensitive to the ascriber's interests and attention when 'what is assertable' or 'what one ought to believe' are not? (The point is made especially pressing by the fact that—as far as I can tell—interests and attention induce just as much conflict in the area of the relevant normative discourse as with knowledge ascription itself.)[99]

---

[98] There is a general tendency among contextualists to take a more invariantist attitude to normative predicates. Consider, for example, Lewis, who helps himself to facts about what 'one ought to believe' in his discussion, but does not consider at all that claims about what one ought to believe might themselves be highly context-sensitive. See Lewis (1996: 555–6). I am grateful to Richard Fumerton for drawing my attention to this.

[99] I suspect that *if* there is good reason to treat 'know' in a way very different to normative terms concerning assertion and practical reasoning, it is because knowledge ascriptions do double duty in a way that the latter concepts do not: after all, knowledge

Perhaps on reflection the contextualist will propose that the latter are highly ascriber-dependent as well. But such a strategy makes it far more difficult to theorize about the contextual parameters governing 'know' than contemporary contextualists have heretofore acknowledged: in describing how context fixes the semantic value of 'know', one could not appeal to what have been assumed to be context-insensitive normative predicates.[100] But the difficulties are deeper. Assertability conditions and propriety conditions for practical reasoning just don't seem to vary in that way.[101] The practical reasoning considered above is inappropriate, regardless of what an ascriber is attending to, and parallel remarks apply to the propriety of flat-out assertions of lottery propositions (in the setting envisaged). An additional problem is that we expect normative claims to be motivating. If I say to someone 'You ought to do X' and he takes me to be correct, then I expect his judgment to have direct bearing on his (intended) behavior. Were normative claims ascriber-dependent in their truth conditions, it is hard to see how someone's belief in the correctness of normative claims made by others would play a self-regulating role for him.[102]

Given that the relevant normative truths about assertability and practical reasoning seem to be ascriber-insensitive, then why not maintain an intimate tie between the facts of knowledge and the facts of propriety, making the semantics of 'know' ascriber-insensitive

ascriptions both attempt to keep track on who is in a position to assert what (and, relatedly, who to trust) and also who is in a position to use this or that in their deliberations. (I am grateful for a conversation with Keith DeRose here.)

[100] Of course this is only a problem if one uses (rather than merely mentions) normative predicates in one's favored contextualist story. (There is also the option of an account that does without use or mention of normative predicates altogether.)

[101] As noted earlier, we are in general somewhat intolerant of rampant contextualism about normative discourse. When some of us think hard about the starving in the Third World, we are disposed to say of some fairly wealthy citizen S 'S should be giving a lot more money to charity'. When others of us put our attention to other uses, we may be disposed to say 'There is nothing wrong with S's level of charitable donations'. Think how unhappy most philosophers would be with a contextualist treatment of the prima facie conflict according to which each party speaks the truth on account of discrepancies in what is salient to the various ascribers.

[102] I am grateful for a conversation with Michael Smith here.

as well? A test case:[103] You are in the house being asked where your car is. I am outside looking at your car. I have what the contextualist describes as 'pretty high standards' for 'know'; you have what he describes as 'lower standards'. I am thus happy to claim that you do not know where your car is. I am of course happy to claim that I know where your car is, since I am looking right at it, which is good enough, by my standards, to know. I hear you flat-out assert 'My car is parked outside'. Insofar as I am genuinely convinced that you do not know, am I not convinced that you shouldn't flat-out assert that your car is outside? Of course, I may not think you have committed a really egregious act. But if I really am convinced that you do not know where your car is, I will reckon you a little out of line to flat-out assert that it is outside when asked. (Similarly, for example, if I am convinced that X's inductive evidence does not enable him to know that Y will show up for a conference, I will think it a little out of line for X to flat-out assert that Y will show up when asked.) If these convictions really do march in step,[104] then it would seem that contextualism about 'know' puts a good deal of pressure towards a similar contextualism about 'ought to assert'. But insofar as the latter is intolerable, contextualists are left with a real problem. These issues obviously merit further investigation. For now, let us agree that contextualism threatens to disrupt the somewhat intuitive links between knowledge, assertion, and practical reasoning. This is certainly a cost for the view.

2.5 Knowledge and Objective Chance

It is natural to suppose that knowledge of objective chances constrains epistemic probability. As Lewis (1999: 228) notes, 'Whatever

---

[103] I am grateful to Stewart Cohen here.
[104] In further support of this, note that if I think that you are in general entitled to flat-out assert propositions that you do not know, then I will have some considerable

makes it true that the chance of decay is 50% must also, if known, make it rational to believe to degree 50% that the decay will occur.'[105] This is the thought behind what Lewis calls 'the Principal Principle', which consists of the following equation on rational credence:

$$C(A/E) = P(A)$$

where A is a proposition, E specifies the present chance of the proposition and contains no extra 'inadmissible information about future history', and P is a function that gives the present chance of all propositions. The following weaker principle will serve our purposes:[106]

> *The Objective Chance Principle.* If at t, S knows that there is a nonzero objective chance that p at t (where p supervenes on the intrinsic facts about the future relative to t), then, at t, there is nonzero epistemic probability for S that p.[107]

(The principle will have to be restricted to exclude clairvoyants, if there are any, since they may have 'inadmissible evidence'.) The Objective Chance Principle is, prima facie, quite intuitive.[108]

---

inclination to trust you about things that I think you do not know. This threatens to disrupt the plausible idea that, in general, A should only trust B's testimony that p insofar as A thinks that B knows p. (I am grateful to conversations with Stewart Cohen here.)

[105] 'Chance' as Lewis uses it here is glossed as 'objective single case probability: for instance, the 50% probability that a particular tritium atom will decay sometime in the next 12.26 years... If there were no believers, or if our total evidence came from misleadingly unrepresentative samples, that wouldn't affect chance in any way' (1999: 227).

[106] I am grateful for discussions with Daniel Nolan here.

[107] It is a further issue, of course, whether the proper notion of epistemic probability links it in a straightforward way to rational degree of confidence. I set that issue to one side here.

[108] Outraged readers should clear their heads and just run through the inference: There is an objective chance that p will happen. Therefore, p might happen. If the principle is incorrect, then there should be an epistemic reading of the conclusion according to which the inference is faulty. But no such reading occurs to us.

We noted earlier that it is plausible to suppose that if *p* has some nonzero epistemic probability at *t* for S, then S does not know that not-*p* at *t*. But if we combine that claim with the Objective Chance Principle, we can derive:

> *The Chance-Knowledge Principle.* If at *t*, S knows that there is a nonzero objective chance that *p* at *t* (where *p* supervenes on the intrinsic facts about the future relative to *t*), then, at *t*, S does not know that not-*p*.[109]

The contextualist, like everyone else, will wish to accommodate principles about knowledge that are compelling. She may thus wish to endorse this principle. In endorsing it, the contextualist will of course be using the verb 'know'. Which proposition she expresses by the sentence that articulates the principle will thus depend in part on the context in which 'know' is being used. For reasons analogous to those raised in connection with closure, the contextualist may thus wish also to endorse the more general metalinguistic principle:

> *The Metalinguistic Chance-Knowledge Principle.* For every context, any sentence of the form 'If at *t*, S knows that there is a non-zero objective chance that *p* at *t* (where *p* supervenes on the intrinsic facts about the future relative to *t*), then, at *t*, S does not know that not-*p*' is true at that context.

But if the contextualist does endorse this principle, she will quickly discover a tension between it and her preferred diagnosis of our puzzles. Consider versions of the puzzle that deployed quantum mechanics and thus considerations of objective chance.[110] Suppose in a context, the standards for 'know' are not too exacting. It would

---

[109] An even stronger principle *might* be advocated, namely: If at *t* there is a nonzero objective chance that *p*, where *p* supervenes on the intrinsic facts about the future relative to *t*, then, at *t*, S does not know that not-*p*. This principle, combined with an indeterministic physics, yields skepticism about undetermined future events as a corollary.

[110] At least on those interpretations of quantum mechanics where the wave function is treated as describing objective probability.

seem that in such a context, people can count as knowing various (true) deliverances of our best physics and, in particular, that for pretty much any ordinary proposition p that exclusively concerns the future, there is an objective chance that not-p. But if we now hold fixed the metalinguistic version of the Chance-Knowledge Principle, such people will not express a truth by 'I know that p' in that context.[111] The contextualist's motivating idea is that, thanks to contexts with inexacting standards, knowledge ascriptions often come out as true. But if we cleave to the very intuitive idea that knowing that there is some objective chance that not-p is incompatible with knowing that p, we shall find it difficult as contextualists to make good on that motivating idea, at least when it comes to propositions about the future. As one would anticipate, the same kind of problem will make trouble for any nonskeptical resolution of our puzzles. My point here is that the thesis of context-dependence for 'know' does not appear to offer any special escape route.

2.6   The Threat from Conjunction Introduction[112]

The contextualist's strategy, as I have described it thus far, is to preserve the truth of ordinary knowledge ascriptions in combination with closure by appropriate appeal to context shifts. Can this do all the work? That is far from clear. Suppose Joe believes that Alfred will not have enough money to go on an African safari this year. And suppose that, on similar grounds, he believes that Bertha will not have enough money for such a trip. And on similar grounds

---

[111] As Cian Dorr pointed out to me, perhaps the best tactic for the contextualist is to explain away the relevant intuitions via a weaker principle, namely that sentences of the form 'I know that p and there is an objective chance that not-p' are never assertable because the very saying (or entertaining) of such a sentence makes salient a counterpossibility to the situation described by 'p'.

[112] This section borrows heavily from Hawthorne (2002a).

he believes that Caleb will not have enough money for such a trip. In a context in which I am not attending to lotteries, I believe that each of 'Joe knows Alfred will not have enough money to go on an African safari' and 'Joe knows that Bertha will not have enough money to go on an African safari' etc. are all true. Suppose Joe has such beliefs for 5,000 of his friends. And suppose that each of them has a lottery ticket in a lottery with 5,001 tickets. As it turns out, the winner is a nonfriend. Consider the knowledge ascriptions that I believe to be true. The contextualist invites us to think that in the context in which those beliefs are held, the verb 'know' expresses a relation—call it 'K'—that does hold between Joe and propositions of the form 'S will not have enough money to go on an African safari', where S is one of his friends. Suppose Joe has in fact deduced and thereby come to believe that S will lose the lottery, for each friend S. Assuming Single-Premise Closure (SPC), the verb 'know' in my mouth expresses a relation that Joe has to the proposition that S will lose the lottery, for each friend S. Suppose Joe has deduced that none of those 5,000 friends will win the lottery. Assuming Multi-Premise Closure (MPC), Joe Ks that none of those friends will win the lottery. But it seems crazy to suppose that in any context, 'know' expresses a relation that holds between an agent and the proposition that none of 5,000 people will win the lottery when the agent has no special insider information and there are only 5,001 lottery ticket-holders.

And as if that were not bad enough, it is pretty clear that, given the nonskeptical standards for knowledge ascription being deployed by me, if Joe has witnessed the distribution of his tickets, observed each of 5,000 of his friends handing over the money, and seen the one remaining ticket being handed to a nonfriend, then Joe Ks that there are 5,001 lottery tickets, 5,000 of which are owned by his friends. Suppose he has in fact deduced and come to believe that the nonfriend will win. It now turns out that Joe Ks that the nonfriend will win—once again assuming MPC. So the verb 'know' in the original context expresses a relation that holds between Joe and the proposition that his nonfriend will win!

These results are extremely unpalatable. But there is nothing in the contextualist machinery on offer so far to prevent them. We are faced once again with the choice of embracing skepticism, giving up a closure principle, or finding some extra resources to stake out some third position. The contextualist resources that we have considered so far are simply insufficient to help us to see our way through the issue.

Here is a sketch of one style of solution. Let us begin with Lewis's Rule of Belief, according to which any possibility that is accorded sufficiently high credence by the subject—or ought to be accorded such high credence—is relevant to knowledge ascriptions. Now in the case just described, the subject accords high credence—or if he doesn't, he ought to—to the proposition that one of his friends will win the lottery. As it stands, that proposition is not a possibility in Lewis's sense, namely: 'A possibility will be specific enough if it cannot be split into subcases in such a way that anything we have said about possibilities, or anything we are going to say before we are done, applies to some subcases and not to others' (1996: 552). But if the Rule of Belief is plausible, then so too, surely, is the following:

> *New Rule of Belief* (NRB). If, at *t*, S gives—or ought to give— sufficiently high credence to proposition *p*, then at least some subcases of *p* are relevant for S at *t*.

The subject ought to accord high credence to the proposition that one of his friends will win the lottery. This proposition divides into various subcases—some in which Alfred wins, some in which Bertha wins, and so on. By NRB, not all of these subcases can be irrelevant. Suppose that an ascriber is managing to keep from relevance all the possibilities in which, say, Alfred wins the lottery. He cannot, by our principle, also be keeping from relevance all the possibilities in which one of the other friends wins. In short, whether or not they are actually attended to by the ascriber, some friend-winning possibilities must always be counted as relevant to knowledge ascriptions to Joe, since Joe accords—or ought to accord—high credence to the proposition that one of his friends will win.

With this in mind, a solution is ready at hand. When the puzzle was framed, we assumed that there was a single context in which the ascriber's various speech acts were performed and, relatedly, that there was a single relation, K, that was expressed by each deployment of the verb 'know'. This assumption has to be dropped. When the ascriber says 'Joe knows that Alfred will never get rich', the possibility that Alfred will win the lottery is irrelevant. But on that occasion is the possibility that Bertha will win the lottery irrelevant as well? NRB says that at least some friend-winning possibilities will have to be relevant. We may as well say that on that occasion, all the possibilities involving a friend other than Alfred winning were relevant, consistently maintaining that the possibility of Alfred winning was irrelevant. The speech continues: 'Joe knows that Bertha will never get rich'. In this setting the possibility that Bertha will win the lottery is now ignored. But by NRB, some friend-winning possibilities must be relevant. Perhaps the possibility that Alfred will win is not relevant yet—the preconditions of the truth of the earlier speech act can be allowed to remain in force for a short while. But what is clear is that, sooner or later, the possibility that Alfred will win must become relevant in order that the last speech act of the form 'Joe knows that S will never get rich' be true in the mouth of the ascriber. Given NRB, some possibilities whose irrelevance was crucial to the truth of earlier speech acts in our sequence must become relevant by the time of the last speech act in our sequence in order for that last speech act to be true. Assuming that we make the necessary accommodations to allow that each speech act be true (adhering, *ceteris paribus*, to the rules of accommodation that prevail over our language game[113]), we can be sure that some possibilities swing from being irrelevant to being relevant. Accordingly, we can be sure that the semantic value of 'know' varies widely during the conversation. There is no relation K,

---

[113] Here I have in mind the rules articulated in Lewis (1983).

expressed by some use of the verb 'know', such that Joe stands in relation K to each proposition of the form 'S will never get rich', where S is identical to a friend. The details of this solution may have to be adapted to the details of one's preferred framework for contextualist semantics,[114] but the main theme should be clear enough.

The kind of hyperactive context-shifting required by our refined theory will seem utterly anathema to certain readers. Moreover, it is not easy to see how to extend the approach to a case where, instead of temporally distinct speech acts serving as the object of evaluation, we have a case in which a person believes 'Joe knows that S will not win' for each of his 5,000 friends *at the same time.*[115] Nevertheless, I offer the above as the beginnings of a strategy for contextualist accommodation of Multi-Premise Closure. We can at least all agree that it is more difficult for the contextualist to accommodate that principle than might first appear.

2.7   Contextualism and Propositional Attitude Reporting[116]

A disturbing aspect of contextualism is its bearing on the status of propositional attitude reports in which 'know' figures in a that-clause. We can make trouble for contextualism by combining two

---

[114] For example, the toy theory sketched in this paragraph took 'relevant mistakes' to be the key parameter, whereas the discussion of the previous paragraph did not proceed in quite those terms.

[115] In general, it is important to bear in mind that one will typically, at any given time, accept all sorts of knowledge ascriptions that are not uttered.

[116] Let me mention another style of argument against contextualism in epistemology that I shall not be pursuing at length here. In a series of papers Jason Stanley (2000, 2002*a,b*) has advocated a syntax-based test for the acceptability of semantic theories that postulate contextual parameters governing the semantic value of some fragment of the language. The view can be summarized very briefly: Expressions in the language whose semantic value varies from context of utterance to context of utterance fall into two categories: (*a*) a list of simple, paradigmatic indexicals like 'I'; (*b*) expressions which, in the canonical syntax for the language, will have a variable associated with them. When such a variable exists, it will manifest itself in a particular way: sentences that contain

very simple ideas. First, there appears to be a very straightforward mechanism whereby we can combine information about what people believe in combination with information about whether their beliefs are true in order to obtain information about the world. Here are some schemas:

> *True Belief Schema* (TBS). If S believes that *p*, then S's belief is true iff *p*.

> *False Belief Schema* (FBS). If S believes that *p*, then S's belief is false iff not-*p*.

the purported context-dependent expression within the scope of a quantifier will admit of 'bound variable' readings. The idea can be brought out by considering one of Stanley's favorite examples: (1) Everyone went to a local bar. If I utter (1), I may be asserting the proposition that everyone went to a bar local to me. Or, if I have just been talking about someone in another location, I may be asserting the proposition that everyone went to a bar local to that person. Or finally, there are settings in which I may be asserting that each person *x* went to a bar local to *x*. Call this final reading the 'bound variable' reading. (Let me be explicit: When *I* call a reading a bound variable reading, I do not mean to imply anything about the deep syntax of that sentence. We can all agree that, were we to try to make maximally explicit the content of the relevant reading using a first-order language, then we would do so by associating a variable with local— 'local to *x*'—which is bound by a quantifier. The expression 'bound variable reading' alludes, then, to how, as theorists, we would represent the relevant content using a first-order language, but it is neutral on the question of how linguistics should describe the logical form of the sentence.) What Stanley's view implies is that when a term's semantic value varies with context, then, paradigmatic simple indexicals aside, there will be certain sentences in which that expression is controlled by a quantifier that admit of bound variable readings.

We now have the makings of a very general argument against certain theses of contextualism in semantics: If there are no bound variable readings associated with some alleged contextual parameter C, then if Stanley's reasoning is correct, there is no such parameter C. For if there were, it would be marked by a variable in the syntax that would generate bound variable readings. As Stanley is well aware, this outlook makes trouble for standard contextualism about 'knows'. Consider the sentence (2) Everyone knows that Moore has feet. Intuitively, there is nothing like the 'bound variable' reading available. But it is not so clear that Stanley's test is decisive. Consider by analogy (3) It is three o'clock. When said at 3.01 (in the context of a rocket launch, or to someone running to reach an airplane whose doors close at precisely 3.00), (3) clearly expresses a falsehood. But there are plenty of ordinary, less demanding contexts, where intuitively (3) expresses a truth. And this phenomenon cannot be accounted for simply by saying that (3) is vague, for this does not by itself explain the variance in verdicts from one context to another. A standard semantic maneuver is to appeal to a 'width parameter' in

It seems obvious that such schemas govern our use of belief ascriptions. It would be altogether bizarre, for example, to suppose that someone has a belief that he is in London and that the belief is true, and yet for it still to be an open question whether he is in London.

Second, it seems altogether obvious that we take sincere uses of the verb 'know' as a straightforward guide to the contents of what people believe. For example, if Jones says 'I know I have feet' and I reckon that he is being sincere, I will have no hesitation at all in reporting the contents of his mind as follows:

explaining the semantics of (3): In any given context, there will be a period that counts as meriting the title 'three o'clock', but this period may be wider or narrower on one or another occasion of use. It is important to note that Stanley's approach militates against this style of semantics. From his perspective, a width parameter would require a covert variable. And a covert variable would in turn make for bound variable readings of sentences like (4) Everyone went to work at three o'clock, in which the width would vary according to which element is selected from the domain of quantification. But, intuitively, no such bound variable reading of (4) is available, so Stanley would appear to be committed to an invariantism about the width parameter. And if there is a single 'width' to be semantically associated with 'three o'clock', it will surely have to be quite narrow; otherwise, such conditionals as 'Necessarily if it is three o'clock then in a minute it will be exactly one minute past three' will come out semantically false on every occasion of use. So it would seem that Stanley is committed to the analogue of skeptical invariantism for 'It is three o'clock'. Of course, this does not automatically commit him to such claims as 'What is said by "It is three o'clock"' is nearly always false, since it is far from clear that such English locutions as 'What is said' track semantic value. But the view is nonetheless unappealing for the same reasons that skeptical invariantism is. (Skeptical invariantists can obviously make the same moves concerning such locutions as 'What is said' and so on.) Moreover, there is nothing special about three o'clock; exactly the same considerations apply to a large range of natural language expressions. Consider 'circular'. It is plausible to postulate something like a 'tolerance parameter' that dictates what level of imperfection a thing might have and still merit being called 'circular'. Once again, since such a tolerance parameter does not seem to make for bound variable readings, Stanley would seem to be pushed towards skeptical invariantism here as well. It turns out that Plato was right: we can only speak approximate truths when we reckon things in the world of flux to be circular. One who endorses Stanley's view needs to be up-front about these radical consequences and to explain away their costs. Until that task is successfully undertaken, we may remain properly dubious of his framework. Meanwhile, it is far from clear that whenever there is, intuitively, a bound variable reading of the truth conditions of an utterance, that is to be accounted for by positing a variable in the syntax. Here is not, however, the place to pursue matters further.

(1) Jones believes that he knows that he has feet.

Generalizing:

> *Disquotational Schema for 'Knows'* (DSK). If an English speaker E sincerely utters a sentence *s* of the form 'A knows that *p*', and the sentence in the that-clause means that *p* and 'A' is a name or indexical that refers to *a*, then E believes of *a* that *a* knows that *p*, and expresses that belief by *s*.[117]

Of course not all words behave disquotationally in this way. If a speaker sincerely says 'It is raining here', I cannot report the contents of his mind by an ascription of the form 'He believes it is raining here', unless he and I happen to be in the same place. By contrast, it looks very much as if we *do* adopt something like DSK. If, for example, someone sincerely utters 'I know that I will never have a heart attack', we have no hesitation whatsoever in reporting the contents of his mind by claiming that he believes that he knows that he will never have a heart attack. That is how the verb 'know' seems to work.

We are now in a position to state a problem for the contextualist. TBS seems exactly right (as does FBS). DSK seems exactly right. But the contemporary contextualist is forced to reject at least one of those schemas. It is not hard to see why. Grant with the contextualist that there may be situations where the semantic value of 'know' in your mouth is different than its semantic value in mine. Suppose, for example, that the verb 'know' in your mouth picks out a relation

---

[117] Complications are raised by Kripke's (1997) case of Pierre. Suppose that 'London' and 'Londres' are both names for London but Pierre doesn't realize it. Pierre will sincerely assent to 'London is pretty' but will also sincerely assent to 'Londres is ugly' (he has picked up sinister hearsay about 'Londres' and has got a pretty good first-hand impression of London, having visited). Arguably 'Londres is ugly' means that London is ugly, yet it is far from clear that when Pierre sincerely assents to 'I know that Londres is ugly' we can claim that he believes that he knows that London is ugly. In reply: Those who think that the belief ascription 'Pierre believes that London is ugly' is false ought to think that there is a correlative notion of meaning such that Pierre does not quite mean the same by tokenings of 'London' as by tokenings of 'Londres'. Let it be that notion that figures in the principle. (Thanks to Zoltán Szabó here.)

that holds between you and the proposition that you have feet, but that in my mouth 'know' picks out a relation that *does not* hold between you and the proposition that you have feet. The standard contextualist wishes to maintain that in this situation, the belief that you express by the words 'I know that I have feet' is a true belief. Like pretty much everyone else, the standard contextualist assumes something like the following connection between sincere acceptance of a sentence, semantic value, and belief:

> *The True Belief Principle* (TBP). If a speaker sincerely accepts an utterance *u* and *u* has semantic value *p*, then the belief manifested by his sincerely accepting *u* is true iff *p* is true.[118]

Since you sincerely accept and understand 'I know that I have feet', and since the semantic value of that utterance is true, TBP tells us that the belief you manifest by sincere acceptance is a true belief. So if I am a (standard) contextualist I am committed to saying that your belief is true. But DSK enjoins me to say:

(2) You believe that you know that you have feet.

This in turn combines with TBS to deliver:

(3) You know that you have feet.[119]

So standard contextualism, in combination with DSK and TBS would have me conclude that you know you have feet. But this conclusion is altogether forbidden in the setting described. For were I to sincerely accept 'You know you have feet', I would have a false belief since, in the scenario envisaged, the semantic value of the latter sentence is false.

---

[118] See Soames (2002, ch. 6) for related discussion. In order for any such argument to proceed, we need some bridge principle between the talk of semantic value that figures in high semantic theory and more ordinary ways of talking. I have suggested one in the text—TBP. Here is another bridge principle that will do the job: If a person's utterance *u* expresses a belief that *p*, and the semantic value of *u* is a true proposition, then *p*. (Thanks to Ted Sider here.)

[119] It might be argued that, strictly, DSK only licenses (4) insofar as 'you' is given wide scope. That is unimportant here as no one in the imagined setting (whether or not they held a direct reference perspective on 'you') would wish to suggest that the narrow- and wide-scope readings come apart.

What is making all the trouble, note, is the fact that 'know' is not supposed to be flexible with regard to whose standards govern in the way that 'local' is flexible with regards to whose location is relevant. If I am in New York and you are in Paris and you sincerely utter 'I am going to a local bar', and express a true belief, I will not get into doxastic trouble by running through the following inference:

> You believe that you are going to a local bar.
> Your belief is true.
> Therefore, you are going to a local bar.

'Local' can be 'tied' to your location throughout. But I have no similar freedom with 'knows' by the lights of standard contextualism. The point can be made vividly if we help ourselves to the expressions 'know-by-your-standards' and 'know-by-my-standards'. The trouble is that there is no reading available of

(4) You believe that you know that you have feet,

which corresponds to

(5) You believe that you know-by-your-standards that you have feet.

The reason is that the truth of that belief, in combination with TBS, would require a reading of

(6) You know that you have feet.

which corresponds to

(7) You know-by-your-standards that you have feet.

But according to standard contextualism, I can only ever read (6) as

(8) You know-by-my-standards that you have feet.

Conclusion: The contextualist has to do one of the following: (i) detach the notion of semantic value from that of true belief, (ii) give up TBS, (iii) give up DSK, or (iv) allow 'know' to vary like 'local'. I suspect that he will opt for (iii). But this is a significant cost.

That completes my presentation of the argument. It appears, prima facie, to provide considerable embarrassment to the contextualist.

But couldn't an analogue of this argument be raised for, say, all context-dependent comparative adjectives? And wouldn't this show that the argument proves too much? There are disanalogies here that should not be ignored. Suppose I say:

(9) That is flat.

And suppose that you challenge me by pointing to some little bumps. There are three kinds of tactics available to me.

(i) *Concession.* I concede that my earlier belief was wrong and try to find new common ground: 'I guess you are right and I was wrong. It's not really flat. But let's agree that…'

(ii) *Stick to one's guns.* I claim that the challenge does not undermine what I said. I say (9). You point out some small bumps. I say: 'Well, that doesn't mean it is not flat'.

(iii) *Clarification.* I clarify my earlier claim and then protest that your challenge betrays a misunderstanding of what I believe and what I was claiming. There are various sorts of 'hedge' words that can be invoked in aid of this kind of response.

Here are some examples of clarification:

Example 1. 'The glass is empty'. Challenge: 'Well, it's got some air in it'.
Reply: 'All I was claiming is that it is empty of *vodka*'.

Example 2. 'The field is flat'. Challenge: 'Well, it's got a few small holes in it'.
Reply: 'All I was claiming is that it is flat *for a football field*'. (Or: 'All I was claiming is that it is *roughly* flat'.)

Example 3. 'He'll come at 3 p.m.'. Challenge: 'He's more likely to come a few seconds earlier or later'.
Reply: 'All I meant is that he'll come at *approximately* 3 p.m.'.

I want to draw attention to the fact that we have very few devices in ordinary life for implementing the clarification technique when it comes to 'knows'.[120] (Think especially of our lack of clarificatory devices when we have previously said something positive of the form 'I know that *p*'.) We don't have anything like the 'of F' and 'for a G' locutions available. Nor do we have anything like the hedge devices 'roughly' and 'approximately' available.[121] As a consequence, our standard techniques for dealing with epistemic challenges that raise relatively farfetched possibilities are concession and, more rarely, sticking to one's guns. Our epistemic practice runs smoothly not because we have clarification techniques available when responding to challenges, but because we are sparing about raising challenges in the first place.[122]

[120] Cf. Feldman (2001: 77). Granted, we have the locution 'by S's standards'. But in ordinary English this does not work in the manner that the contextualist philosopher intends. An ordinary person might say 'By Hitler's standards, all non-Aryans are bad', but in no way intend to suggest that 'All non-Aryans are bad' was true in Hitler's mouth. There are other adjuncts too that are sometimes appended to 'knows': 'He knows, in effect'; 'He knows with reasonable assurance'; 'He knows for certain'; 'He knows full well'; 'He pretty much knows'. But these are rarely put to the service of the clarification technique: If I say 'I don't know' at one time and someone later complains 'You did know', it is not common practice to reply along the following lines: 'It's true that I knew. But what I meant back then was that I didn't know for certain'. (Insofar as 'I don't know for certain' plays an excusatory role, it is probably best understood along the lines of 'I didn't hit him hard', where the point is not to deny that one hit). It is even more obvious that I standardly have no ready means of reconciling apparent conflict by indicating that my earlier self attached 'lower standards' to 'know': if I say 'I know' at *t₁* and then accept at *t₂* a claim of the form 'I didn't know at *t₁*', there is little I can do in ordinary discourse to clarify my earlier remark so as to avoid criticism of my earlier self, especially in a situation where my current self is not willing to gloss 'I didn't know' as 'I didn't know for certain'. I thus have no easy means of indicating that my earlier self attached 'lower standards' to 'know'. (I am grateful for conversations with Alan Prince, Peter Ludlow, and Keith DeRose here.)
[121] This isn't anything particularly special about 'knows'. The same could be said for the verb 'hits'. In general, when the hedge devices are unavailable, contextualist semantics will seem more foreign. (Note, by the way, that the fact that greater force is required for a dinosaur's motion counting as a hit than it is for a human's motion counting as a hit provides no evidence for *ascriber*-dependence for 'hit'. Nevertheless, I would not be at all surprised if philosophical reflection could make a convincing case for ascriber-dependence for 'hits'.)
[122] I do not wish to say that the contrast between 'flat', 'empty', and 'know' is altogether sharp. Even in the case of 'flat' and 'empty' we have some inclination to

Given that this is how our practice works, it is not surprising that contextualist semantics will seem foreign and that, relatedly, DSK strikes us as true. For it is through the clarification technique that sensitivity to context-dependence is manifested.

Consider now a comparative adjective, say 'tall'. The following disquotational schema for 'tall' is clearly unacceptable:

> *Disquotational Schema for 'Tall'.* If an English speaker S sincerely utters something of the form 'A is tall' and 'A' refers to *a*, then S believes of *a* that *a* is tall.

Suppose I am a coach discussing basketball players. Since by 'tall' I mean 'tall for a basketball player' I cannot report an ordinary English speaker as believing that Michael Jordan (who is about 6 foot 6 inches) is tall on the grounds that such a person sincerely uttered 'Michael Jordan is tall'.

Similar remarks undermine the following schema for 'ready':

> *Disquotational Schema for 'Ready'.* If an English speaker S sincerely utters something of the form 'A is ready' and 'A' refers to *a*, then S believes of *a* that *a* is ready.

The schema is unacceptable. At *t* Sally utters 'Joe is ready', meaning that Joe is ready to take a driving test. If I am later in a setting where the conversational participants are discussing whether or not Joe was ready to give up smoking at *t*, then it would be unacceptable in that setting to report 'Well, Sally believed that Joe was ready'. Our practice betrays no commitment to the disquotational schema for

---

regard ourselves as in a more enlightened perspective concerning flatness and emptiness (with regard to our former self) when we pay attention to small bumps and drops. There is then some corresponding inclination to treat our former self as making mistakes. But there is a much stronger inclination to reckon ourselves more enlightened with regard to our former self (on the topic of knowledge) when possibilities of error become salient. There is, correspondingly, less tendency towards clarification when it comes to 'know'. (I do not know about the explanatory order here. Is it that these tendencies explain why we do not have much by way of clarificatory devices. Or is it the other way around?)

'ready' and 'tall'. But it very much betrays a commitment to such a schema for 'knows'. The behavior of 'know' does not then seem analogous to that of familiar context-dependent predicates.[123]

How should a contextualist in epistemology respond to all this? The most promising strategy would be to adopt a view that invokes *semantic blindness*: There is a real sense in which users of the word 'know' are blind to the semantic workings of their language.[124,125]

---

[123] Semanticists distinguish 'gradable' from 'non-gradable' predicates, where a scale is taken to be fundamental to the content of a gradable predicate, not so for a non-gradable predicate. Standard diagnostics for a gradable verb fail for 'know': we do not say 'X knows that p more than Y knows that p' nor 'X knows that p as much as Y knows that p' nor 'He so knows that p that…' nor 'Y knows that p less than X knows that p'. Stanley (unpub.) suggests that contextualists in epistemology have gone badly awry in using gradable predicates as the model for 'knows'. The connection of gradability to context-dependence merits further investigation. (For a good introduction to the topic of gradability, see Rusiecki 1985. For further discussion, as it relates to the current topic, see Stanley (unpub.), who has independently arrived at conclusions rather similar to those reached here.)

[124] See Schiffer (1996) for related discussion.

[125] An interesting kind of exception to the true belief schema is provided by styles of belief reporting that have directly quotational elements—when Quine's (1990) 'de voce' readings of belief ascriptions are in play. (This point was brought to my attention by David Lewis, as was the 'adobe' example.) Someone knows that he does not live in a mud hut but confuses the words 'adobe' and 'abode'. The sentence 'He thinks that he lives in an adobe' will, in some settings, be an effective way of communicating his belief. An example closer to our current topic: I can say 'You see that really tall person over there? The basketball coaches think that he isn't tall at all'. Once again, in a suitable setting, such a belief report will seem perfectly acceptable. But in this setting, we are not at all intending to report that the basketball coach has a false belief. How does this bear on our true belief schema? We have a few choices: (i) We can claim that this is not, despite appearances, a case to which the schema applies. Analogy: I cannot treat 'If Jones believes that he is happy then Jones's belief is true iff he is happy' as an instance of the schema if the first tokening of 'he' is accompanied by a demonstration of Bill, the second by a demonstration of Frank. Or else (ii) we can allow directly quotational styles of belief reporting as a kind of exception to the true belief schema. (I shall not adjudicate here.) So why not say that when we use 'know' in belief ascriptions we are nearly always doing something rather like the directly quotational style of belief reporting? The trouble is that insofar as we are doing that, then we cannot treat the truth of a pair of claims of the form 'S doesn't know that p' and 'S believes that he knows that p' as a basis for thinking that S has a false belief. But it is quite clear that we *do* think of that as a basis for thinking that S has a false belief. Obviously, there are very difficult issues raised by the style of belief reporting that we are considering. A full treatment would, *inter alia*, require a decision on what to say concerning those cases from 'A Puzzle about Belief' where 'our normal apparatus for the ascription of belief is placed under the greatest strain and may even break down' (Kripke 1979: 907).

English speakers proceed as if DSK were correct. But it isn't. While those speakers are, at least implicitly, well aware of the context-dependence of 'tall', the same is not true for 'know'.[126,127]

Why posit contextual parameters that we are blind to?[128] Why dispute common sense about attitude ascriptions? Perhaps *some* dispute with common sense is inevitable. As Peter Unger writes:

> On many matters, common sense is inconsistent; we do not actually have our unreflective thoughts so perfectly in line all the time. So, in particular, it is with matters of semantics: On the one hand, we believe that most statements ordinarily made with 'flat' and fellows are true; on the other, we believe that the semantics of these terms and statements is not only relevantly simple but relevantly independent, or interest-free. Common sense would have it both ways, but that is impossible. (1984: 38–9)

This thought may apply with yet more force to the case of 'know'. Think back to our puzzles. Which view *are* we going to adopt if it is not the contextualist one?

---

[126] The contextualist may be encouraged in this regard by the evidence presented by Nichols, Stich, and Weinberg, (forthcoming), which suggests that both cultural and socioeconomic differences make for significant discrepancies in epistemic intuitions concerning the application of 'know'. Example: East Asians were far less inclined to withhold 'know' from standard Gettier cases. One possible diagnosis is that there are idiolectical differences to which we are blind and that make homophonic translation of 'know' problematic. Of course, these data do not in themselves demonstrate the existence of the sorts of context-dependent mechanisms that the contextualist in epistemology typically proposes. But they do make potential trouble for the disquotational schema for 'knows' and so may lessen the cost of contextualism. (On the other hand, one who wished for an ambiguity-based resolution of Nichols, Stich, and Weinberg's data should at least feel somewhat uncomfortable. After all, it is hard not to be sympathetic with Kripke on a related matter: 'I would be very surprised to be told that Eskimos have two separate words, one for (say) Hintikka's 'strong' sense of 'know,' another for his 'weak' sense.' (1977: 402).

[127] Somewhat more speculatively, we might conjecture that, simple indexicals aside, if contextualism is true of *any* fundamental piece of the lexicon in our language of thought, we are likely to be semantically blind to that fact: for we will find it difficult to make explicit to ourselves what we are thinking in a way that makes for explicit recognition of the contextual parameters at work. In conversation, Jerry Fodor worried that this has the unacceptable consequence that we lack proper authority concerning the contents of our own thoughts, which will in turn disrupt the fundamental asymmetry between how I figure out what *you* are thinking and how *I* figure out what I am thinking. Such worries certainly merit investigation.

[128] Thanks to Brian McLaughlin here.

Certain features of color and weight might provide a suggestive analogy here. Ordinary speakers are not aware of such facts as that things only look brown and olive when certain contrast colors are in view, that things that are hard to lift on earth are easy to lift on the moon,[129] and so on. In order to get a plausible distribution of truth values, a semantics for that discourse may, in light of those facts, end up positing parameters that are not built into the deep psychology of ordinary competence (in addition to the parameters that are tacitly recognized).[130] The overall best story about the distribution of semantic value may thus cut against judgments about when to use homophonic translation methods for, say, color predicates. Correlatively, the correct semantics may end up claiming that certain cases of apparent disagreement are illusory.[131] Obviously, we do not wish to posit semantic blindness when we don't have to. Other things being equal, a semantic theory that didn't claim semantic blindness on the part of competent speakers would be a better theory. But still, it *may* be that in the case of, say, color predicates, the best theory, all things considered, is one that does posit semantic blindness. Similar thoughts extend, *mutatis mutandis*, to 'know'.

Let me close this section with one final thought, related to the claim of semantic blindness (and its costs). Contextualists tend to focus on knowledge ascriptions. But if one expands one's focus from what is said to what is believed, their view may seem less appealing. For simplicity's sake, imagine we have a belief box that contains

[129] Imagine that an ordinary person is shown an object and told that it is heavy. He is transported to the moon and attempts to lift the object for the first time. Upon finding it easy to lift, he may well be inclined to think 'They said it was heavy. But it is easy to lift. It isn't heavy at all. They were wrong'.

[130] Thus we tacitly recognize that when an animal is covered in paint, we may correctly say that 'It is red', describing the color of the paint, but we may also correctly say that 'It is brown', describing the color underneath. But we cannot, in one context, say 'It is red and brown'. Thanks to Zoltán Szabó here.

[131] For what it's worth, one moral the contextualist should draw from all this is that, unlike syntax, the semantic working of our language may be as obscure to us as a whole range of metaphysical questions about the world itself. Philosophy of language is no first philosophy.

sentences of English. To believe that p requires (in this simple model) that one have a sentence in one's belief box that expresses the proposition that p. Suppose a speaker notices that it is raining and says 'It is raining here'. If the speaker wants to *preserve* that information in the belief box, it won't do to encode 'It is raining here' as a permanent inhabitant of the belief box, for the sentence will change its content as the speaker moves through time and space. Better to encode the information by a sentence that is not shifty in this way. Perhaps 'It was raining there' (accompanied by a mental snapshot or file of the relevant spatiotemporal location). Or 'It was raining by the Eiffel Tower at noon on May 4th'. If contextualism is true, then a similar problem confronts us in preserving the information we get from knowledge reports. And here, no such easy fix seems available. Suppose that Joe says 'I know that p', and at the time of utterance he expresses the same relation as you do by 'know'. You accept what he says. The sentence 'Joe knows that p (plus a date index)' goes into your belief box. But now suppose that your standards for knowledge rise. Your belief about Joe's knowledge will now come out false—as will, presumably, hundreds of other once true beliefs— unless you somehow update the sentences in your belief box. Moreover, you will no longer have a cognitive hold on those true propositions that your belief box once truly expressed and that, as a result, you once truly believed.

Similarly, if the standards for knowledge fall, many beliefs that deny knowledge will now come out false and much true information will be lost, unless updating occurs.[132] Suppose further that we are semantically blind in the way suggested: the semantic content of 'know' shifts, but our language organ does not supply us with a standards index—analogous to a dating method—with which to enrich knowledge ascriptions that are tokened in the belief box. Then shifting semantic values for 'know' would spell disaster—in the ways just outlined—for our belief set.

---

[132] Of course, I am taking liberties with use and mention here (as I have in many other places). But I assume that this is no impediment to understanding.

In sum: if the package of contextualism and semantic blindness is correct, it is very unclear, on the one hand, how we could manage to preserve information in memory, and, on the other, how we could avoid finding ourselves with hundreds of false beliefs on account of failure to update in line with shifting standards.

2.8 Scorecard

I can offer no final verdict on any of the main views that I shall be discussing in this monograph. But it is worth noting that we have encountered a number of dimensions along which the merits and flaws of the competing views may be evaluated.

It is natural to begin with something of a datum, one that constrains much of the theorizing that we are examining, namely: Very many ordinary positive knowledge ascriptions are true. Lewis thus writes: 'It is a Moorean fact that we know a lot. It is one of those things that we know better than we know the premises of any philosophical argument to the contrary' (1996: 549). We thus have what we might call

(1) the Moorean Constraint.

But the discussion so far has brought to light of number of other prima facie attractive principles, which it would be natural to try to respect. Notably:

(2) the Assertion Constraint (knowledge is a norm of assertion)
(3) the Practical Reasoning Constraint (knowledge is a norm of practical reasoning)
(4) Single-Premise Closure
(5) Multi-Premise Closure
(6) the Epistemic Possibility Constraint (if the epistemic probability for S that p is not zero, then S does not know that not-p)

(7) the Objective Chance Principle
(8) the Disquotational Schema for 'knows'.

Perhaps certain readers will find some of these principles altogether uncompelling. And readers will certainly disagree about how their importance is to be weighted. I have suggested that Single-Premise Closure is pretty much nonnegotiable, but will not venture to offer a relative weighting for the other principles.[133] What I can do—in the service of clarity and future inquiry—is to offer a scorecard for each of the main views that I shall undertake to consider in terms of (1)–(8) above, leaving it to the reader to pursue matters from there. A scorecard is hardly intended to replace the substance of the text—but some may find it useful nevertheless. The scorecard for one who offers a contextualist solution to our focal puzzles is roughly as follows: the Moorean Constraint is well satisfied; Single-Premise Closure can be respected; the Assertion and Practical Reasoning Constraints are not respected, though replacement principles that retain some of their spirit can be offered; the Objective Chance Principle and the Epistemic Possibility Constraint cannot be jointly respected; the Disquotational Principle for 'knows' cannot be respected; the status of Multi-Premise Closure remains problematic—its compatibility with the current style of approach remains unclear.

Even granting that we have identified a variety of costs for a contextualist treatment of our puzzles, it is not yet clear whether or not they are costs worth paying. A proper evaluation of contextualism's merits requires careful consideration of its invariantist competition. That is the task of Chapters 3 and 4.

---

[133] Nor do I pretend that (1)–(8) provide some kind of exhaustive list. José Benardete has suggested to me the following vague but very compelling constraint: Knowledge, whatever it is, is something worth wanting and having ('the Value Constraint'). We also would like many of the ordinary *negative* verdicts about knowledge to come out as true, including verdicts to the effect that this or that true conviction is nevertheless not a piece of knowledge ('the Negative Verdict Constraint'). And so on.

3 SKEPTICAL AND MODERATE INVARIANTISM

3.1 Introduction

ACCORDING to the *invariantist*, the semantic value of 'know', and accordingly the extension of 'know', does not vary across contexts of use.[1] It is time to look at approaches to our puzzle that are compatible with invariantism. As noted in Chapter 2, the thesis that 'know' is context-dependent, even if correct, is not obviously the key to the epistemological puzzles raised by lotteries. So certain of the solutions on offer in this section might be embraced, perhaps with minor adjustments, by the contextualist as well.

There are two very different kinds of invariantism. The *skeptical invariantist* claims that the semantic value of the word 'know' is such that all—or nearly all—ordinary positive knowledge ascriptions of the form 'S knows that *p*' are false. The *moderate invariantist*, on the other hand, claims that the semantic value of the verb 'know' is such that very many of the positive knowledge ascriptions that we make in daily life are true. We shall look at each in turn, though the second style will engage most of our interest.

3.2 Three Varieties of Skeptical Invariantism

The skeptical invariantist claims that the semantic value of the word 'know' is such that all or nearly all ordinary positive

---

[1] Leaving aside uses of 'know' which take a noun phrase as direct object.

knowledge ascriptions are false. In effect, the verb 'know' (semantically) brings with it extremely demanding standards. It is clear enough, then, what the skeptical invariantist will say about our motivating puzzles: In every case, it is false that the ordinary proposition is known and, as a result, there is no asymmetry between knowledge of ordinary propositions and knowledge of lottery propositions.[2] I shall discuss three versions of this view. The first version says that when we make knowledge claims, we assert something false but we do not realize that we are; the second version says that when we make knowledge claims, we assert something false and we realize that we are; the third version says that when we make knowledge claims, we don't even assert something false.

Skeptical Invariantism 1: Error Theory

All versions of skepticism hold that (i) the semantic value of 'know' is invariant[3] and (ii) all or nearly all positive knowledge ascriptions are false. The error theory supplements this pair of commitments with the claim that (iii) ordinary people generally believe the propositions expressed by their knowledge ascriptions. On such a view, in order to know that p, one must satisfy incredibly demanding epistemic standards that are rarely if ever met. But ordinary speakers of English are blind to this fact about their own semantics. (Otherwise, they wouldn't believe the propositions expressed by their knowledge ascriptions.)

Does this mean that they do not know what the word 'know' means? Well, yes and no. We can take Williamson's (1994) epistemicism as an analogy here. According to that view (simplifying a little), some claim of the following form is true but unknowable:

---

[2]   Of course, it is possible to occupy some ground intermediate between the skeptical and moderate invariantist. Perhaps the cases that involve the future are ones where the ordinary proposition is not known, whereas certain other cases—especially those that involve perception and memory and thereby represent paradigmatic instances of knowledge—are ones where the ordinary propositions are known and where the lottery propositions, despite appearances, are known (or at least knowable). The reader is welcome to explore such hybrid views.

[3]   Again, setting aside uses of 'know' that take a noun phrase as direct object.

'is bald' is true of someone if and only if that person has fewer than *n* hairs on his scalp. But we do not know which claim of that form is true. Suppose the number is in fact 16. Then it is true that someone is bald if and only if he has fewer than 16 hairs on his scalp—but we are blind to that fact. Does that mean that we do not know what 'bald' means? Well, we know that 'bald' is true of someone iff he is bald. It's just that we do not in addition know that someone is bald iff he has fewer than 16 hairs on his scalp. As Williamson is well aware, knowing what the word 'bald' means, in the ordinary sense, does not entail knowing such equivalences.[4]

The error theory skeptic can adopt a parallel approach. We know that 'know' means know, so we pass the (relatively undemanding) tests for linguistic competence with 'know'. But (at least most of the time) we do not recognize that we know something only if certain extremely demanding standards are met. Thus we form beliefs and make assertions as if knowledge were easy to come by, with the result that, on the topic of what we know, we end up saying and believing much that is false.[5]

Skeptical Invariantism 2: Exaggeration[6]

'Know' has a semantic value that imposes very demanding standards. Because we recognize this, we are not so foolish as to believe that we know anything, except perhaps in very exceptional

---

[4] See Williamson (1994: 209–12). This is but one example of a very general phenomenon. Similar considerations apply to all sorts of other cases where failing to know certain necessary connections is compatible with knowing the meaning of a term.

[5] For comparison, most of us think that people in the past made many moral claims that were mistaken, but we don't think they did not know what 'good' meant. The fact that they thought that it was morally acceptable to have slaves, for example, or morally unacceptable for women to have equal civil status to men shows that they made moral errors (with alarming regularity)—but it does not show that they failed to understand the meanings of moral terms. (I am taking for granted here that moral claims are truth-value apt.) This involved semantic ignorance *of a sort*. They did not know that 'bad' was true of slavery. And so on. But this hardly meant that they did not know that 'good' meant good and so on. (Moreover, all ignorance involves semantic ignorance of *that* sort.)

[6] This view has been put forward by Jonathan Schaffer (forthcoming). I am particularly grateful for correspondence with Schaffer on this topic, which saved me from a number of serious errors.

cases.[7] (Perhaps our own existence and our own current phenom-
enal states provide such exceptions, perhaps not.) Just as (nearly)
all positive knowledge ascriptions are false, so too are (nearly) all
belief attributions with positive knowledge ascriptions in the that-
clause. It is false that I know that there is a table in front of me. And
it is false that I believe that I know that there is a table in front of me.

Do I ever assert that I know things? The exaggeration model says
that I do. I claim to know this and that, and in so doing, I engage in
harmless exaggeration. When someone is doing pretty well epistemically, I harmlessly exaggerate by claiming that she knows;
when someone thinks she is doing pretty well epistemically, I
harmlessly exaggerate by claiming that she thinks that she knows.

The proponent of this view will need to supplement its bare
bones with a suitable pragmatic story. If I say 'I know I will be living
in Syracuse' then, by the lights of this theory, the semantic value of
the sentence uttered is false, but I nevertheless successfully convey
true information.[8] Similarly, 'I believe that I know that I will be
living in Syracuse this summer' is by the lights of this theory false,[9]
but assertable. By contrast, presumably, if I say 'I know I will not be
one of the unlucky people to have a heart attack this year' then, at
least in most contexts of conversation, the utterance is inappropriate: not only will the semantic value be false, but I will convey
misleading information. (The same goes for 'I know I will lose the
lottery'.) The contrast needs to be explained. When is an exaggeration harmless? When isn't it? Since, by hypothesis, the semantic
value of 'know' is invariant, some pragmatic story needs to be told
here.

---

[7] One might worry that verbs like 'recognize' and 'understand' imply knowledge, so
that the skeptic should not help himself to them. This worry runs quite deep, I think,
but I shall not pursue it here.

[8] Consider, meanwhile, 'I don't know whether or not I will be living in Syracuse' said
in a situation where I have excellent reason to think I will be. According to this model,
such a claim would be true but misleading. (Supposing the claim 'I know I will be living
in Syracuse' is standardly used to convey q via the exaggeration p; then the negation of
that claim will serve to convey not-q via the truth that not-p.)

[9] Since according to this theory, we do not believe that we know anything (except
perhaps in very exceptional cases).

Grice (1989*a*) taught us that conversation is governed by an overarching Cooperative Principle—'Make your conversational contribution such as is required, at the stage at which it occurs, by the accepted purpose or direction of the talk exchange in which you are engaged' (p. 26). Among the maxims of conversation is that of Quality, under which falls the submaxim 'Do not say what you believe to be false'.[10] But, Grice observed, we can communicate effectively even if we flout 'some maxim at the level of what is said' in cases where 'the speaker is entitled to assume that that maxim, or at least the overall Cooperative Principle, is observed at the level of what is implicated'.[11] Some proposition q is conversationally implicated in saying p just in case (roughly) it is reasonable to take the speaker as fulfilling the overarching Principle of Cooperation in saying p only if we suppose that he thinks that q. As Grice himself notes, exaggeration is explained nicely by such a framework. To take a simple example: You ask me what Bob is like and I say 'He's never done anything for anyone else in his entire life'. The semantic value of this sentence is false. (I assume that the appeal to domain restriction isn't enough to salvage truth here.) If you, the hearer, think that I, the speaker, am trying to be informative and so on, you will take it that I think that Bob does very little for others.[12] I thus use a falsehood (that Bob has never done anything for anyone else) to convey a truth (that Bob is selfish). Depending on the facts (and, in particular, on whether I really was being cooperative), what I say may be a harmless exaggeration—or it may be genuinely misleading. I shall not pursue the details further here.

The coherence of the exaggeration model turns, *inter alia*, on some subtle issues about the nature of assertion. Suppose the only beer in the fridge is a pack of very expensive imported ale that I have bought as a birthday gift for my uncle. If my roommate asks 'Is

---

[10] If knowledge is the norm of assertion, it would seem that the basic Maxim of Quality is 'Only assert what you know to be true'. (Cf. Williamson 2000: 243.) The remarks that follow apply here as well.

[11] Grice (1989*a*: 33).

[12] I abstract away from tricky issues concerning how to fill out the relevant 'derivation'.

there any beer in the fridge?' then in answering 'No' I assert a harmless falsehood. After all, my roommate would hardly complain about my answer if, upon discovering the bottles, he was informed of their intended destination.[13] But the envisaged scenario here is different. We all, by hypothesis, mutually recognize that we know nothing (or next to nothing) and that the semantic value of pretty much any knowledge ascription is a falsehood. So the information I convey when I make a knowledge ascription does not include the proposition that I know something. Under those circumstances, can I even be reckoned to *assert* the falsehood that is posited as the semantic value?[14] Suppose, by analogy, I look at a very long swimming pool and utter the words (exaggerating) 'That pool is a mile long'. Granting that the proposition that the swimming pool is a mile in length is in some sense 'displayed', am I actually *claiming* that the swimming pool is a mile in length? There is some intuitive pull to deny this.[15] Such considerations put pressure on this second brand of invariantist to shift to a third position.

Skeptical Invariantism 3: Unasserted Semantic Value

While the semantic value of a knowledge ascription is nearly always a falsehood, we rarely believe *or* assert the semantic value of such

---

[13] I assume that appeal to domain restriction will not help here. More difficult in that regard is a situation where there is a large puddle of beer in the salad crisper and I similarly answer 'No'. Even here there is some inclination to say 'Harmless falsehood'. After all, the beer in the crisper *could* be poured into a glass and drunk. On the other hand, the answer 'Yes, but it's a birthday gift' feels much more acceptable than 'Yes, but it's in a big puddle in the salad crisper'. (Consider also the case where beer is kept in frozen blocks in the freezer.)

[14] A test case. You and I enter a party. It is fairly deserted. I say 'There is no one here'. Did I *assert* a falsehood? Is there some proposition such that it is false and I *claimed* that it was true?

[15] Intuitions are, admittedly, a bit shifty here. A Gricean may insist that the mechanism of hyperbole works via the fact that one does *assert* something false—that is what the violation of Quality consists in. The proponent of the third view will maintain that the Maxim of Quality is only *apparently* flouted and that this is sufficient to generate the implicature. We should not be too quick to foist a view on Grice himself. For more on Grice's own use of 'say', see Grice (1989c, essays 5 and 6).

ascriptions. Like the proponent of the exaggeration model, the proponent of an unasserted semantic value view owes us an account of why we so readily make (i) false knowledge ascriptions and (ii) false belief ascriptions concerning what is believed to be known. In making good on this debt, the proponent of the third model will presumably proceed much like the proponent of the second, by providing a pragmatics that makes our practice intelligible.[16] The relative merits of the second and third views turn, of course, on general questions about the nature of exaggeration.

3.3   In Favor of the Error Theory

Problems with the Second and Third Views

To my eye, the first version of skepticism is by far the most plausible. Whereas all three are committed to saying that we know very little, the second and third involve additional commitments about what we correspondingly believe. According to such views, no one—not even the philosophically unsophisticated—ever believes that he knows such ordinary propositions as that Manchester United beat Coventry City 2–1, or that the plane from Detroit is late, or that the towels are in the dryer. (Recall that according to those views, not only are nearly all knowledge ascriptions false, but nearly all claims to the effect that someone believes that he knows something are false as well.[17]) Some further considerations:

---

[16] The reader will notice that there is much in common between this view and contextualism. After all, the proponent of this view agrees with the contextualist that what is communicated when I say 'S knows that *p*' varies across contexts of utterance. Where they disagree is in what they take the semantic value of such an utterance to be. Unger (1984) claims that there is no fact of the matter underlying such disputes. *Perhaps* a persuasive case can be made that this issue is merely terminological. (Though see n. 17 below.) (On the other hand, a 'no fact of the matter' thesis concerning the debate between error skepticism and contextualism strikes me as altogether unpromising.)

[17] One might try to salvage the view by claiming that we are rarely guided by considerations of literal truth when issuing or assessing knowledge claims, and hence

1. [18] The analogy to exaggerations that is crucial to the second model is extremely strained. In ordinary speech we have devices for making it clear that we are not exaggerating when we make a claim. One use of 'literally' is to do just that: 'He is literally going to die any day now' will, in many settings, be a much better way of conveying that someone is about to die than the bare 'He is going to die any day now'.[19,20] If knowledge ascriptions were ordinarily hyperbolic, one would expect this exaggeration-canceling use of 'literally' to be available. But it isn't. When we say that someone thinks that she knows that p, we have no reluctance in saying that she literally thinks that she knows that p. Moreover, we do not say such things as 'I don't literally know that there is a table in the room, but I do literally know that $2 + 2 = 4$'.

Another sign of exaggeration is that there are conventional preferences for using certain expressions over other, synonymous ones, for the purpose of exaggerating. Thus one might exaggerate the length of a swimming pool by saying 'It was a mile long' but not

that our judgment that it is odd to say 'No one believes that she knows that her towels are in the dryer' does not provide evidence of its falsity. If assertability and truth regularly come apart, and if our intuitions are responsive to assertability rather than truth, then our intuitions that we believe that we know certain things may tell us little about what we in fact believe that we know. I find such maneuvers rather dizzying. Moreover, in discussions of the semantics–pragmatics divide, there remains a place for (albeit fallible) *direct intuitions* of semantic truth value regarding sentences. (For more on the notion of 'direct intuition' that I have in mind, see Kripke 1977.) And in the case of the kinds of belief ascriptions at hand, we have a direct and relatively unshakable intuition that very many of them are true (and not merely that we convey useful information in uttering them). I am grateful for discussions with Ernie Lepore here.

[18] I am grateful to Timothy Williamson here.

[19] Of course, the term 'literally' may have other uses, as in, 'I am literally dying of thirst, dude', as said by a laid-back American (Jonathan Schaffer's example), and H. W. Fowler's 'The 300,000 Unionists ... will be literally thrown to the wolves' (from *Webster's Dictionary*). As Ted Sider pointed out to me, though, there is some room for claiming that these examples do not point to a different use. Perhaps the whole point of these speeches is that 'literally' is a device for representing oneself as not exaggerating, and so its use here serves as a device for exaggerating all the more! Cf.: 'The swimming pool was a mile long. I'm not exaggerating'. I take it, though, that context and cues normally tell us whether the net intended effect is to reinforce an exaggeration or to cancel it.

[20] Consider also the exaggeration-canceling role of 'in fact', used as a verb modifier: 'The swimming pool was in fact a mile long'.

by 'It was a mile in length'. Correlatively, an unwillingness to say 'It was a mile in length' is a good sign that an utterance of 'It was a mile long' was an exaggeration. But we are quite willing to replace 'S knows that p' with such synonymous expressions as 'It is known by S that p' and 'S has the knowledge that p' and so on. Finally, and relatedly, when we exaggerate in saying something of the form 'x is F' we are typically unwilling to say various ostensibly entailed claims. Thus, when we exaggerate, we are happy to say 'It is a mile long', but not happy to say 'It was over three quarters of a mile long'—the exaggerated use disrupts inferential liaisons. But when we say that S knows that p we are typically happy to endorse ostensibly implied weaker claims such as 'S has good reason for thinking that p' as well. So, in short, none of these tests deliver the verdict that ordinary claims involving 'know' are exaggerations

2. Both the second and third pictures put strain on the very notion of semantic value. As a springboard, we can begin with the following plausible constraint on the semantic value of a sentence, offered by Scott Soames:

> [C+] A proposition p is semantically expressed by s only if p is included in the information a competent speaker would assert and intend to convey by an assertive utterance of s in any context c in which s is used with its literal meaning by conversational participants who understand s, provided that (i) s is not used metaphorically, ironically, or sarcastically in c, and (ii) the presumption that the speaker intends to commit himself or herself to p is not defeated by conversational implicature to the contrary. (2002: 60)

But C+ is insufficiently general for our purposes, for we do not merely say things of the form 'S knows that p' in the context of conversation with others; we use representations of that form in our own silent deliberations, in our own silent practical reasoning, and so on. In this regard, it seems that an analogous constraint on semantic value is generated by conditions of conscious acceptance:

[C++]   A proposition *p* is semantically expressed by *s* only if
for any context in which a competent speaker consciously accepts *s*, that speaker would thereby manifest a judgment that *p*, provided that *s* is not used
metaphorically, ironically, or sarcastically in *c*.[21]

The second and third pictures are not outright incompatible
with principles of this sort. After all, the relevant kind of skeptic
can advert to caveats (i) and (ii) in Soames's principle and to the
exception clause in C++. But this leaves the skeptic with the task
of justifying his contention that knowledge ascriptions have the
semantic value that he claims that they do—a contention that is
hard to defend. Consider an ordinary person silently reflecting in a
sober way on whether someone knows something. On the views in
question, her conscious acceptance of a sentence of the form 'S
knows that *p*' will not involve the literal use of 'know'. Now we can,
perhaps, tell a story according to which some phrase is always used
nonliterally, even in the context of inner judgment. (Consider: 'This
line is taking forever; I'd better switch to a different one' as said to
oneself, silently.) But that story will inevitably involve considerations about how the lexical components behave in other linguistic
environments. When such stories can be plausibly told—as they
perhaps can be for sentences like 'This line is taking forever' and 'I
wouldn't touch him with a ten foot pole'—they will appeal to a
crucial contrast between the sentence's literal meaning (elicited
from compositional considerations about how the sentential constituents normally contribute to the meaning of a sentence) and the
proposition that is normally judged to be true when a speaker
consciously accepts that sentence. But no such story can be told
for 'know', since on the view in question, its use is invariably
hyperbolic, and since, unlike 'taking forever', it does not have
lexical constituents that have a sober use in other contexts. And if

---

[21] We can allow that sentences sometimes have metaphorical, ironic, or sarcastic
uses even in one's inner life. Note that the principle corresponds to Kripke's (1997)
'disquotation principle' (though not in its 'strengthened form').

the semantic value of 'know' rarely if ever plays a role in the propositions that are conveyed and believed when knowledge ascriptions get used, then where does its purported semantic value come from? The suspicion remains that both the second and third views posit too great a gap between semantic value and linguistic practice.[22]

A Misleading Analogy

An analogy is sometimes drawn[23] between embracing skepticism about knowledge, and embracing an austere invariantist semantics for absolute comparative adjectives. (Where, following Unger, 'F' is absolute just in case the following schema holds: if x is Fer than y then y is not F.[24]) On such a view, the semantic value of (nearly) all positive ascriptions of any such adjective is false. Consider, for example, an invariantist semantics according to which 'flat' means *absolutely* flat, having *no curvature or bumps whatsoever* (where there is no restriction on the relevant quantifier domain). There are two versions of this approach. According to the first, we do not realize that 'flat' means absolutely bumpless or curveless; as a result, we falsely believe that many actual objects are flat. According to the second, we commit no such mistake: when we use sentences of the form 'S is flat' to communicate information, we realize that their semantic value is false. Call the first the 'error approach', the second the 'pragmatic approach'. For any semantics that makes some class of ordinary utterances come out as invariably false, we have such a choice. Consider, for example, a view according to

---

[22] As Karson Kovakovich has pointed out to me, even if there were a community that began life with a term 'know' such that moderate-standard propositions (so to speak) were pragmatically conveyed rather than semantically expressed by sentences containing it, there is still the concern that, over time, the propositions conveyed would be fossilized into the semantics.

[23] Notably by Unger (1975, 1984).

[24] Cf. Unger (1975, ch. 2). Unger also claims of absolute terms that the pair 'is F' and 'is absolutely F' are synonymous. As noted earlier, we should recognize, following Lewis (1983: 245), that such observations do not in themselves force an austere invariantist semantics upon us.

which 'It is *n* o'clock' always means 'It is *precisely n* o'clock'. We might take an error approach, according to which our semantic blindness causes us to take on false beliefs almost hourly; or we might take a pragmatic approach, according to which our time-related utterances, though almost always false and almost never believed, usefully convey that the time is as close to *n* o'clock as people care about in the context of conversation.

In the case of austere invariantism concerning absolute comparative adjectives, it is the pragmatic approach that is normally in view.[25,26] And it is this approach that underlies the second and third versions of skeptical invariantism described above. But for the reasons just surveyed, neither of these versions of skepticism can be plausibly maintained—though we feel no parallel hesitation in the case of absolute comparative adjectives. That we are drawn to an error view in the one case and a pragmatic view in the other suggests that the analogy between 'know' and absolute comparative adjectives may not be so fruitful for the skeptic after all.

3.4   Evaluating Error Skepticism

The prima facie appeal of an error-skeptical treatment of our puzzles should be obvious. When someone confronts us with a lottery proposition, we are strongly inclined to make a concession speech concerning the ordinary proposition that entails it: 'I guess I was wrong: I didn't really *know* that *p*'. On the most natural reading, this seems to be an admission that one previously believed something false (namely, that one knew that *p*).[27] And as we have seen,

---

[25] 'We often say what is easiest rather than what directly expresses our most relevant beliefs' (Unger 1984: 26).

[26] The reader may wish to consider how the constraints on semantic value just considered bear on the pragmatic approach to 'flat', 'three o'clock', and so on. I shall not pursue the issue here, however.

[27] Contextualists may claim that the use of 'really' is a sign of shifting standards. But there are plenty of cases where 'really' doesn't work that way. If I say 'OK, I didn't really

Single-Premise Closure is extremely compelling. So, on the face of it, lottery considerations provide a compelling argument against most ordinary claims to know.[28,29]

In what follows, I shall briefly consider some problems that seem to confront this appealing version of skeptical invariantism. I do not pretend that any are decisive. We should take care to distinguish *error skepticism*—the thesis that all, or nearly all, ordinary positive knowledge ascriptions are false (though believed to be true)—from the *error skeptic*, one who believes that thesis. Certain arguments that might be leveled against the skeptic—in particular arguments to the effect that the error skeptic holds self-defeating commitments—

work all evening, I went to the movies' or 'OK, I guess she doesn't really like me', these are vehicles for retracting a previous speech, not for shifting the standards associated with the predicate in question. (As Ryan Wasserman has pointed out to me, it is worth exploring further the role of intonation contour and focus in such constructions.)

[28] Note that if one embraces an error theory about ordinary 'would' counterfactuals—see Chapter 1 n. 9—this is likely to make error skepticism seem even more compelling.

[29] In a recent piece Timothy Williamson has suggested that the ordinary concept of danger can help to clarify the concept of knowledge: just as one is in no danger of drowning when in a desert, one is in no danger of error when one knows something (2000: 32). To press his point, the skeptic can usefully use the concept of danger to his advantage: for even if the metaphysical possibility of our being brains in vats does not show that our ordinary beliefs about the external world are in danger of being false, isn't it plausible to suppose that lottery-style considerations do? On any given night, after all, there is some danger that my car will be stolen from my driveway: given this danger, do I really know that it is parked outside? At the same time, linking knowledge to danger may also provide grist to the contextualist mill. For there are contexts where we would say to someone who has parked their car in a safe neighborhood 'Don't worry, there is no danger of your car getting stolen', where it is nevertheless true that cars sometimes get stolen in that neighborhood. A proper evaluation of these matters requires, *inter alia*, further exploration of the relevant notion of danger. Williamson (2000) suggests that the notion of danger (*a*) is objective and (*b*) can apply even in a deterministic world (and is thus not to be assimilated to a notion of objective chance that treats every nonactual future event in a deterministic world as having zero chance of occurring). But as against (*a*) we should note uses of the concept that are clearly sensitive to epistemic context, especially in application to the past. (Someone does not show up. I say 'There is a danger that something terrible has happened to him'.) And as against (*b*), consider a Laplacean demon in a deterministic world who notices that a meteor will just miss the earth. Earth dwellers assert 'There is a danger that the meteor will hit us'. It would, intuitively, be appropriate for the demon to correct them: 'No there isn't. There is no danger whatsoever that it will hit you'. Further investigation is called for.

may not cut any ice against the thesis of error skepticism. (After all, it is open to us to adopt an agnostic attitude towards error skepticism: even if it is somehow self-defeating to believe it, it doesn't follow that one ought to believe its denial.[30])

The Objection from Common Sense

It is often maintained that skepticism flies in the face of common sense and that we can, with G. E. Moore, reject it on those grounds alone. But the appeal to common sense is something of a double-edged sword. After all, doesn't common sense tell us that we don't know that we will lose the lottery, that we don't know whether we will have a sudden heart attack, and that we don't know whether our car has been stolen overnight? The whole point of our puzzle is that common sense pushes us in different directions. A war of words deploying the 'It is common sense that' operator seems to have no clear victor. So let us pursue a slightly different tack, following the lead of Paul Grice.

In 'Common Sense and Skepticism' Grice raises the following question: 'Is it logically possible for it to be true that most people would usually, or more often than not, use an expression "p" to describe a certain kind of situation, and yet be false that "p" is a correct description of that situation...?' (1989*b*: 151). Grice then points out that the skeptic will have to maintain that it is. In actual fact, the scenario described by the question is obviously logically possible. It is obviously possible that everyone assent, say, to the sentence 'Franklin was the inventor of bifocals' even if someone else invented them and Franklin took credit,[31] or that everyone accept

---

[30] One is reminded of the ancient skeptic Sextus Empiricus, who tells us 'it must further be remembered that we say that we neither affirm nor deny anything of the things said dogmatically about non-evident things—for we yield only to those things which move us affectively and necessarily to assent' (Hankinson 1995: 281). Hankinson goes on to note that Sextus never commits himself to the normative claim that one ought to suspend judgment on non-evident things (p. 282). A good deal turns, note, on the distinction between the evident and the nonevident.

[31] Cf. Kripke (1980).

'Henry VIII loved Catherine of Aragon more than anyone' on the basis of misleading information. Likewise, a computational flaw in some mathematical proof or engineering calculation might go unnoticed and on that basis a community might assent in unison to '*p*' even though '*p*' expresses a falsehood. (Everyone at a given time might assent to 'The *Titanic* would not be sunk by collision with an iceberg' on the basis of faulty calculations.)

Community-wide error about some empirical matter of fact is not surprising at all; nor is community-wide confusion on the basis of computational error. What is a little harder to make sense of, perhaps, is a situation where the semantic value of '*p*' is invariably believed to hold of a certain kind of situation—and yet this is due neither to any error in calculation nor to any mistake about the basic empirical facts.[32] This, I suspect, is the issue that Grice is getting at. To take a simple example: if all English speakers agree that 'big number' applies to the number 1 million, it is hard to make sense of how they could be wrong. Likewise, it might be argued, it is hard to make sense of the skeptic's suggestion that we are all wrong about ordinary knowledge ascriptions, though we are fully apprised of the facts, and have not made any calculational errors.[33] I suspect that when philosophers appeal to common sense in repudiating

---

[32] One might worry here about what the notion of 'basic empirical fact' really comes to, as it is being used here. I will set that issue aside.

[33] I note in passing that there is a case to be made that something akin to a calculational error may go on in certain knowledge ascriptions. Daniel Kahneman, Amos Tversky, and others have begun the task of identifying the heuristics that we use in calibrating judgments of risk and danger, pointing out that such heuristics may lead to gross miscalibration in certain settings. Insofar as such heuristics in turn affect our knowledge judgments, then systematic error about knowledge may be put down to a calculational error of sorts. (See Kahneman, Slovic, and Tversky 1982; Kahneman and Tversky 2000). A number of findings from these works may offer special encouragement to the skeptic: We have a marked tendency to view ourselves as 'personally immune to hazards' (see Slovic, Fischhoff, and Lichtenstein 1982); we are overconfident with regard to 'general knowledge items of moderate to extreme difficulty'—even to the extent of often being willing to make 'probability 1' and 'probability 0' claims in settings where there is very significant risk of error (see Lichtenstein, Fischhoff, and Phillips 1982); we reckon possible futures that do not strike us as 'representative' as significantly less likely than futures that do so strike us as such, even where the chance of each is demonstrably the same (see Kahneman and Tversky 1982). And so on.

skepticism, what they often have in mind is something like this objection.

In addressing the issue, Grice imagines the following case:

> Suppose a state of society in which our linguistic behavior were such that all of us, on most occasions when we wished to describe a situation involving a rose, used expressions such as 'that is a cauliflower' (or other suitable expressions containing the word 'cauliflower'); and all of us on all occasions also used expressions containing the word 'cauliflower' to describe cauliflower situations. Suppose, however, also that on all those occasions when we had before our minds the thought both of a rose and a cauliflower (for example, when our attention was drawn to our practice of using the word 'cauliflower' in descriptions both of rose situations and cauliflower situations), we then called a rose 'a rose' and refused to call it 'a cauliflower'... (1989*b*: 151)

Grice notes that there are various semantic perspectives one might adopt here. According to one thesis, 'cauliflower' is ambiguous; there is no semantic conflict between one's earlier ascription of 'cauliflower' to roses and one's later refusal to so ascribe it. According to another, the meaning of 'cauliflower' is uniform, and either the earlier ascription or the later refusal is incorrect.[34]

As Grice notes, analogous moves are available in the case of skepticism. This raises two key questions. First, are there lines of thought that render us (appropriately) unwilling to assent to the kinds of positive knowledge ascriptions to which we habitually assent? Second, insofar as we find ourselves unwilling to so assent, what semantic perspective should we take with respect to our earlier selves? The standard contextualist in epistemology, notice, occupies the analogue of the first position on 'cauliflower' (so long as we are not overly meticulous about the distinction, whatever it comes to, between context-dependence and ambiguity). Such a contextualist standardly concedes that in the face of skeptical lines of thought we ought to dissent from ordinary positive know-ledge ascriptions. She will then point out, with Grice, that one

---

[34] I might mention that Grice (1989*b*: 151) takes seriously the possibility that the issue is epistemically undecidable.

cannot infer skeptical invariantism from the fact that no one knows anything (or hardly anything)—even if it is a fact—since that fact can be explained well enough by supposing that we are in a context where the standards attaching to 'know' are unusually high, without pretending that they are uniformly high across contexts.

For the sake of argument, let us grant the existence of lines of thought that make assertoric endorsement of ordinary knowledge ascriptions inappropriate. If we have gone that far with skepticism, is it at least very tempting to eschew an ambiguity-based salvage of earlier ascriptions in favor of an error thesis. After all, if we habitually predicate 'F' of some situation, but upon prolonged rational reflection find ourselves disinclined to predicate 'F' of that situation, then we should hardly feel bound to insist that our earlier, unreflective use of 'F' was correct. Or so it would seem. Even if one does not endorse some sort of constitutive equivalence between the extension of a term and the deliverances of idealized reflection, it hardly seems a stretch to allow that the deliverances of such reflection are a better guide to the extension of a term than our ordinary habits.[35] Granted, the contextualist will insist that a change in meaning occurs during the reflective process. But what we are after is an argument *why* this should be so. The point can be illustrated even with the case of 'big' given earlier.[36] Suppose we encounter a tribe such that if you ask its members 'Is 37 a big number?', they say 'Yes' (same for 38 and 39), but if you ask them 'Is 40 a big number' they are uncertain and even incline towards 'No'. They universally agree that if x is greater than y and y is 'big' then x is 'big' too. When they reflect on their practice, they notice the glitch—recognizing, perhaps, that they had a slight tendency to

[35] If the skeptic's candidate referent for 'know' were particularly natural vis-à-vis the competitors, then he would have an extra argument as well: Other things being equal, joints in nature trump gerrymandered properties when it comes to reference (see Lewis 1999). It is not so clear, however, that the skeptic is particularly well placed to use eligibility considerations in his favor. (I see much more clearly how this might work in favor of an 'absolutist' semantics for 'flat'.) The matter certainly merits further investigation.

[36] I am grateful to conversations with Tim Williamson here.

allow how long it takes to say the number in their native language to play a role in their brute unreflective judgments. Upon reflection, they decide that 40 is 'big' after all. In this case an error perspective on the earlier claim '40 is not big' seems perfectly in order. This is quite compatible, of course, with acknowledging that their prior widespread disposition to apply 'not big' to 40 was evidence—even quite good evidence—that 'is not big' was true of 40. To take a more familiar example: we are quite willing to allow that rational reflection might induce us to dissent from an ethical sentence that previously received widespread assent. (The fact that everyone in a community uses terms like 'good' or 'just' to describe certain activities—keeping slaves, for example—is far from decisive evidence that those terms apply.)[37] And when this happens, we are quite ready to embrace an error view over an ambiguity view. (In general, apparent normative disagreement is rarely handled via an appeal to ambiguity.)[38]

It thus appears that there are situations where '*p*' is habitually used to describe a situation and yet, despite there being no ignorance of the relevant empirical facts and despite there being no computational error, a mistake is made. There will also be cases, of course, where we begin with a widespread commitment to '*p*' but on reflection find there to be competing considerations for and against '*p*', and then shift from belief to agnosticism. Cases that fit this mold will not be hard to contrive and may serve as an even better model for the skeptic.

Nothing I have said here indicts the idea that widespread application of a term to a situation in which there is no empirical illusion

---

[37] I am grateful to Brian Weatherson here.

[38] As Tamar Gendler pointed out to me, an interesting case study is provided by 'disgusting': We are inclined to judge certain things clean and nondisgusting until we look closely at them; when we do, we realize that they are crawling with microscopic vermin. Even though additional empirical information becomes available, when we use the microscope, it's not clear (to say the least) that this is the perspective we want to privilege when contriving a semantics. Interestingly, though, there is a marked tendency in untutored practice (i) to translate homophonically across perspectives and (ii) to treat the microscope as giving us enlightenment on the matter.

and no straightforward computational error is pretty good evidence that the term is true of that situation. (Hence the Moorean Constraint on the scorecard.) Moreover, it is undoubtedly true that dispositions to apply predicates are constitutively relevant to extension: without pretending to have a complete metaphysics of meaning at our disposal,[39] it seems pretty clear that a correct metaphysical account of why a predicate like 'thin' has the extension that it does will advert to dispositions to apply that term under certain perceptually presented circumstances. Nevertheless, a commitment to ordinary practice should not be overstated.

The Impermanence of Skeptical Attitudes

Consider some of the analogies just presented. Having detected a glitch in their use of 'big' and corrected it, members of the tribe will presumably remember to call 40 'big' in the future. Having reached a certain ethical insight, one will presumably learn to be critical of the opposing position. But things do not appear to proceed this way in the case of the skeptical arguments under consideration. Suppose I come to think that I do not know whether I will have a heart attack in the near future, and on this basis, I conclude that I do not know what I will be doing next summer. Even as I form the skeptical belief, I realize that I will not remain committed to it for long. If the skeptic is to maintain that his arguments provide us with a powerful reason to forever refrain from believing positive knowledge ascriptions, how is he to explain our willingness to lapse—doxastically as well as assertorically—into those very ascriptions?

David Hume offered a kind of answer to this question: Our nature sees to it that reason loses its grip on us, so that we are able in a short while to believe something which we now have compelling reason to think is false: "'Tis happy, therefore, that nature breaks the force of all skeptical arguments in time, and keeps them from having any considerable influence on the

---

[39] Kripke (1982) shows very well how simple-minded accounts are bound to fail.

understanding.'[40] (Consider by analogy the biases in risk assessment and decision-making induced by the heuristics that are invariably deployed by the human mind for such purposes. One would hardly expect such biases to disappear from our practice simply on account of their having been pointed out to us.[41])

So what should we make of a Hume-embellished error skepticism? Recall that we need to distinguish the question of evaluating the skeptical thesis from that of evaluating the skeptic who positively endorses it. There are special worries about the latter: after all, once one has allowed that nature frequently leads one to find opinions compelling that would be abhorrent to the detached light of reason, it becomes a pressing matter *which* perspectives signal the distractions of nature at work, which not. Why be so confident that nature is not playing a distracting role when skeptical intuitions are forceful? (Perhaps it is in our nature to *underestimate* our knowledge and it is for that reason that the lottery argument confuses us.) Even if this kind of worry undermines the skeptic (who is positively committed to skepticism), it does not yet quite tell us whether and why to outright reject the relevant version of skepticism (even though, no doubt, it provides some negative evidence).

Assertion, Practical Reasoning, and Skepticism

A real trouble spot for skepticism arises from the normative connections between knowledge, assertion, and practical reasoning. Let us begin with assertion.

There are two versions of error skepticism that we might consider here. One version affirms that knowledge is the norm of assertion, a second version denies it. Let us consider each in turn.

Let us say that a theory is *weakly self-defeating* if it entails that one oughtn't to assert it, *strongly self-defeating* if it entails that one ought to assert its negation. The first version of error skepticism, in its

---

[40] *Treatise*, I. iv. 1 (1968: 187).
[41] For discussion of the techniques available for 'debiasing', see Kahnemann, Slovic, and Tversky (1982, pt. VIII, 'Corrective Procedures').

perfectly global form—one according to which all positive knowledge ascriptions are false—is weakly self-defeating: if it is true, then one oughtn't to assert it. It is not strongly self-defeating: it does not say that one ought to assert its negation. Asserting a weakly self-defeating theory is a bad idea: it is tantamount to asserting a claim of the form '*p* and I shouldn't believe *p*', for if *p* is a weakly self-defeating theory, the first conjunct entails the second. But that does not obviously tell us that there is anything wrong with suspending judgment on this version of error skepticism.[42] Moreover, slightly less global versions of error skepticism might not even be weakly self-defeating.[43]

I do not then think that considerations of self-defeat indict a view that combines error skepticism with knowledge as the norm of assertion. But what does make trouble for that view is the sheer implausibility of its claim that assertions are always (or nearly always) improper.[44] Given that it is hard to take seriously the suggestion that all assertions are improper, the second version of error skepticism (that denies that knowledge is the norm of assertion) is likely to seem the more plausible. Such a view need not deny that we *think* that knowledge is the norm of assertion. It merely needs to say that insofar as we think this, we are wrong, and that some alternative normative theory is correct. Perhaps for

[42] Nor even, strictly speaking, that one shouldn't believe it. From the fact that one shouldn't assert *p*, it does not straightforwardly follow that one shouldn't believe it. (Thanks to Karson Kovakovich here.)

[43] Distinguish conditional from unconditional global skepticism (in their error-theoretic invariantist versions). Conditional global skepticism takes the form: If people are using 'know' in the ways I think then error-theoretic skeptical invariantism is true. Unconditional global skepticism takes the form: Error-theoretic skeptical invariantism is true. Suppose one's skepticism did not extend to a priori matters. Then one might at least allow oneself to know conditional global skepticism. (Thanks to Ted Sider here.)

[44] Nor can one easily try to allay the concern with revisionary language. Suppose someone suggested that we dispense with the concept of what one ought to do and opt instead for some successor concept ought*, allowing, for example, that knowledge isn't the norm* of assertion. As noted earlier, we do not find it intuitive, when confronted with apparent normative disagreement, to explain the disagreement away by appeal to ambiguity. If someone used a term 'ought*' as their guide in this way, we would inevitably translate 'ought*' by 'ought', 'norm*' by 'norm', and claim that such a person is denying that knowledge is the norm of assertion.

an assertion to be proper, it merely has to be as close to knowledge as the context demands. It might even be maintained that assertions of the form '*p* and I do not know it' are appropriate, despite our impression to the contrary: our sense of an impropriety is grounded in the mistaken conviction that an assertion is proper only if it is known. While such a view is not manifestly absurd, its abandonment of the intuitive connection between knowledge and assertion surely has to be reckoned a cost.

Let us turn now to practical reasoning. It is radically implausible to suppose that such reasoning is always improper. The Ancient Skeptics, apparently, aimed for a life from which practical reasoning was absent, supplanted by habits and mechanized routine. Here is Hankinson's bleak description of the way of life that the Skeptic seeks:

a Skeptic might heed a warning not to eat a poisoned breakfast without its being true that he acts directly upon the semantic content of the warning. The warning affects him but not, or at least not directly, because it is the warning that it is. ... Comparison with programmed responsive machines is instructive. ... Skeptics are automata of the same type. ... The Skeptic may still reason—what has gone is any tendency to act on the basis of those reasons taken as reasons. The Skeptic will come to derive impressions from the breakfast which do set it apart from ordinary non-toxic cases. He may even perform tests upon it which, from our Dogmatist's perspective, we would describe as confirming the view that it was poisoned—the important point is that, for such a sequence of behavior to be action guiding, the Skeptic need not so represent it to himself. Rather he simply follows out a routine, acting on the basis of commemorative signs.[45]

Whatever our views on the nomic possibility of human beings becoming the kinds of skeptics that Hankinson describes on behalf of Sextus, it is clear that the above descriptions do not even begin to strike us as descriptions of a kind of being that we ought to become. Once again we should give more credence to a version of error skepticism that denies that knowledge is the norm of practical reasoning—as opposed to one that maintains that all practical reasoning is improper. Such a theory might tell us, for example, that it is acceptable to use a premise in practical reasoning just in case it is as epistemically probable as the deliberative situation demands. But, as in the case of assertion, we need to reckon this revisionism as a cost.

Knowing Probably p

The thesis that nearly all ordinary knowledge ascriptions are false is in principle compatible with the thesis that one can know that probably *p* for very many ordinary propositions *p*: despite being unable to know ordinary propositions, one can know very many claims of epistemic probability. Thus it is open to the error skeptic to take the line offered by Nelkin (2000) to our puzzle—one is merely in a position to know that the ordinary proposition is probably true. (Nelkin is talking about the particular case of lotteries: he does not seem to be fully aware of the generality of the problem.) I expect this view to have significant appeal to many readers. I am not, however, much appeased by it. When one supposes, say, that one knows that one will probably be at a meeting in a week, one normally assumes that one knows, flat-out, a good deal about one's current environment. But if one responds to each version of our puzzle by conceding that one does not know the ordinary proposition, then any such assumption is incorrect. We should not, then, look past the fact that ordinary beliefs about what we know turn out false, by the lights of this view. Nor should we look past the fact that this view, like other versions of error skepticism, has to choose between disrupting the intuitive connection between knowledge and assertion and defending the implausible normative claim that nearly all assertions are improper.

There is another basic problem. Supposing that one is skeptical enough to suppose that one knows hardly anything, flat-out, about the external world. Why suppose that one is nevertheless in a position to know this or that claim of epistemic probability? If the facts of the world are so epistemically elusive, why should the facts of epistemic probability be so epistemically secure?

What of the tie between knowledge and practical reasoning? Here matters are a little more complicated. There are Bayesians who reckon it normatively desirable to confine oneself to probabilistic premises in practical reasoning—unless the premises are a priori certain.[46] Their idealized Bayesian reasoner is one that we strive to approximate as best we can and, to the extent that we fall short, we are subject to normative criticism. From such a perspective, it is a normative blemish on our part that we often use practical syllogisms with premises that are neither probabilistic nor a priori knowable (albeit a minor blemish, insofar as it does not yield behaviors that diverge from one recommended by an expected utility calculation performed by the idealized Bayesian version of ourselves). Given the probabilistic version of error skepticism, there remains the prospect of defending the intuitive connection between knowledge and practical reasoning.[47]

There are deep questions here concerning the proper role of the idealized Bayesian reasoner just described in the normative evaluation of human beings, ones that I cannot fully engage with here. But I strongly suspect that there is room for a normative framework more directly tied to human reasoners (that is, to the human epistemic situation, rather than idealized Bayesian reasoners), that such a normative framework is the one most familiar to us, and that the concept of knowledge has its place within that more familiar normative framework. This is a framework in which in any given practical environment, many empirical propositions will properly be taken for granted and will serve to narrow down one's epistemic state space to worlds in which the negations of the propositions do not hold (and hence where the epistemic probability of those contingent propositions is zero). And it is a framework in which a proposition that is properly taken for granted in one

---

[46] I am thinking here of the Bayesian who thinks of updating in terms of Jeffrey conditionalization (see Jeffrey 1983).

[47] Thanks to Brian Weatherson here.

practical environment is not so treated in a different practical environment (and hence where our epistemic life does not—and should not—unfold in a way that approximates Bayesian conditionalization).[48] In the 'Practical Environment' section of this chapter, I shall begin an account of how the concept of knowledge is located within such a framework.

Here is one final consideration, which is independent of the previous one. Let us suppose that the error skeptic of the current stripe has succeeded in identifying some relation K,[49] such that we only at best K that probably *p*, for this or that empirical *p* (and perhaps even for this or that mathematical *p* and this or that experience-describing *p*).[50] We now have to make a semantic decision concerning 'know'. We may say that 'know' expresses K, so that error skepticism is right. Or else we may say that (at least in some contexts), sentences of the form 'S knows that *p*' are true iff *p* and the person designated by 'S' Ks that probably *p* (in which case either contextualism or moderate invariantism is true). Are we so sure that the error-skeptical semantic strategy is preferable? The familiar pressures towards a non-skeptical semantic treatment apply with equal force here.

A Final Worry[51]

I end with a general problem for all types of skeptical invariantism. That style of position is often motivated by considering comparative

---

[48] I do not take diachronic Dutch book and Reflection arguments lightly. But nor do I find them decisive. I lack the space to pursue these matters here. See Williamson (2000, ch. 10) for a helpful discussion of Bayesian conditionalization and the dynamics of our epistemic life. I note one key theme: while the idealized Bayesian reasoner has perfect access to his or her degrees of belief, an analogous thesis cannot hold for evidential probability (at least in the human case), due (among other things) to the fact that knowing is quite compatible with not knowing that one knows.

[49] See, though, the next section.

[50] I note that if one doesn't at least K various propositions describing one's experiences, then it will be particularly hard to combine a knowledge = K thesis with the plausible view that epistemic probability is a matter of how well supported this or that proposition is by what one knows. (For more on the latter, see Williamson 2002.)

[51] Similar themes are discussed in Lawlor (forthcoming).

adjectives—'flat', 'empty', and so on—and in particular those comparative adjectives for which claims of the form 'That is F, but
something else is Fer' have an air of unassertability. Regardless of
the ultimate merits of an invariantist semantics for those 'absolute'
comparative adjectives, it is clear enough what the candidate invariantist semantics would look like, since it can and has been explained
using the comparative version of the adjective:

> Something is flat iff nothing could possibly be flatter.
> Something is empty iff nothing could possibly be emptier.[52]

But it is not so clear that we have nearly as secure a grip on what
the candidate high standard semantic value for the verb 'knows' is
even supposed to be. Let me make two points in this connection.
One obvious difference between the verb 'knows' and comparative
adjectives (beyond the fact that one is a verb and the others are
adjectives!) is that there is no analogous comparative use of 'knows'.
We can say 'She knows more than he' but that does not mark a
comparison between individual pieces of knowledge.[53] So we
cannot readily use the model of the 'absolute' comparative adjective
as a basis for articulating a super-high standard of application.
Speaking with maximal abstractness: mastery of the comparative

---

[52] Note that if, as Jason Stanley (2000) has urged, there is a contextual parameter
associated with 'The cup is empty' marked by a hidden 'of x', many of the issues raised
by skeptical invariantism will still remain: will a cup that contains a single drop of
vodka falsify an ascription of the form 'That is empty of vodka'? The analogue of the
skeptic will refuse to allow properties like being a drinkable quantity of vodka to be
among the candidate values along the relevant parameter.

[53] Admittedly, we say 'He knows better than anyone', but this construction has
limited usefulness in the current context. For one thing: while 'a is flatter than b' does
not entail that a is flat, 'S knows that p better than anyone' entails that S knows that p.
Moreover, I think Dretske is roughly correct in taking 'such constructions to be
describing not better knowledge, but more direct, more compelling kinds of evidence'
(2000*b*: 48). (I note in passing that there is reason to think that there is a rough and ready
ranking of categories of evidence that is common to humans. See Palmer (2001).
Especially interesting here are the data provided by languages with 'evidentials',
markers for the kind of evidence that one has for one's assertion.) Note also that
Stanley (unpub.) argues that the 'better than anyone' construction is idiomatic on the
basis of the dubious intelligibility of such constructions as 'doesn't know better than
anyone that p' and 'knows better than three people that p'.

use of a comparative adjective requires a conceptual grip on some kind of scale. Where the scale has an upper bound, it will provide the basis for a concept that applies to a thing iff it is at that upper bound. In the case of 'flat' and 'empty', it is clear that we associate the relevant kind of scale with the adjective and thus, whatever we think of the actual semantics for 'is flat' and 'is empty', we can perfectly well understand a very demanding notion of 'perfectly flat' and 'perfectly empty'. The question at hand is whether our mastery of 'know' has a scale of the required kind as a conceptual backdrop; and with no comparative use of 'know' to rely on, it is very much an open question whether our mastery of 'know' is dependent on a scale, let alone one with an upper bound.[54] Second, most efforts to articulate a 'super sense' for 'knows' presume an independent grip on the concept of evidence. So, for example, the skeptic might say that in order to know p, our evidence has to entail p. Recent work in epistemology suggests that the concept of evidence cannot be understood independently of the concept of knowledge: Williamson (2000) has persuasively argued that one's evidence is all and only the propositions that one knows. If that is right, then the evidence constraint does nothing by way of articulating a demanding conception of knowledge. For if evidence is what one knows, then by anyone's standards, one's evidence will have to entail p in order for one to know p. (Similar points may well apply to attempts to explain the skeptic's conception of knowledge that deploy the concept of 'objective certainty'.)[55] Similarly, it might be said that if one super-knows p, it must be the case that p, where the 'must' is here used as a vehicle of epistemic modality. But if epistemic modals connect with the concept of knowledge in the way that I have presumed, this once again does nothing by way of

---

[54] Thanks to Jonathan Vogel here.

[55] Moreover, if the concept of evidence is crafted in such a way that it is not analytic that one knows one's evidence, then why should a proposition's being entailed by one's evidence necessitate one's knowing it in any way at all. The evidential constraint is thus at best a necessary condition on the super-sense of knowing, and it remains unclear what to add to the necessary condition to round out one's conception of what the super-knowing comes to.

delineating a super-sense for 'know'. If 'It might be that p' just means that p is consistent with what I know, then *of course* my knowing that p entails that it must be that p and that it is not the case that it might be that not-p. Skeptics and nonskeptics alike should all agree with that. The content of the 'super-sense' of 'know' remains a mystery.[56]

Most textbooks concede to the skeptic that we have 'Cartesian certainty' about hardly anything, taking the central issue to be whether 'know' expresses the relation that the skeptic expresses by 'Cartesian certainty', or instead something rather more modest. It is standardly agreed that 'Cartesian certainty' would be rather nice if we had it, and that it's something of a disappointment that we don't. We presume that God, if he exists, does have it (though we can't quite understand what that would be like)[57] and try to craft suitably mundane goals for ourselves. Framing our dispute with the skeptic in this way may be to concede more than is necessary. Even leaving aside whether it is the denotatum of 'knows', it remains an open question whether the skeptic even has a coherent positive conception of a relation that some of us hope to (but rarely do) have to propositions.

3.5   Scorecard

It is clear enough that a number of the structural constraints on the concept of knowledge are perfectly compatible with skepticism.

---

[56] Nor will my current concern be alleviated by maintaining that knowledge (in the super-sense) requires being sure or being psychologically certain. Granted, 'being sure' and 'being certain' admit comparative uses for which the notions of being absolutely certain and being absolutely sure are clear enough. But the skeptic does not think that the high standards that he associates with 'know' consist merely in a requirement of being sure. So even if such a requirement could be defended, it would not give us a secure grip on what the skeptic is after.

[57] We might thus be tempted to fall back on the hypothesis that (as José Benardete put it in conversation) Cartesian certainty is unachievable for mind *qua* mind.

Indeed, skepticism uses them to its advantage: Single-Premise Closure, in combination with the apparent datum that we do not know lottery propositions, yields skeptical results. The Objective Chance Principle, in combination with the Epistemic Possibility Constraint, puts pressure on any claim to know the future. The Disquotational Schema blocks contextualist peacemaking. And Multi-Premise Closure makes any claim that one can know lottery propositions look particularly implausible, given the manifest absurdity of any claim to know long conjunctions of them. The costs, meanwhile, are clear enough: The Moorean Constraint is obviously violated. Skepticism is also at odds with the intuitive normative connections between knowledge, assertion, and practical reasoning that we have described. The scorecard is not obviously terrible. But we should carefully examine alternative approaches.

3.6　The Successful Moorean

Consider a thesis of the form 'No one knows any F-type proposition' that precludes knowledge of some ordinary proposition *p*. Call such a thesis a 'skeptical thesis'. Error skepticism will entail all sorts of wide-ranging skeptical theses. Of course, it is not merely skeptical invariantists who allow that far-ranging skeptical theses can express truths. Contextualists allow that too. But while inferences from

> We know that *p*

to

> Contextualism about the verb 'know' is incorrect

are altogether unacceptable (since the contextualist hardly insists that skeptical standards prevail in all contexts), the inference from

> We know that *p*

to

> Skeptical invariantism is false

is perfectly acceptable. So if the former can be known and one can build on one's knowledge by deductive inference, it seems that the latter can be known too.

Assuming epistemic closure, it isn't true that anyone who knows that p will be in a position to deduce that a skeptical thesis that indicts knowledge of p is false. The falsity of that theory can be deduced from 'S knows that p'. But it cannot be deduced from 'p'. But if S knows that he (or someone else) knows that p, then, assuming closure, if that person deduces that the skeptical thesis is false, comes to believe it is false on that basis, and retains his knowledge that p throughout, he will thereby come to know that the skeptical thesis is false. And, once again assuming Single-Premise Closure, he will thereby be able to come to know that skepticism is false.

I have criticized general theses to the effect that common sense is never wrong (with this or that qualification). We should thus not applaud one who rejects skeptical theses on the basis of any such generalization about common sense. But what of the more flat-footed Moorean who uses 'Some people know p' as a basis for deducing the falsity of the skeptical thesis? We should not expect the Moorean to be able to change the mind of someone who has suspended judgment about anyone's being able to know p. But what of the Moorean himself? Is there any special reason to think that this is not an acceptable way to come to know that the skeptical thesis is false? Insofar as someone comes to know that a skeptical thesis is false in this way, let us call that person a 'successful Moorean'. Is the successful Moorean an impossible creature?

Assuming Single-Premise Closure, there seem only three grounds upon which one might say that the successful Moorean is an impossible creature (or at least a humanly impossible creature). (1) One might think that insofar as the successful Moorean knows someone knows p, it is inevitable that the successful Moorean already knows that error skepticism is false. Given that in general one needn't know the a priori consequences of what one knows, I don't see any compelling reason to believe this. (2) One might think that while the successful Moorean might know *p*, the act of performing the inference to the conclusion that skepticism is false inevitably destroys the knowledge that *p*: hence the retention clause invoked by Single-Premise Closure is not satisfied. We shall take a sympathetic look at a weaker version of this idea later: but the suggestion that such an inference *must* destroy knowledge (at least in all human cases) is overblown. (3) One might think that knowledge that someone knows that *p* is impossible (or at least humanly impossible).

It seems that only (3) can be taken very seriously. If the successful Moorean is humanly impossible, that is because second-order knowledge of ordinary propositions is humanly impossible. However, it seems to me that insofar as humans can know a wide range of ordinary propositions, humans *can* have such second-order knowledge. Suppose we agree that humans can know such ordinary propositions as that other humans are happy, that other humans *want* a certain result, that other humans achieved what they wanted, that other humans are *noticing* a certain event, and so on. Grant that we can know such things and it seems extremely strained to suppose that we can never know that other humans *know* this or that. Thus it appears that insofar as the successful Moorean is humanly impossible, that can only be because some far-ranging skeptical thesis is true. The point is limited but important: if wide-ranging skeptical theses are false, then the Moorean route is not an illegitimate way of knowing that they are false.

Of course, that does not mean that skeptical theses have no further interest for the successful Moorean. Such a character might pursue certain issues concerning *why* the skeptical thesis is false even if she knows that it is false. She might still, for example, want to wonder exactly how to diagnose the puzzlement generated by the problems we began with. Assuming that we do know many ordinary propositions, what exactly do we say about our epistemic position with regard to lottery propositions? Do we know them in many cases after all? Are we thereby in a position to assert them and use them in practical reasoning after all? Does the intuitive connection between objective chance and knowledge fail to hold after all? And so on. The successful Moorean will further have to make a choice between some version of contextualism and some version of moderate invariantism. The successful Moorean who finds no interest in all of these questions will scarcely seem like a philosopher at all. (Not that everyone has to be a philosopher.) The discussion that follows—devoted to the details of moderate invariantism—should thus be of interest even to those philosophers who consider themselves successful Mooreans.

3.7   Simple Moderate Invariantism

We shall begin with a moderate invariantist treatment of our puzzle that is very straightforward—if a little flatfooted—then move on to consider some more sophisticated—some will say sophistical—versions of that view.

The 'simple' moderate invariantist claims that in nearly every case that we have been considering, we *do* know the relevant lottery propositions. If I hold a lottery ticket, I believe that it will lose; and that belief has sufficient credentials to count as knowledge. The same goes for my belief that I will not be one of the unlucky people to have a fatal heart attack in the near future. And so on. The proponent of this view would not pretend that the ordinary channel to such knowledge is via deduction from ordinary propositions, though she would be happy to accept such a route as a perfectly acceptable way to extend one's knowledge to lottery propositions in those cases where the relevant ordinary propositions are known and the relevant lottery propositions are not known already. It is to be conceded, of course, that in those cases where one holds a winning lottery ticket, one does not know that the ticket will lose: knowledge attributions are factive. (So too in cases where one is destined to have a fatal heart attack.) But in the standard case in which one thinks one will lose the lottery, the following conditional is true:

> The lottery ticket will lose ⊃ One knows the lottery ticket will lose.

Moreover, if one were to believe a number of propositions of the form 'S's lottery ticket will lose' in a given lottery, then the set of conditionals taking the following form will be true:

> S's lottery ticket will lose ⊃ One knows that S's lottery ticket will lose.[58]

It is very clear that the proponent of this view will deny Multi-Premise Closure. In a 10,000 ticket lottery, one can know many propositions of the form 'Ticket N will lose'. But it seems outright absurd to suppose that one can come to know the conjunction of those propositions by deduction. To allow that is to allow that one can know which ticket will win: after all, the proponent of this view, generous in his allotment of knowledge, will hardly wish to deny that one can in such a case know that 1–10,000 are all the tickets in the lottery. Combine that with, for each *x* that is a loser, the knowledge that *x* will lose, and one can deduce the winner. Now the source of the problem hardly seems to be that performing deductions from known premises destroys one's knowledge of them. (For example, it hardly seems that conjunction introduction destroys knowledge of the conjuncts.) Hence the proponent of this view will have to allow that there can be cases where premises are

---

[58] Might the simple moderate invariantist claim that while one often knows one will lose the lottery one isn't well placed to know that one knows that one will lose the lottery? This is not a plausible position: assuming simple moderate invariantism, it seems easy enough to know that one knows. (Note the curious tendency of philosophers to treat 'I know that I know' claims as epistemically elusive while treating 'I know that he knows' claims as epistemically mundane. Thanks to Stewart Cohen—drawing on a conversation with Saul Kripke—here.) I suspect that if one is to defend the view that one knows but does not know that one knows in this case, it will have to be because it is very hard to know that anything like simple moderate invariantism is true. I shall not explore the matter further here.

known, a conclusion deduced and believed thereby, knowledge of the premises retained, and yet the conclusion not known. Multi-Premise Closure is thus abandoned.

What of the connection between epistemic possibility and knowledge? Can the proponent of simple moderate invariantism maintain that 'It might be that not-p' said by S at t is true only if it is not the case that S knows that p at t? If so, then he is committed to saying that when someone holds a lottery ticket that will go on to lose, the claim 'I might win' is false in that person's mouth. Consider, moreover, a plausible and standard structural constraint on any notion of probability: if p and q are incompatible, then the probability of their disjunction is equal to the sum of the probability of their disjuncts (the principle of finite additivity). Assume that at t, prior to the draw, each holder of a losing ticket is known to S and that it is known to S that one of 1–10,000 will win. In fact #7 will win. It follows that '#7 might lose' is false and '#7 must win' is true in the mouth of S. Not only are such claims very strange in their own right: if such claims are true, it becomes extremely unclear why a person cannot, after all, know who the winner is going to be by deduction from the premises. Presumably, then, the proponent of simple moderate invariantism will hold that we are mistaken in our unreflective subscription not only to Multi-Premise Closure but also to the thesis that a subject's knowing p entails zero epistemic chance for the subject that not-p. Rather, she will suggest, when our attention is drawn to some positive epistemic chance that not-p, we erroneously infer that we do not know p. In the lottery case in particular, parity reasoning makes salient the epistemic chance of the lottery proposition's falsity—which in turn makes salient the epistemic chance of the negation of those ordinary propositions that entail it. But the inference to the conclusion that we do not know one or the other is a mistake, based on a faulty piece of folk theory.

What of the connections between knowledge, practical reasoning, and assertion? The proponent of this view needn't deny that one ought to assert p only if one knows p. But the explanatory power of that conditional will be severely attenuated given his perspective. It is clear that, in very many settings, we think that we oughtn't to assert that a lottery ticket will lose. And a plausible explanation of this is that we think one oughtn't to assert what one doesn't know. The simple moderate invariantist will either have to reject the claim that one oughtn't to assert that a ticket will lose, or he will have to provide a new basis upon which to ground that normative claim. Since the first of these options seems deeply unpromising, the simple moderate invariantist will need to provide us with a new normative self-conception.[59]

Let us turn to practical reasoning. Here again, the view in question need not deny that one ought only to use what one knows in practical reasoning. But once again, the explanatory power of that dictum will be radically affected by the view. Consider our paradigmatically bad piece of practical reasoning, wherein one sells a ticket for a cent on the grounds that it will lose. Our natural thought is that such reasoning is bad because one doesn't know the premise in question. This explanation cannot be accepted by the simple moderate invariantist. For on such an account, the reasoning does turn out to be reasoning from known premises. Nor can the problem be traced to the structure of the reasoning: as we noted earlier, when one learns the winning number and sells the ticket for a cent to someone who does not know that the number has been announced, the reasoning will be reckoned acceptable, even though its structure is exactly the same.

---

[59] One option is to propose the following normative constraint (one that we entertained at the end of Chapter 1): If one believes that one does not know that *p* then (even if one does) one shouldn't assert that *p*. The simple moderate invariantist can say that when people deploy parity reasoning, that leads them to think they do not know this or that lottery proposition (even though in many cases they do). Combine this fact with the normative proposal and the unassertability of the lottery proposition is explained well enough. (But what of someone who embraces simple moderate invariantism and stops thinking that he does not know lottery propositions. Is it now acceptable for him to assert the true ones?) An alternative (and even less promising) approach would insist that the lottery propositions are assertable in the ordinary case, and that we merely think they are not because we think (often incorrectly) we do not know them, and then misapply the original norm of assertion.

Presumably, the proponent of this view will turn to epistemic probability as the key to evaluating practical reasoning. Given that, on this view, knowledge does not entail epistemic probability of 1, epistemic probability will trump considerations of knowledge when it comes to evaluating practical reasoning. Where the difference between zero probability and a small probability makes no difference, we can use the concept of knowledge to effectively evaluate the reasoning. But where that difference makes a difference, the concept of knowledge is too blunt an instrument. Thus, presumably, in the case where one sells a ticket for a cent, the rationality of the action will depend upon the expected utility of keeping the ticket as opposed to the expected utility of the sale. Knowing that the ticket will lose doesn't settle the issue. The rationality of the action will be gauged, *inter alia*, by judging whether it conforms with an expected utility calculation performed on the agent's values and epistemic probabilities. Since the information that someone knows p does not tell one whether the epistemic probability of not-p is small or zero, and if small, how small, those cases where such matters of detail will make a difference to what one ought to do by the lights of an expected utility calculation will be cases where considerations of knowledge will fail to provide the key to evaluating practical reasoning.[60]

While the view has a certain theoretic elegance, its counter-intuitiveness should not be underestimated. Stewart Cohen (1999) considers a case where people have consulted an itinerary to find out whether a plane stops in Chicago but, owing to the importance of the matter, feel the need to check with an airline agent as well. Cohen notes that prior to checking, the following speech is very odd 'Okay, we know the plane stops in Chicago, but still, we need to check further'. He notes, quite rightly, that 'It is hard to make sense of such a claim'.[61] But if the view under consideration is correct, then such a claim is perfectly in order—at least when the chance of error upon reading the timetable is sufficiently low as to be compatible with knowledge, but where the expected utility of consulting an airline agent—and thus lowering the chance of error further with little effort—outweighs the expected utility of not doing so. The strain on our ordinary use of 'know' is evident.

Scorecard

The costs and benefits are easy enough to identify: the Moorean Constraint, Single-Premise Closure, and the intuitive tie between epistemic and objective chance are easily respected. Yet our use of the concept of knowledge to evaluate assertion and practical reasoning is, at least to some extent, called into question. And there is an obvious tension with Multi-Premise Closure and the intuitive connections between knowledge and epistemic possibility. Beyond that, of course, many particular denials of knowledge in ordinary life get reckoned false, since the point of the view is that knowledge is much easier to come by than we realize. The scorecard is not a particularly happy one. Can we do better?

3.8   Harman

I wish to consider next some suggestions by Gilbert Harman that, in effect, offer some refinements to simple moderate invariantism. Since Harman's suggestions are among the most thoughtful on the problems at hand, I shall quote them in some detail.

Harman's discussion in *Thought* includes as a backdrop the following picture of inductive inference:

Our 'premises' are all our antecedent beliefs; our 'conclusion' is our total resulting view...Induction is an attempt to increase the explanatory coherence of our view, making it more complete, less ad hoc, more plausible. At the same time we are conservative. We seek to minimize change. We attempt to make the least change in our antecedent view that will maximize explanatory coherence. (1973: 159)

He then goes on to to offer the following abstract remarks:

Consider the case in which there are N explanations of various aspects of the evidence, each very plausible considered by itself, where however it is known that only N−1 are correct. Competing possible conclusions must specify for each explanation whether or not that explanation is accepted. A particular explanation will be accepted not simply because of its plausibility when considered by itself but only if it is included in a total inferable explanatory account. We will not be able to infer that all N explanations are correct, since, I am assuming, that would greatly decrease coherence. (1973: 160)

This picture is then applied to a lottery scenario:

Similarly, we will be able to infer that a particular ticket will fail to win the grand prize in the next New Jersey lottery only if there is a total resulting view containing this result that is to be preferred to alternative total views on grounds of maximizing coherence and minimizing change. The claim that a particular ticket fails to win will be part of an inferable total view only if that claim adds sufficiently more coherence than do claims that other tickets fail to win. Otherwise that total view will not be any better than a different total view that does not contain the claim that the first ticket fails to win …

… If we are simply interested in the question of whether a particular ticket will win or fail to win, we cannot include in our total view the conclusion that the ticket will fail to win, since it would not be correct to say that in such a case we know the ticket will lose. On the other hand, if we are primarily interested in a quite different question whose answer depends in part on an answer to the question of whether this ticket fails to win, we may be able to include the conclusion that it does fail in our total view, since we can often come to have relevant knowledge in such cases. Thus we might infer and come to know that the butler is the murderer because that hypothesis is part of the most plausible total account, even though the account includes the claim that the butler did not win the lottery (for if he had won he would have lacked a motive). Or we might infer and come to know that we will be seeing Jones for lunch tomorrow even though our total view includes the claim that Jones does not win the lottery (e.g. because if he won he would have to be in Trenton tomorrow to receive his prize …)… (1973: 160–1)

In his later *Change in View*, meanwhile, he voices the idea that the order of inference matters:

Can one infer something simply because it is statistically highly probable, given the evidence? That would be an inference from an explanation, an inference to a conclusion of the form h because e, which we have seen is a possible sort of inference. But to suppose one can make such an inference on statistical grounds would seem to yield the lottery paradox. Although one believes that one ticket will win, one could also infer from any ticket in the lottery that that ticket won't be the winning ticket.

There is no actual contradiction here. To say one can infer this of any ticket is not to say one can infer it of all. Given that one has inferred ticket number 1 will not win, then one must suppose the odds against ticket number 2 are no longer 999,999 to 1, but only 999,998 to 1. And after one infers ticket number 2 won't win, one must change the odds on ticket number 3 to 999,997 to 1, and so on. If one could get to ticket number 999,999, one would have to suppose the odds were even, 1 to 1, so at that point the hypothesis that this ticket will not win would be no better than the hypothesis that it will win, and one could infer no further. (Presumably one would have to have stopped before this point.) But the order of inference really matters here, since one could have inferred that ticket 999,999 won't win if only one had made this last inference early enough. (1986: 70–1)

Harman remarks shortly thereafter that we are not inclined to call any of the lottery beliefs knowledge in this story, conceding that 'I have no idea how to account for our reluctance to attribute knowledge in cases of this sort.' [62] But let us in any case consider whether

[62] We might also note in passing an idea that is canvassed but not endorsed in *Thought*: 'The lottery paradox can be avoided if a purely probabilistic rule of acceptance is taken to be relevant not to the acceptance of various individual hypotheses but rather to the set of what we accept. The idea is that the probability of the whole set must exceed .99. We are free to choose among various hypotheses saying that one or another participant in a lottery loses as long as the probability of the conjunction of all hypotheses accepted remains above .99' (1973: 119). Generalized, this tells us that for any set of beliefs that we opt for, the probability of the total set should be maintained above a certain threshold. As regards our current concerns, it remains unresolved what we should say when the rule is violated: surely we do not want to claim in such a case that no belief in the set is known. The basic idea surely merits further consideration. (See Swain 1970.)

the ideas contained in the above passages help us to improve upon simple moderate invariantism.

There are two basic ideas in the above passages. Consider the set S of singular propositions that say of each *x*, where *x* is a ticket in a lottery, that *x* will lose. Let S' be the set of all the true propositions in S. One idea—articulated in *Change in View*—is that while it is never acceptable to come to believe each member of S, it is acceptable to come to believe some (presumably smallish) subset of S. (Note that the idea is not that one can, simultaneously, acceptably believe each member of the set but not the conjunction.) Applied to the topic of knowledge, one might try out the corresponding idea that while one cannot come to know every member of S', one can come to know a small subset of them. While it is natural to think that if we are now in a position to come to know of any particular member of S' that it is true, then we are in a position to come to know each of S', the current analysis suggests that this is an illusion. From this perspective, it might be suggested that the grip of parity reasoning is due partly to our making this conflation. The other idea—articulated in *Thought*—is that in order to properly come to believe some member of S', one must have some reason for preferring it over any other arbitrary member of S'. Moreover, there are often grounds for such a preference; some member of S' may be an a priori consequence of some proposition *p* that is important to our total view of the world, whereas the same cannot be said for various other members of S': witness the murderer and lunch examples. If that is right, then there is something even more fundamentally wrong with parity reasoning, which relied on the idea that there is no appreciably greater reason to think that one ticket will lose over another. Appealing to this analysis, one might suggest that when we are confronted with a set of lottery propositions S', we tend to lose sight of the fact that the commitments of our 'total view' may provide us with better reasons to believe some than others.

Neither idea in isolation will seem particularly compelling. Suppose we take on board just the first, allowing, for example, that for any member of S', one can know on statistical grounds that it is true, though one cannot simultaneously know this of each of a large subset of S'. Suppose I then come to believe on statistical grounds that #7 will lose. You also come to believe on statistical grounds that #7 will lose. But on analogous statistical grounds you also come to believe that #6 will lose, #5 will lose, and so on. Can I really take seriously the idea that I know that #7 will lose but you don't? Consider now the second idea alone. Suppose I have generally excellent grounds for thinking that Arnie is a 'loser' and will never get rich, that Barbara will be having lunch with me in New Jersey, that Carlos won't be able to afford an African safari, and so on. For each of a large set of ticket-holders, the proposition that their ticket will lose can be justified not merely by statistical considerations about lotteries, but by various aspects of my world view that play independently important roles in my picture of things. Does that mean that in such a case I can know a very large subset of S', perhaps all of it? As it stands, this seems like an uncomfortable consequence.

Perhaps in combination the two ideas are more helpful: one can only know a small subset of S', and only if one has special reasons—connected with the rest of one's total view—to privilege that subset over the rest. Would this improve upon simple moderate invariant-ism? This is not clear. Many of the original problems remain. Suppose we allow on these grounds that I know that the holder of ticket #7 will lose because I know that she will be meeting me for lunch. We now have to explain why it still seems problematic for me to assert that she will lose, and why it still seems wrong for me to use that fact as a premise in practical reasoning when someone offers to buy the ticket for a penny. Let us grant with Harman that interests are important to which beliefs are acceptably included in one's total view and thus, for example, that my interest in my lunch appointment was crucial to my acceptably coming to include 'Ticket #7 will lose' in my total view. But once included, we are given no guidance as to whether or not that belief should be subsequently discarded when I am given the opportunity to buy ticket #7 for a penny. According to the suggestion at hand, once 'Ticket #7 will lose' gets included in one's total view, one will then reckon the chance of it losing as 1. (And presumably, if one does know, one will then be correct.) If so, what would be wrong with the envisaged practical reasoning were the opportunity to arise?

Harman's ideas offer some a strategy for defending Multi-Premise Closure (and also for defending the intuitive links between knowledge and epistemic possibility). It does seem absurd to know the conjunction of S′. Harman accounts for this without, it would seem, challenging Multi-Premise Closure: for on his account, while one can know some member or other of S′, no one is in a position to simultaneously know each member.

But worries concerning Multi-Premise Closure are not so easily put to rest. Suppose I believe that Arnie will lose the lottery and that I will not have a fatal heart attack soon and that your car was not stolen and that.... It seems intolerable to suppose that I can know such a conjunction. Parts of one's total world view, drawn from disparate doxastic pockets, may be combined to form what appear to be conjunctions that strike us as likely to be false and hence unknowable.[63] Similarly, suppose that I think Arnie will lose lottery A and Barbara will lose a different lottery B and Carlos will lose yet a further lottery C, each for the kinds of reasons that Harman deems appropriate. It will seem utterly absurd that I could know a long conjunction of such propositions[64]—but Harman's strategy offers us no insight as to why. Only when the threat from conjunction introduction is imagined to come from lottery propositions connected to one specific lottery can Harman's strategy clearly help.

---

[63] In correspondence Harman suggested (as I read him) a sort of holism whereby such use of the 'disparate pockets' would render them epistemically troublesome (and hence not known) when they otherwise would be known.

[64] Nor is the Harman line particularly helpful with preface-style examples. Consider the Philosophy Conference example described earlier, where there is pressure to think that I am not in a position to know of 150 people that they will all be at the APA. For each person that one considers, the most coherent world picture includes his or her conference participation. (Thanks to Brian Weatherson here.)

Consider further a kind of problem endemic to nearly all styles of coherence theories, namely the difficulty they confront in saying what is known when coherence constraints are violated. Suppose I overreach by Harman's lights: I form the belief that Barbara will lose the lottery (since it is part of my total view that Barbara will be having lunch in New Jersey), that Carlos will lose (since he will not be going on an African safari any time soon), and so on. You do not overreach. You believe that Barbara will lose (it being part of your total view that Barbara will be having lunch with me in New Jersey), but you stop there. The Harman of *Thought* allows that you know that Barbara will lose, but that I have gone awry—having violated coherence constraints, I cannot know each of the relevant set of things I believe. But do I know *any* of the set? The account does not leave us well placed to answer this question. Note in this connection a theme voiced a little while earlier: it would be very strange in such a case to claim that you know that Barbara will lose but that I do not. (Similarly, if I have not yet overreached and now know that Barbara will lose, I would not find the conditional 'If I come to believe that Carlos will lose, I will no longer know that Barbara will lose' very compelling.)

One wonders finally what exactly the coherence constraints are that Harman has in mind. He mentions one constraint in the quoted passage from *Thought*: One shouldn't believe every member of S. But that by itself does not explain what is wrong with believing each member of S'. The quoted passage from *Change in View* offers an implicit suggestion: if at *t* one's credence in *p* is pretty high, then it is illegitimate to switch to a world view in which not-*p*. As one adds members of S' to one's belief set, the credence in nonmembers goes down so that, at a vaguely determined point, it becomes illegitimate to add members of S' to one's world view. But that does not explain why it would be incoherent to add every member of S' all at once.

It should further be remembered that standard lottery cases are somewhat special in that (i) there is a guaranteed winner and (ii) the chance of one ticket winning is higher conditional on another ticket losing than it is unconditionally. Many of our puzzle cases are not like that. Suppose I think before looking at a monthly soccer summary that there is a tiny but not negligible chance of any given soccer result containing a misprint—say 1 in 4,000. I open up a monthly soccer summary, scan the soccer scores, and sequentially commit 2,000 soccer scores to memory. In fact there is no misprint. Would Harman here want to say that it was fine for me to believe some subset of those soccer reports, but not acceptable to believe each of them? Note here that even though the beliefs were formed sequentially, the kind of reasoning manifested by the *Change in View* passage is irrelevant here, since the chance of one result being a misprint is not intuitively higher conditional on another being a nonmisprint than it is absolutely. In that case, then, is it acceptable to believe each of them and, via deduction, have as part of one's total view the belief that the monthly soccer summary does not contain a misprint?[65] Does he want to say that such a belief is known in that case? We are given no real guidance.

In sum, while the allusion to 'interests' in the *Thought* passage strikes me as suggestive, and will be explored somewhat in what follows, the details of Harman's suggestions do not appear to me to offer a resolution of our puzzles that improves much on the (troubling) picture offered by simple moderate invariantism.

---

[65] Assuming I also know that there are no other soccer scores in the summary than the 2,000 in question.

4 SENSITIVE MODERATE INVARIANTISM

4.1 From Ascriber-Dependence to Subject-Dependence

THE contextualist invited us to suppose that variations in the ascriber can affect the truth value of knowledge ascriptions even if we hold fixed the subject of the ascription. Thus, on her account, the relation expressed by the verb 'know' on an occasion of use will depend upon, *inter alia*, what is salient to the ascriber and perhaps also upon what the interests of the ascriber are; upon whether there is a good deal at stake for the ascriber that turns on the truth value of the proposition that figures in the knowledge ascription; and so on. It is this ascriber-dependence that forces the thesis of context-dependence. For it forces the conclusion that two ascribers may be looking at a single subject at the same time and one truly say 'He knows that p', another 'He doesn't know that p'. Contradiction is avoided by claiming that the verb 'know' expresses different relations in the mouths of each ascriber.

It is worth inquiring whether there really are pressing grounds for admitting ascriber-dependence. For suppose instead that the kinds of factors that the contextualist adverts to as making for ascriber-dependence—attention, interests, stakes, and so on—had bearing on the truth of knowledge claims only insofar as they were the attention, interests, stakes, and so on of the subject.[1] Then the relevance of

[1] Cohen (1998) is clear about the distinction between rules of relevance that are 'speaker-sensitive' and those that are 'subject-sensitive'—indeed I have borrowed the terminology of sensitivity from him—but doesn't explore the possibility of transforming the speaker-sensitive rules offered by the contextualist into subject-sensitive rules.

attention, interests, and stakes to the truth of knowledge ascriptions would not, in itself, force the thesis of semantic context-dependence. Here is the picture. Restricting ourselves to extensional matters, the verb 'know' picks out the same ordered triples of subject, time, and proposition in the mouths of any ascriber. However, whether a particular subject–time–proposition triple is included in the extension of 'know' depends not merely upon the kinds of factors traditionally adverted to in accounts of knowledge—whether the subject believes the proposition, whether that proposition is true, whether the subject has good evidence, whether the subject is using a reliable method, and so on—but also upon the kinds of factors that in the contextualist's hands make for ascriber-dependence. These factors will thus include (some or all of) the attention, interests, and stakes of that subject at that time. In what follows, I wish to explore this picture—call it 'sensitive moderate invariantism'—in a preliminary way, indicating how it may help with our puzzles.[2] I shall describe two sorts of mechanisms that arguably bear on the truth of knowledge claims, ones that are akin to contextualist machinery, except that they are conceived of as making for subject-sensitivity.[3]

4.2   Salience[4]

A Contextualist Challenge

Our contextualist claimed that if a kind of mistake is salient to the ascriber, then there is a default presumption that it is relevant to

---

[2] There are likely to be principled limits to what can be said here. The verb 'know' is a lexical and conceptual primitive for which no traditional analysis is likely (though that is not to deny that interesting necessary conditions on knowledge may be discovered). Moreover, any temptation to use the notion of probability in exploring our current subject will likely be unhelpful or circular insofar as we keep to the Epistemic Possibility Constraint. More generally, it is confused to think that a relatively manageable theory of the detailed semantic workings of our language is cognitively available to us.

[3] Mechanisms for what? For the contextualist, the candidate mechanisms are mechanisms for shifting the semantic value for 'know'. For the sensitive moderate invariantist, the candidate mechanisms are mechanisms for making knowledge come and go.

[4] Conversations with Stewart Cohen were particularly helpful in writing this section.

the knowledge ascription. Let us transform this into a claim about subjects. In its strongest form, a subject-sensitive salience constraint might take the following form: If S thinks that *p*, but a certain counterpossibility is salient to S, then S does not know that *p*. A weaker version would insert '*ceteris paribus*' into the consequent. I do not propose to quibble over these details just now.

Let us begin with a thought experiment raised by Stewart Cohen in support of contextualism and briefly adverted to earlier. On the basis of a printed itinerary, Smith believes that a certain flight has a layover in Chicago. John and Mary observe Smith consulting the itinerary, and hear him assert that he knows that the flight stops in Chicago. But it matters a great deal to John and Mary whether or not the flight will stop there. Worried that the itinerary contains a misprint or has been recently changed, they decide to check further. Let us accept Cohen's contention that they are prudent to do so.

One diagnosis of the case that Cohen considers is that the claim 'Smith knows that the flight stops in Chicago' is straightforwardly true. But against this he complains:

> Yet if Smith knows on the basis of the itinerary that the flight stops in Chicago, what *should* they have said? 'Okay, Smith knows that the flight stops in Chicago, but still, we need to check further.' To my ear, it is hard to make sense of that claim. Moreover, if what is printed in the itinerary is a good enough reason for Smith to know, then it is a good enough reason for John and Mary to know. Thus John and Mary should have said, 'Okay, *we* know the plane stops in Chicago, but still, we need to check further.' Again, it is hard to make sense of such a claim. (1999: 58–9)[5]

Let us look at the case through the lens of a subject-sensitive salience rule. Clearly, certain counterpossibilities to the proposition that the flight stops in Chicago are salient to John and Mary but not to Smith. Assume that Smith knows the proposition. It might still be the case that John and Mary do not know it on account of the fact that certain possibilities are salient to them. So from the assumption that Smith knows, it hardly follows, *pace* Cohen, that John and Mary should have said 'Okay, we know…'.

---

[5] Similar issues are raised by DeRose's 'Bank Cases' (see DeRose 1992, forthcoming).

But isn't the first segment of Cohen's complaint still pertinent? Doesn't this view imply that John and Mary ought to say 'Okay, Smith knows that the flight stops in Chicago, but still, we need to check further', or, worse still, that they ought to say 'Smith knows and we don't'? It does not. If we cling to the idea that knowledge is the norm of assertion, then if John and Mary are to properly assert 'Smith knows that the flight stops in Chicago', they will have to know that Smith knows that the flight stops in Chicago. Since knowledge is factive, they will then have to know (or at least be in a position to know by simple deduction) that the flight stops in Chicago. But, by hypothesis, they do not know that the flight stops in Chicago (since certain counterpossibilities are salient to them). A similar diagnosis accounts for the prudence of their checking further: Since they do not know that the flight stops in Chicago, they are not in a position to use 'The flight stops in Chicago' as a premise in their practical deliberations. So Cohen's suggestion that the case provides something like a proof that contextualism is the only serious option to skepticism can be challenged.

Anxiety-Provoking Inferences

Let us now consider our puzzles directly. When we deploy parity reasoning, certain counterpossibilities to lottery propositions and to those ordinary propositions that entail lottery propositions become salient. According to the current perspective, this will place us in a position where we know neither the relevant lottery propositions, nor the ordinary propositions that entail them. Thus, once the possibility of his winning the lottery becomes salient to someone (remember—salience is not mere attention), then that person knows neither that he will lose the lottery nor that he will not be able to afford an African safari. Does this make trouble for closure? It does not. Suppose someone knows at t_1 that he will not be able to afford an African safari in the near future. Single-Premise Closure says that if he performs a competent deduction, thereby believing at some later time, t_2, that he will not win the lottery, *retaining all along* his knowledge that he will not be able to afford an African safari, then that person knows at t_2 that he will lose the lottery. But if the counterpossibility of winning the lottery becomes salient to him sometime during the reasoning process, then knowledge of the relevant premise gets destroyed. In that case, Single-Premise Closure does not entail that the person knows he will lose the lottery, even if the latter can be deduced from something that he currently believes.

Generalizing, we can say that certain inferences are what we might call *anxiety-provoking* for certain subjects. In certain settings, as a matter of psychological fact, certain kinds of counterpossibilities are made salient to us. And in these circumstances, the current brand of sensitive invariantism predicts that performing the relevant inference will destroy knowledge of the premises, rather than producing knowledge of the conclusion.[6] Insofar as someone knows an ordinary proposition, but finds the inference to some entailed lottery proposition anxiety-provoking in this sense, that person will know the premise but be incapable of coming to know the conclusion.

This is not to say, of course, that *anyone* who believes a lottery proposition is such that certain counterpossibilities will be salient. It is open to the proponent of this position to allow that in certain contexts, one can know a lottery proposition. (Perhaps these include some of those settings described earlier, where people are happy to assert a lottery proposition, and are untroubled by counterpossibilities.)[7]

---

[6] Note that in the American Model Penal Code the risk that salience may affect matters is somewhat averted by stipulatively defining 'known' as 'practically certain' (see American Law Institute, Model Penal Code, 2.02 (2)(b)(ii)). The role of the concept of knowledge in legal settings is well worth extensive investigation.

[7] The same may be true of brain in a vat hypotheses. The preacher who asserts 'We are beings whose lives make a difference to each other. We are not the beings of the Matrix, isolated in pods from one another, who merely imagine that we are making a difference to each other's lives' may well be one who entertains the brain in a vat hypothesis without it thereby standing as a salient counterpossibility.

Suppose that thinking about lotteries makes a certain counter-possibility to the African safari proposition salient. Should I now say 'Up to five minutes ago, I knew I wouldn't have enough money to go on an African safari, but not any more'? The points raised against Cohen apply with equal force here. If at the later time I don't know the ordinary proposition, then I cannot assert that I used to know it, since knowledge is the norm of assertion. To properly assert that one used to know that p, one needs to know p now. The sentence 'I used to know that I would not be able to afford to go on an African safari' may in fact be true, but it is not proper for me to assert it.

Note that it is extremely intuitive to suppose that someone who is in the midst of parity reasoning about a lottery proposition is not in a position to assert that proposition; and that he does not at that point know the lottery proposition would seem to be a natural and compelling explanation for this normative datum. Our current version of moderate invariantism, unlike simple moderate invariantism (with or without Harman's refinements) can embrace this explanation with open arms. It also seems clear that in the context of a conversation where some counterpossibility to a lottery proposition has been made salient, one is in no position to assert an ordinary proposition that entails it; and it seems that the obvious explanation is that one does not at that point know that the ordinary proposition is true. Once again, this explanation can be endorsed by the current view.

Pessimism and Projection

This is not to say, of course, that there are no counterintuitive consequences to this version of sensitive invariantism. As far as I can see, every candidate story about our puzzle has counterintuitive results. This is no exception.

There is one way that *all* moderate invariantisms will depart from ordinary practice. Once we have gotten ourselves into the frame of mind of thinking 'I do not in fact know whether or not I'll be able to afford the safari', as we frequently do when we use parity reasoning, we are not only unwilling to say 'However I used to know that'; we are positively willing to say 'I never did know that'. And, if pressed, we are willing, moreover, to say that 'I was mistaken in thinking that I did know that'. But moderate invariantism allows that ordinary people do know all sorts of ordinary propositions—so it is inevitable that any form of moderate invariantism will be committed to saying that reflection on lottery propositions induces an excessively skeptical frame of mind. The moderate invariantist holds that we often *do* know things of the form 'That table will be there for a while', and, correlatively, that the cast of mind I get in when I use parity reasoning drawn from quantum mechanics (one in which I say that no one knows what the future will bring) is a cast of mind in which I am excessively pessimistic about what people know. The contextualist, of course, is not so committed: she can maintain that in the so-called 'pessimistic' frame of mind, our standards are high, and so we are exactly right to say 'No one knows things like that'. For the contextualist, the mistake arises only when we go to say to ourselves 'So ordinary people are wildly mistaken in their knowledge ascriptions'.[8]

Despite this departure from ordinary practice, subject-sensitive moderate invariantism has the beginnings of an explanation about why we are sometimes excessively pessimistic in our attributions of knowledge. After all, on such a view, when certain counterpossibilities are salient to us, it is perfectly correct to say *of ourselves* that we do not know the relevant propositions. What we need to account for in addition is our tendency to overproject our own lack of knowledge to others. In so doing, we might helpfully appeal to the psychological literature on heuristics and biases.

---

[8] Note also that if we were to discover that someone had sold a lottery ticket, and had asserted 'I know it will lose', then we have a very strong intuition not merely that it is correct for us to say 'He didn't know that' but, moreover, that he himself said something false. Standard contextualism does a good job at accommodating the first intuition, but has to explain the second one away by appeal to semantic blindness.

Psychologists in that tradition emphasize the role played by the 'availability' heuristic as a distorting influence on our judgments of risk: in many cases, our estimation of the likelihood of an event is affected by the ease with which we can recall or imagine it.[9] So, for example, when a certain scenario is made vivid, the perceived risk of that scenario may rise dramatically. In this regard, it is a widely documented phenomenon that 'a recent disaster or a vivid film' may, as Slovic, Fischhoff, and Lichtenstein emphasize, 'seriously distort risk judgments' as, for example, when 'Recently experienced floods appear to set an upward bound to the size of loss with which managers believe they ought to be concerned.'[10] They go on to note that a 'particularly important implication of the availability heuristic is that discussion of a low-probability hazard may increase its memorability and imaginability and hence its perceived riskiness' (1982: 465).[11] Applied to the issue at hand, the availability heuristic may help to explain our tendency to skeptical overprojection. When certain non-knowledge-destroying counterpossibilities are made salient, we overestimate their real danger; as a result, we may find ourselves inclined to deny knowledge to others in cases where there is in fact no real danger of error.[12]

Whatever our favorite conjectures about the psychological mechanisms at work (I do not wish to speculate further here), one thing seems clear and very important: we do have some tendency to suppose that, as more and more possibilities of error become salient to us, we are reaching an ever more enlightened perspective. Thus

---

[9] Similar suggestions are canvassed by Vogel (1990: 52). I do not at all intend that availability take up all the explanatory burden (nor, I presume, did Vogel).

[10] Kates, quoted in Slovic, Fischhoff, and Lichtenstein (1982: 465).

[11] See also Johnson, Hershy, and Meszaros (2000), who found that people were willing to pay more for flight insurance that provided life insurance in case of terrorism than for flight insurance that provided that same amount of life insurance in case of death 'for any reason', remarking that 'events associated with 'terrorism' … would be more vivid and available than events suggested by the inclusive phrase "any reason"' (p. 228).

[12] For related discussion, see Vogel (1990). This kind of diagnosis will seem particularly natural to those who are happy to insist on a conceptual tie between the concept of knowledge and such concepts as being safe from error and being in danger of error. (See Williamson 2000; Sosa 2000.)

when we consider someone who is not alive to these possibilities, we have a tendency to let our (putatively) more enlightened perspective trump his.[13] This tendency, when left unchecked, leads to skepticism. And even if we are convinced that skepticism is not correct, it is far from clear that we are capable of fully eradicating our tendency to find it compelling. Given this unhappy circumstance, it seems likely that our cognitive relationship to a nonskeptical semantics will always be a complicated one (as the last few thousand years of epistemology would seem to confirm).[14]

Note that the picture we have been considering yields a rather different picture of conversational dynamics than the one embraced by contextualists. Suppose I voice a set of knowledge ascriptions. As the conversation unfolds, counterpossibilities are made salient by my interlocutor, so that I come to give voice to a new, apparently conflicting and more skeptical set of knowledge ascriptions. Here are three candidate descriptions of the conversational dynamics. (*a*) Semantic accommodation.[15] I begin by assigning one semantic value to 'know', but as time proceeds, I shift to a new semantic assignment in order that my ways of talking line up better with that of my interlocutor(s). (*b*) Testimonial accommodation. My interlocutor represents himself as knowing that I might be wrong. I am in general disposed to trust my interlocutors, so I come to believe that I might be wrong about this or that and bring my beliefs about what is known into line with these newly formed beliefs about epistemic modality. (*c*) Availability. My interloctutor paints an extremely vivid picture of certain kinds of error. I come to believe that I might be wrong, not because I trust the interlocutor, but because my tendency to make use of the availability heuristic lies beyond my conscious control.

---

[13] We of course have something of this tendency with 'flat', 'disgusting', 'empty', and 'solid', but it is far less entrenched in these cases, as I illustrated in Chapter 2. The relevant similarity and differences certainly deserve further investigation.
[14] I have heard similar thoughts voiced in conversation by Stewart Cohen, Richard Fumerton, and Timothy Williamson.
[15] See Lewis (1983).

The contextualist uses (*a*) to explain the conversational dynamics. It is far from clear that this is preferable to an explanation that proceeds by way (*inter alia*) of one or both of (*b*) and (*c*).

Residual Costs

Let me now turn to examining the costs of the current approach. I have earlier indicated some ways in which a moderate invariantism that exploits salience may have an edge over simple moderate invariantism. This is not to deny that there are, intuitively speaking, special oddities to the former view. We don't normally embrace thoughts along the lines of 'Just maybe, the only thing stopping me knowing is that I am worrying too much'. Nor, having come to know *p*, do we embrace thoughts of the form 'If I had been less anxious back then, more committed to *p*, less worried about alternatives, I would have known *p* back then'. Nor, having got worried about *p*, do we think to ourselves 'If *p* is true then I knew *p* before I got worried'.[16] But on the current view, such thoughts are often warranted.[17,18] We

---

[16] Stewart Cohen, Troy Cross, and Cian Dorr all pressed this point in conversation. Suppose I'm a contestant in a spelling bee. I do know the spelling of the word before I'm asked, but under pressure my confidence wilts. I might well think with respect to the spelling about which I'm now unsure that, if it's right, I knew it when I was more confident of it than I now am. By contrast, when I muse about lottery success, I'm not inclined to say that when, in the past, I was sure I would never get rich this year, I knew that I wouldn't. A natural picture is that in the spelling bee case, one is merely worried that one does not and never did know, but in the lottery case, once parity reasoning kicks in, one positively thinks one does not know and never did. (Thanks to Jonathan Vogel here.)

[17] In *On Certainty* Wittgenstein writes 'When we say we *know* that such and such, we mean that any reasonable person in our position would also know it, that it would be a piece of unreason to doubt it' (1969: 325). If the salience of a counterpossibility does not manifest unreason but does destroy knowledge, then it would seem that the sensitive moderate invariantist would have to dispute this albeit natural thought.

[18] Another worry, raised by Stewart Cohen, merits further consideration: If the current approach is correct, then in order to know that S now knows that *p*, I would have to be in a position to know whether or not some counterpossibility to *p* is now salient to S. But do I really have to be able to do the latter in order to know propositions of the former sort? If S thinks about skeptical alternatives from time to time, but is not now doing so, am I now precluded from knowing that S knows some humdrum proposition on account of the fact that I am in no position to know whether now is one of the times when S happens to be entertaining skeptical possibilities?

may also note that insofar as the sensitive moderate invariantist embraces the Epistemic Possibility Constraint, he will likely find it difficult to accommodate van Fraassen's somewhat appealing Reflection Principle, which tells us that expected epistemic probability should equal current epistemic probability. Suppose that certain counterpossibilities are currently salient and hence my epistemic probability that p is merely .8. Suppose I know that after I dine and play backgammon, such possibilities will no longer be salient to me. Of course I do not now know that I will know p then, since I do not know p now. But, from the current perspective, I may well be highly confident that if p is true, I will know it at that point. For I may think that *if p* is true, the only thing stopping me from knowing it now is, crudely, anxiety. In short it may be that I assign roughly .8 to the proposition that my epistemic probability will be 1 post-backgammon. If p is false, I will still expect to have some non-zero epistemic probability of p post-backgammon: after all, conditional on p being false, it may well be quite unlikely that at that time I will be in a position to know that it is. So my expected epistemic probability will outstrip my current epistemic probability. I leave it to readers to judge for themselves whether such a violation of Reflection is altogether disastrous.

Note finally that one may complain that the kind of view that we are considering is unfair to thinking people: the philosopher who worries about being a brain in a vat, etc., will know less than the dullard who doesn't. The worry is finessed by the contextualist, who can claim that it turns on a conflation of use and mention. Not so for the sensitive moderate invariantist. One can certainly soften the blow by pointing out that the philosopher is not in a position to *assert* that the dullard knows something he does not. Moreover, intuitions about rather similar cases often deviate from the ones maintained by the objector. Consider the 'thinking person' who worries that his memory is deceiving him and that he has forgotten to turn the stove off. Is it so strained to suppose that, owing to self-induced anxiety, he no longer knows that he has turned the stove off? Consider, meanwhile, the 'dullard' who does not suffer from such anxiety. Is it so strained to suppose that he retains knowledge of having turned off the stove?[19] The case against the view we are considering is certainly far from one-sided.

Another vexed issue is this: To what extent does salience of counterpossibility, anxiety, and so on, merely render one's knowledge temporarily unavailable for practical and theoretical reasoning (as opposed to destroying it)?[20] After all, it is not so strained to describe many of the cases under consideration as ones where one merely has anxiety-induced reluctance to put what one knows to work in one's cognitive labors. When is knowledge rendered inert owing to a (perhaps irrational) unwillingness to put something that one knows to use? When instead is it destroyed? I shall not attempt to resolve these questions here.

4.3   What is Salience?

I turn now to an issue that has been largely suppressed but that is nevertheless extremely important. What is it for the possibility of error to be salient anyway? Recall from Chapter 1 that it is not helpful in this context to identify the salience of error with the mere entertaining of an error-describing proposition.

It is plausible that salient counterpossibility of error is a certain kind of intellectual seeming. Some proposition seems to be true. (That is not to say I automatically believe it: we do not doxastically endorse all intellectual seemings.) But what proposition is it that seems to be true when the possibility of error by some subject S is salient? Not some proposition of metaphysical modality, to the

---

[19] Suppose, by analogy, there were an oracle who could resolve skeptical doubts. The philosopher goes running to the oracle to find out if the world was created, complete with pseudo-memories, five minutes earlier. Is it really so strange to suppose that the philosopher, before arriving at the oracle, does not know he has been around for a while even though the dullard does know? (Informants varied wildly in their reactions to such cases.)

[20] I am grateful for discussions with Adam Sennet here.

effect there is some metaphysically possible world where an error is made. Rather, I would suggest, it is a claim of epistemic possibility that is tied to the epistemic subject. The content of the intellectual seeming associated with the salient possibility of error is basically this: For all the subject knows, p! There is now nothing puzzling whatsoever about the claim that the salience of the possibility of error induces retraction of a knowledge claim. This is just a special case of the claim that its intellectually seeming that p induces us to retract propositions that are incompatible with p.[21] (Notice that on this construal, contextualist proposals about salience as the mechanism whereby semantic shifts occur are fairly uninformative: they amount to the proposal that, other things being equal, if a negated knowledge ascription seems true, it is true.)

With this conception of salience in place, we can refine on our earlier discussion by distinguishing *three* different ways in which one might try to explicate the knowledge-undermining role of salience.[22]

(i) *The Belief Removal Model.* First, salience might destroy knowledge that p by destroying belief that p. It seems to one that it might be that not-p (where the 'might' is here one of epistemic modality). This in turn induces one to stop believing that p, which, if knowledge requires belief, entails that one now does not know that p. So long as knowledge requires belief, there is no doubt that knowledge can be destroyed in this way; the question is whether belief is extinguished in the cases that we are considering, and thus whether this mechanism is the one that explains the veridicality (assuming for now they are veridical) of many ordinary claims of the form 'I do not know whether or not I will win the lottery'. On the face of it, this is not so plausible, since there seems to be a perfectly reasonable sense of 'belief' in which one believes one will lose a lottery even when the possibility of error is salient in the relevant sense.

---

[21] There is also a success sense of 'salience', which will require that the intellectual seeming be veridical.

[22] Conversations with and comments from Jim Pryor were helpful here.

There is a variant on the current proposal that is worth considering. Suppose that an especially strong kind of conviction—something like *being sure*[23]—is a condition for knowledge.[24] One might think that insofar as the possibility of a certain kind of error is salient, this erases the kind of flat-out conviction required for knowledge. If all that were right, it would be natural to suppose that it explains why knowledge is absent in cases where the possibility of error is salient.[25]

(ii) *The Evidential Model*.[26] Its seeming to me perceptually that *p* provides me with evidence for *p*.[27] Similarly, if it seems to me that I might be wrong (in the sense explained) then, plausibly, that very seeming provides me with evidence that I might be wrong, and thus evidence that I do not know that *p*. Perhaps, even if I knew that *p*, the

---

[23] Cf. Ayer (1956).

[24] As a further variant on the current theme, one might consider Williamson's (2002) distinction between outright belief and high subjective probability. Perhaps some case could be made that outright belief is often destroyed by the salient possibility of error even though subjective confidence is not.

[25] Insofar as one defends this kind of view, one has to confront the fact that we are often willing to ascribe knowledge to someone even when they vacillate or hesitate in consciously endorsing the proposition that they are claimed to know. In response, it might be suggested that we do often adopt a tiered conception of the human mind, allowing that there may be an underlying certainty, complete conviction in a proposition, below the surface of conscious indecision. Radford (1966) describes a librarian who has never made a mistake about the location of a book but who dithers about her answer, hesitating, unsure. It may be argued that it is only because we suppose utter conviction at some level that we are willing to ascribe knowledge. If we learned that no matter how deeply we go into the librarian's psyche, we find nothing more than credence slightly above .5 in all the correct answers that she had given, that may well shake our willingness to ascribe knowledge. On the other hand, if one thinks that knowledge requires being sure (at some level), then one will be somewhat hard pressed to make sense of such locutions from daily life as 'know with some confidence', 'know with some reasonable certainty', 'know with reasonable confidence', 'know with reasonable certainty' (where it seems, for example, that if S knows with reasonable confidence that *p*, then S knows that *p*). Philosophers rarely use such locutions but ordinary people do. I shall not explore the issue further here. (I am grateful to Peter Ludlow for discussion on these points.)

[26] I am particularly grateful to Jim Pryor here.

[27] At least assuming that I know that that is how things seem to me.

seeming provides evidence that destroys knowledge.[28] Here is the rough and ready principle at work:

> *Defeat.* If, at *t*, I get evidence that I do not know that *p*, and I have no effective means for rebutting that evidence, then I do not know that *p* at *t*.

(This of course must be distinguished from a weaker principle according to which, when I get evidence that I do not know that *p*, and cannot 'rebut' it, then I do not know that I know that *p*.[29])

The Defeat Principle, as stated, does not strike me as particularly plausible.[30] Suppose a student is presented with an argument to the effect that he knows nothing and cannot rebut that argument. Is it really plausible that at that time, he does not know anything? If someone on a train presents me with Zeno's arguments that motion is impossible and, while not knowing how to answer them, I choose to ignore them, do I then not know that I am moving? When the possibility that I have left the cooker on becomes salient and yet I ignore it, shaking off the anxiety without trying to justify this to myself, is my knowledge really disturbed? The answer in all three cases seems to be 'No'; it seems that one can know *p* while having nothing very useful to say about certain

---

[28] Epistemologists often distinguish different kinds of 'defeaters' for a belief that *p*. Sometimes one gets evidence that is directly suggestive of the falsity of *p*, and this in turn destroys knowledge that *p*. Sometimes, instead, one gets evidence that one's relevant epistemic mechanisms are inadequate, and this in turn destroys knowledge that *p*. Presumably, if the salience of error (in the sense given) is a defeater for my knowing that *p*, it is a defeater of the second sort (though of the first sort with respect to my knowing that I know that *p*).

[29] For the record, I don't even find the weaker principle very plausible (unless knowing *p* automatically counts as 'rebuttal', which is hardly the intended meaning of the principle).

[30] Again, I assume that 'rebutting' is not to be read in such a way that knowing *p* automatically counts as a rebuttal of evidence against *p*.

counterconsiderations that one recognizes as having some evidential force.[31]

While offering a somewhat elegant diagnosis of our puzzles, it
remains unclear whether any model of knowledge in the vicinity of
Defeat will fit well with our intuitions about cases. But it remains
true that there are plenty of cases where we think knowledge *is*
destroyed by excellent counterevidence. Given that an intellectual
seeming that one does not know *p* is at least some evidence that one
does not know *p*, we should not dismiss entirely the idea that
salience destroys knowledge by providing counterevidence. I
shall not pursue the matter further here.

(iii) *Authority*. It may be suggested that our negative verdicts about
knowledge in our own case are decisive on account of a constitutive
first-person authority. If I believe of myself that I do not know, then,
automatically as it were, I do not know. On this model, the relevant
intellectual seeming (that it might be that not-*p*) requires doxastic
endorsement to destroy knowledge, but once that endorsement
occurs, loss of knowledge inevitably follows. It might be suggested
that this is a case of a more general phenomenon where our first-
person negative verdicts have authority: If one thinks one isn't
happy, one isn't happy, if one thinks one doesn't believe that *p*, one
doesn't. And so on. The claimed constitutive authority for first-
person verdicts does not seem at all plausible to me, and especially
so in the knowledge case. (Consider the simple case of someone who
believes that he doesn't know what the answer to a question is and
yet quickly discovers that he has known the answer all along.)
Perhaps the relevant authority claim can be weakened enough to
make it plausible without rendering it utterly vacuous.[32] I shall not,
however, pursue the authority idea further here.

---

[31] Of course if knowledge delivers probability ı, then one has to be careful. If I know
p and *q* is purported evidence against *p*, then the conditional evidential probability of
not-*p* on *q* will be zero. In what sense then is *q* evidence against *p*? This is just a special
case of the problem of 'old evidence' familiar in discussions of Bayesian epistemology. I
shall not undertake to examine solutions to that problem here.

[32] Though I doubt it.

4.4   Practical Environment

I earlier introduced the sensitive moderate invariantist as one who claimed that the extension of 'know' 'depends not merely upon the kinds of factors traditionally adverted to in accounts of knowledge—whether the subject believes the proposition, whether that proposition is true, whether the subject has good evidence, whether the subject is using a reliable method, and so on—but also upon the kinds of factors that in the contextualist's hands make for ascriber-dependence'. Our discussion of salience has not proved to be a particularly promising way of making good on that view. For it may well be that the most promising version of a subject-dependent version of the thesis that salience destroys knowledge proceeds via that idea that salience destroys belief (or whatever kind of conviction is required for knowledge). This idea hardly takes us beyond the factors traditionally adverted to in accounts of knowledge, given the centrality of the belief condition to standard accounts. From this perspective, the only mistake made by the simple moderate invariantist is to suppose that belief of the suitable type is invariably present in the puzzle cases we have been considering.

More importantly still, I do not think it plausible to suppose that an appeal to salience will, at least by itself, resolve our puzzles. Here is one way to make this especially clear. Suppose someone is dogmatic. When he infers lottery propositions, counterpossibilities are not salient to him (on any of our candidate glosses of 'salience'). He infers that he will lose the lottery on the basis of some ordinary proposition and does not worry about alternatives. He then uses the conclusion of that inference as a basis for his assertoric and deliberative practices. Surely there is something out of line with such a dogmatist. But the account so far provides us with no resources for explaining why. The sensitive moderate invariantist should concede the limitations of the salience framework.

There is an analogy to be drawn here with the contextualist. Lewis is aware that the truth of a knowledge ascription has to depend not merely on what an ascriber is ignoring, but also on what he *ought* to be ignoring. Likewise in the case of subject-sensitive knowledge ascriptions: whether a subject knows some proposition depends not merely on which counterpossibilities he *does* ignore, but also on what he *should* ignore, and the problem with the dogmatist is that he ignores things he should not. But what is to be said, at least in a preliminary way, about the matter of which counterpossibilities ought to be ignored by a subject? Here I turn to the second kind of mechanism that I wish to discuss.

When introducing the connection between knowledge and practical reasoning, we noted a case where a lottery proposition serves as a premise for a manifestly bad piece of practical reasoning, and where it seems quite obvious that the explanation for why the practical reasoning is bad is that one does not know the premise to be true. Recall, then, the following case of an intuitively awful piece of practical reasoning:

> (i) You are offered a cent for a lottery ticket that cost a dollar, in a 10,000 ticket lottery with a $5,000 first prize and reason as follows:
>
> I will lose the lottery.
> If I keep the ticket I will get nothing.
> If I sell the ticket, I will get a cent.
> So I ought to sell the ticket.

It is important to notice that one can easily construct analogous cases where it is an ordinary proposition and not a lottery proposition which figures as the key premise. Thus consider the following:

> (ii) You are offered a lottery ticket in the above lottery for the price of a penny and reason as follows:
>
> I will not have enough money to go on an African safari this year.
> So, if I buy the lottery ticket I will lose.
> So I should not buy the lottery ticket.

Or again:

(iii) You are offered life insurance and reason:

I will be going to Blackpool next year.
So I won't die beforehand.
So I ought to wait until next year before buying life insurance.[33,34]

Two points of clarification. First, consider the following reasoning:

(iv) Someone dares you to eat poisonous toadstools and you reason as follows:

I will be going to Blackpool next year.
So if I take the $10,000 dare to eat those poisonous toadstools they won't kill me.
So I ought to take the dare.

Someone who reasons as (iv) describes is using the belief that she is going to Blackpool in a way that makes it likely to be false. By contrast, someone who, say, turns down lottery tickets on the basis described in (ii) is not using the African safari belief in a way that is likely to render it false. Indeed, in some sense it makes the belief more likely to be true if one uses it as a basis for turning down lottery tickets.

Second, our sense that these instances of practical reasoning are bad has nothing to do with assuming that certain counterpossibilities

---

[33] Of course, if the belief about a Blackpool vacation is true, then the life insurance will not come in handy. But this is beside the point. Such a belief, whether true or not, should not be used in practical reasoning of that sort. I assume that the reader shares that intuition very strongly, at least on one very obvious reading of 'should'. (There may be a reading of 'should' where this is not so. When all the evidence suggests that the Cadillac is behind door A and I later find that it is behind door B, I might later say 'I should have taken B', and perhaps there is a reading on which that is true.)

[34] Supposing the quantum-mechanical chance of a desk evolving into a desk façade in the next two seconds is a trillion to one. Ten trillion people are each offered a bet such that one person (drawn at random from the pool of 10 trillion people) gets a cent if the desk in front of the bet-taker isn't a façade and everyone in the pool loses a dollar if it is. If every person in the pool takes the bet and one loses, should we say that all but the latter were epistemically laudable for taking the bet?

are salient to the reasoner. If the reasoner is so dogmatic as to ignore such counterpossibilities in these practical settings, that hardly makes us think better of the reasoning.

In these deliberative settings, then, it is intuitive to suppose that the practical reasoning is flawed and that this is because the premise—whether it is an ordinary proposition or a lottery proposition—is not known.[35] How can we respect this intuition without embracing skepticism? Only by allowing what we might call 'practical environment' to make a difference to what one knows. We now have before us the outlines of a second mechanism that may be introduced by the sensitive moderate invariantist. The basic idea is clear enough. Insofar as it is unacceptable—and not merely because the content of the belief is irrelevant to the issues at hand—to use a belief that p as a premise in practical reasoning on a certain occasion, the belief is not a piece of knowledge at that time. Thus when offered a penny for my lottery ticket, it would be unacceptable to use the premise that I will lose the lottery as my grounds for making such a sale. So on that occasion I do not know that I will lose. Meanwhile, when you are offered life insurance, it would be unacceptable for you to use your belief that you are going to Blackpool as grounds for refusal.[36] So on that occasion you do not know that you are going to Blackpool.

Allowing such a mechanism will make knowledge come and go with ease.[37] One is offered a lottery ticket. At that point one doesn't know that one will be unable to afford a trip to Mauritius.

---

[35] Of course, the reasoning also manifests tendencies that would be likely to get the reasoner into trouble in other situations, and reveals a flaw in the reasoner in that way too. But this additional observation does not seem to lessen our confidence that the premise is not known in this situation.

[36] This should be distinguished from a different phenomenon, namely one where the offering of a bet straightforwardly provides one with relevant evidence for or against a proposition. When I claim to be healthy and my doctor says 'Let's make a wager on that', the offer of a bet obviously gives me evidence against my good health. Not so when I am offered life insurance. Indeed, if anything, that is a sign of good health—if I had seemed to be at death's door, the insurance agent might well have been less willing to provide the insurance.

[37] It is also worth reflecting on the fact that for pretty much any proposition of which we are convinced, we will be inclined to accept a bet against it given the right odds and reckon ourselves perfectly rational in doing so. (For example, I would happily

One buys the ticket, forgets about the lottery, and goes to the bookstore. One chooses the 'local destination guide' over the much more expensive 'worldwide guide', reasoning from the premise 'I won't be able to afford to go to an exotic destination'. At that point you do know that you will be unable to afford a trip to Mauritius. Someone comes and offers you a penny for the lottery ticket. At that point you don't know. And so on.[38,39,40]

Of course it is very tempting to give the following explanation: the difference between the bookstore decision and the other decisions is that in the bookstore case the chance for the subject that he will win is small enough so as to be irrelevant to the practical issues at hand: he can safely disregard the small epistemic chance that he would win. Tempting indeed. But if there is always a chance for the subject that he will win, then—assuming the Epistemic Possibility Constraint—one *never* knows one will lose. Skepticism triumphs. If we are to avoid yielding to skepticism, then we must either

bet a penny against a billion dollars on not having being born in England, and on the falsity of the law of noncontradiction.) In exploring these issues further, we should consider whether knowledge of any proposition can be destroyed by environments in which a suitable bet is offered. One option, of course, is to think that the sketched connection between knowledge and practical reasoning is only roughly correct, where this might still allow it to do work along the lines sketched in the body of the text. Readers are welcome to explore such middle ground.

[38] Note that in such a setting I might make comparative likelihood assessments of pairs of propositions that I would ordinarily say I know to be false: 'I'm more likely to go on an African safari than on the QE II since even if I won the lottery, there's the problem that my wife gets seasick …' (Thanks to Richard Fumerton here.)

[39] Of course there will be lots of indeterminacy besetting questions about when, exactly, knowledge comes and goes, and, more generally, about the cutoff between the practical environments that destroy knowledge and those that do not. One should here deploy one's favorite theory of vagueness.

[40] As Timothy Williamson pointed out to me, this picture makes for some intuitively odd counterfactuals. There will be cases where someone does not know that *p*, but we can assert 'If the stakes had been lower, he would have known that *p*' or 'If he hadn't been offered a penny for his lottery ticket, he would have known that *p*'; and so on. There is no denying the intuitive cost. The question is whether, all things considered, it is a price worth paying. (Consider, in this connection, the following counterfactual, said of a person looking at a barn in fake barn country: 'If there hadn't been those fake barns nearby, he would have known that he was looking at a barn'. Hear it afresh and you will certainly find this counterfactual odd as well.) Note also that contextualism will, for its part, likely make for the truth of such odd-sounding *indicative* conditionals as 'If my stakes are low, he knows, but if they are not, he does not'.

adumbrate a notion of epistemic chance that is not tied to knowledge in the way that the Epistemic Possibility Constraint describes,
or else resist the gloss just given, insisting that, when in the bookstore, there is no epistemic chance for you that you will be able to
afford a trip to Mauritius.

There are thus two ways to develop the practical environment
constraint. One approach gives up the Epistemic Possibility Constraint, allowing that knowledge that p is compatible with a small
epistemic chance that not-p. There is a natural way to spell out the
practical environment constraint on such a picture: if there is a small
epistemic chance that not-p, one knows p only if one is in a practical
environment where the difference between a small epistemic
chance that not-p and zero epistemic chance that not-p is irrelevant
to the matters at hand. A second option is one that cleaves to the
Epistemic Possibility Constraint: when one knows p, there is zero
epistemic chance that not-p. In that case, glosses of the practical
environment idea in terms of epistemic chance will be circular and
uninformative. Instead, one will consider the question of what kinds
of practical reasoning we ought and oughtn't to engage in as sufficiently fundamental to be intractable in terms of a prior notion of
epistemic probability. One's goal, in that case, will not be to offer an
analysis of knowledge in terms of epistemic probability and decision-making. Rather it will be to insist that, contra the simple
moderate invariantist, changes in deliberative environment can
make a difference to whether one knows a given proposition. One
will learn to live with a circle: In a deliberative environment where
one ought to use p as a premise, one knows p. When one knows p, the
epistemic chance for not-p is zero. When the epistemic chance of
not-p is nonzero, one shouldn't use p as a premise in practical
reasoning. Why should this circle require a more basic anchor?[41]

---

[41] I should note in passing that while the practical environment constraint might be
combined with a salience constraint of the sort described in the previous section, it
need not be. Those that are unconvinced of, say, the destructive powers of salient
counterpossibilities as such might still reckon practical environment a source of
subject-sensitivity.

It is worth drawing attention to a theme that is by now familiar. One advantage of this version of sensitive moderate invariantism over (standard) contextualism is clear enough: suppose S uses 'I will be in Blackpool next year' as a premise in (illegitimate) practical reasoning. An ascriber, unaware of the practical reasoning to which that premise is being put, asserts 'S knows that he will be in Blackpool next year'. By standard contextualist lights, that ascription is true. Further, if the ascriber says 'If S is now acting on the premise that he will be in Blackpool next year, he is acting on the basis of something he knows to be true', she will have said something true. The reason for this is that the practical environment of the subject is not given any constitutive role to play in the truth conditions for knowledge ascriptions. The connection between good practical reasoning and the truth of knowledge ascriptions has been lost. Not so for our sensitive moderate invariantist.

Meanwhile, considerations of practical environment provide one clue as to why we may be overly pessimistic in our knowledge ascriptions. When we claim that no one can know that he or she will lose the lottery, part of what is going on is that we realize that no one is in a position, in advance of the lottery draw, to acceptably sell a lottery ticket for miminal return. We sense well enough that in that kind of deliberative setting, the cognitive division into subcases typified by parity reasoning is recommended, and that brute reliance on a lottery proposition in one's deliberations is out of the question. And it is extremely natural to think that if anyone did know that he was going to lose the lottery in advance of the draw, that person would be in a position to reasonably sell the ticket whatever the sale price. If the practical environment idea is right, then that line of thought, while very natural, is flawed: if knowledge is destroyed by certain practical environments, any thought that knowledge will bring with it the capacity to perform certain cogent pieces of reasoning in those environments will be incorrect. For those will count among some of the very environments in which such knowledge would be destroyed.[42]

We now have the beginnings of a diagnosis for our epistemological puzzlement. We underestimate the contribution of practical environment to the truth of knowledge ascriptions. The picture just given is compatible with the idea that most ordinary knowledge claims come out true. But when we reflect as philosophers, it does not occur to us that issues about practical environment may be relevant to the truth of those ordinary ascriptions. We are insensitive, and attempt to evaluate knowledge ascriptions out of context. In particular, we fail to consider the deliberative context of the subject.[43] No wonder we get confused.[44]

4.5 Practical Reasoning and Misleading Evidence[45]

In Chapter 2, I considered a puzzle associated with Saul Kripke that uses Single-Premise Closure to generate the odd-sounding result that if I know that p, I can know that all future evidence against p

[42] The reader may note some analogy here to the topic of 'junk knowledge', discussed earlier.

[43] Shades of pragmatism? I leave pursuit of such analogies to others.

[44] Be that as it may, there is no avoiding the intuitive cost of this kind of view. As Stewart Cohen urged in conversation, it seems that the view will have to allow that I can truly say 'I know that I won't be able to afford an African safari but you don't know that you won't', simply on account of the fact that you are right now being offered a lottery ticket and I am not (I have already bought mine). Can I even know that to be true? (If so, we cannot mollify the objector by claiming that the relevant truth is unassertable.) Perhaps attending to your environment will raise the possibility of my winning a lottery prize to salience. But what if I am dogmatic? (Recall that mere attention to a possibility should not be enough to destroy knowledge.) Another possibility: If we are not sufficiently discriminating to be able to gauge whether a contextualist or subject-sensitive treatment is true in these cases, then even if the subject-sensitive account is right, we are unable to know that it is right and hence unable to know that 'know' applies to us in those cases which turn on the difference between rival accounts. So perhaps I am unable to know that I know in Cohen's case, owing to my lack of discriminatory abilities with regard to the concept of knowledge. I leave it to others to explore these matters further.

[45] I am grateful for discussions with Stewart Cohen and Ram Neta here.

will be misleading. I there endorsed a solution to that puzzle that relied on treating that knowledge as 'junk knowledge'.

But there is a residual puzzle concerning practical reasoning. Suppose I am offered a pill that will make me ignore future evidence against p. If I know that p, it would seem that I can reason as follows: All future evidence against p will be misleading. So I would do well to ignore it. So I should take the pill.

But there is, intuitively, something wrong with this exercise of practical reasoning. Contrast two cases. (i) A pill has been developed that immunizes takers against propaganda against p. The pill gives the brain special powers—that of recognizing misleading counter-evidence to p. I know that p and to protect my knowledge, I take the pill. (ii) A pill has been developed that immunizes takers against *all* evidence against p. I know that p and reason that all evidence against p is misleading. On that basis, I reason that the effect of the pill will be to immunize me against propaganda against p. I take the pill.

Intuitively, the pill-taker in case (i) is acting acceptably—but not the pill-taker in case (ii). How is this to be explained? Accept the framework described in the last section and, at least schematically, a solution is ready at hand: in the practical environment described by case (ii), one does not know that p. Consider the reasoning: 'p. But the pill will cause me to ignore all evidence against p. So all evidence that the pill will cause me to ignore will be misleading evidence. So (unless the pill has no other untoward effects) it would be a good thing for me to take the pill'. Intuitively, this would be an acceptable piece of practical reasoning if the premise was known. Intuitively, the reasoning is unacceptable. The 'practical environment' framework has the advantage of respecting both intuitions.

4.6 Multi-Premise Closure

Do these reflections help to salvage Multi-Premise Closure (MPC)? The path is still a difficult one. Let us grant that all sorts of ordinary propositions can be known in the appropriate practical environments and with appropriate salience requirements satisfied. MPC suggests that on those occasions, if one competently deduces long conjunctions of those ordinary propositions, one can come to know those long conjunctions. After all, why should the mere activity of conjunction introduction destroy knowledge of the conjuncts?[46]

There are at least two objections that we ought to consider. First, there is the objection based on what might be called the *Preface Intuition*: for almost any long conjunction of empirical beliefs that one might have, one is in a position to know on inductive grounds that the conjunction is likely to be false. For the moderate invariantist, MPC does not sit well with the Preface Intuition. For if MPC is correct, one can come to know some long conjunction p. If the Preface Intuition is correct, one can come to know that p is probably false. But it seems altogether bizarre to suppose that one can come to know both that p and that p is probably false. The Preface Intuition has to be explained away. Second, we can make special trouble for MPC via certain lottery-style cases. Suppose it is allowed that in the appropriate practical setting, I can know that Amelia will never get rich and know that Bartholomew will never get rich and so on, for 5,000 friends, each of whom has a ticket in a 5,001 ticket lottery where only ticket #7 is owned by a nonfriend. Assume MPC and I will be able to know a conjunction that will be true only if #7 wins. But isn't it outrageous to suppose that anyone can know such a thing in advance of the lottery draw? Better, it seems, to endorse the skeptical hypothesis that no one ever really knows any of the conjuncts.

How, then, could the moderate invariantist hold onto MPC? A first step will be to maintain the Epistemic Possibility Constraint. For if knowledge is compatible with small epistemic chances of

---

[46] Those who think of knowledge in terms of safety—freedom from error in close worlds (see Williamson 2000; Sosa 2000)—can supplement all this with the simple logical consideration that if there are no close worlds where one makes a mistake about p and no close worlds where one makes a mistake about q then there are no close worlds where one deduces the conjunction from the conjuncts and is mistaken about the conjunction.

mistake, there is no prospect whatever of MPC being correct, since small epistemic chances add up. As for the twin arguments of the last paragraph, the best hope, I think, is to lean heavily on the idea of practical environment. In those settings where we intuitively think of putting long conjunctions to work—where some practical issue at hand turns on the whole long conjunction—knowledge is destroyed. So in any setting where the long conjunction is of practical relevance, we do know that it is probably false. It is only when our knowledge is idle that we know long conjunctions through MPC. And so the intuition that we know all such long conjunctions to be probably false (where 'probably' is being used as an epistemic modal) is an understandable overprojection from practical cases.[47] A parallel diagnosis is offered for the second case, though here the pill is even harder to swallow. In any circumstance where we imagine the conjunction of 'loser' beliefs being put to work (say, as a basis for spending a lot on lottery ticket #7), knowledge of the conjunction is destroyed. But in cases where it is idle, we do have such knowledge.

But it is not clear that an appeal to practical environment can do all the work. Begin with a thought that drives Preface intuitions: knowledge is destroyed when someone is given excellent evidence against p, even if the evidence turns out to be misleading. This does not turn on whether the recipient of the evidence is responsive to it. If someone ignores the evidence and carries on believing the relevant proposition, knowledge is still destroyed. Return to the APA case of Chapter 1, in the version where someone comes in and announces 'I'm not going to tell you who, but one of the people on the list has just died'. Suppose I hear that and ignore it, even though I have every reason to trust the informant (who is in fact speaking falsely on this occasion). I deduce and come to believe the long conjunction that says of 150 on the list that they will be at the APA. Given that excellent counterevidence (misleading or not) destroys knowledge, I do not know the conjunction. But what of my

---

[47] Think back to the faulty intuitions generated by cases of 'junk knowledge'.

knowledge of the conjuncts? It seems something of a stretch to suppose that my knowledge of each individual conjunct is destroyed, especially in the case at hand, where my conviction is intact. Consider, similarly, a case where someone shows me a list of 1,000 propositions, each of which I in fact know, and gives me misleading evidence that one item on the list is false (without telling me which). Assuming that my conviction in each of the 1,000 propositions remains intact, it seems farfetched to suppose that my knowledge of each is destroyed. But my knowledge of the conjunction is certainly destroyed. Allow that I might have come to believe the conjunction by deduction from the conjuncts, and we seem to have a counterexample to MPC.

Suppose one were to treat MPC as an analytic girder. What is one to say here? I can think of only one promising strategy, borrowing from discussions of vagueness: the news that destroys the knowledge of the conjunction renders it determinate that one does not know all of the conjuncts, but for each conjunct, it is indeterminate whether the news destroys knowledge of that conjunct (where 'determinate' and 'indeterminate' are to be understood in accord with one's favorite theory of vagueness). This cluster of claims, note, is compatible (given standard logics of determinacy) with the further claim that it is determinate that I know nearly all of the *conjuncts*. MPC is retained without wholesale skeptical concession.[48,49,50]

---

[48] If knowledge of some of the conjuncts was much safer than others, one might refine the proposal by allowing that the safer knowledge was unimpugned: it is determinate that knowledge of some conjunct is destroyed and determinate that it is not one of the safer pieces of knowledge.

[49] One interesting issue is whether one should treat the case differently when the conjunction is not believed on the basis of deduction from the conjuncts. Might one make a case here that no knowledge of the individual conjuncts is destroyed? Perhaps so, if the only reason in the original case for claiming that it is determinate that one's knowledge of some conjunct is destroyed is that one was determined to treat MPC as a fixed point, a 'penumbral connection' (in Fine's 1975 sense).

[50] Assuming that indeterminate propositions cannot be known, this approach would lead one to suppose that in the cases we are considering, one cannot, for any conjunct, know that one knows it. But that would seem to be a happy consequence of the approach.

For anyone drawn to such a line, a further embarrassment lies in wait, one that relies on the idea that small risks add up to big risks, using this time the concept of objective chance in place of epistemic chance. Suppose, as nonskeptics, we allow that knowing p is compatible with there being a small objective chance that not-p. If MPC is correct, then since small objective chances add up to large objective chances, we shall have to allow for truths of the form 'S knows that p and it is overwhelmingly objectively likely that not-p'! Suppose, to illustrate, there are $2^{10,000,000}$ coin-flippers $f_1 \ldots f_n$. Each is poised to flip a fair coin a million times. I consider each coin-flipper in turn and form the belief that he will not toss heads a million times in a row. In fact, things are such that none of the coin-flippers will toss heads a million times in a row. Assuming MPC and my knowledge of each premise (each of which is intuitively just as much a piece of knowledge as my knowledge in the Heartbreaker case from Chapter 1), I can know a conjunction that claims of each coin-flipper that she will not flip heads a million times in a row. While in any particular case, it would be very surprising that a coin-flipper toss a million heads, it is, by contrast, both objectively unlikely and intuitively quite remarkable that none of the coin-flippers tosses heads a million times in a row—certainly not the kind of thing that one can know.[51]

Whatever one says, certain deeply held intuitions will have to yield: I shall not adjudicate here whether, all things considered, it is MPC that should be relinquished.

4.7 Scorecard

Sensitive moderate invariantism has a fairly promising scorecard. It respects the Moorean Constraint and Single-Premise Closure. It

---

[51] One might try the indeterminacy-based salvage here too. Hold MPC fixed and add the rule that when it is objectively likely that the conjunction is false, it is determinate that one does not know one of the conjuncts, though indeterminate which conjunct is not known.

offers the best hope yet for respecting the intuitive links between knowledge, assertion, and practical reasoning. And it offers *some* prospect for maintaining Multi-Premise Closure. As a species of invariantism, it can respect the disquotational schema for 'knows'. As we have seen, it can also be developed in a way that respects the Epistemic Possibility Constraint. We should acknowledge, though, that if developed so as to respect the Epistemic Possibility Constraint, it will have a hard time with the Objective Chance Principle. For assume both the Epistemic Possibility Constraint and the Objective Chance Principle. Then, supposing we know there are small objective chances of pretty much any description of the future, we will not know ordinary propositions about the future.

The Objective Chance Principle is not the only sticking point for the sensitive moderate invariantist. We have, along the way, noted a range of intuitive oddities that such a view will yield—and there will no doubt be many more that I have not brought to the fore.

4.8   Concluding Remarks

Closing Reflections

It is striking that the puzzles with which we are struggling do not disturb us very much in ordinary life. Why is this? After all, as we have seen, ordinary common sense delivers apparently inconsistent verdicts across conversational contexts. Why does this not bother us? In broad outline, the answer is obvious enough. When we find ourselves in one practical environment, we do not look back to what we said in very different practical environments for guidance in forming our current epistemic verdicts. When offered life insurance, I do not feel the force of my earlier claims to know things about my own future. It's not that I look back on those claims and evaluate them as incorrect; it's that I am so constituted as to simply ignore them. And this tendency is even more striking in the reverse case. When I say that I do know *p* although my earlier self, concerned with life insurance, claimed not to know *p* (or some *q* entailed by *p*), it's not that I evaluate my previous self as having been overcautious—I simply ignore him.

What I have been trying to do in the current work is to achieve some kind of unified semantic perspective on knowledge claims made in myriad settings: Which apparent inconsistencies are genuine? Which knowledge ascriptions are actually correct? This attempt to take in the gamut of knowledge ascriptions in one sweep, as it were, is precisely what we don't do in ordinary life. This is why the puzzlement that grips us here eludes us (for the most part) there. The smooth functioning of ordinary epistemic discourse in a person's life, despite apparent diachronic inconsistencies, is indeed a striking fact. But it is not one that by itself solves our puzzles, nor one that unmasks them as mere pseudo-puzzles.

So which of the views presented here is the right one? Some readers, faced with the range of competitors, will be inclined to think that there is no fact of the matter as to which is correct, embracing some kind of noncognitivism that denies statements of knowledge any truth value. They will, perhaps, insist that the concept of knowledge is incoherent[52]–strictly speaking, tokenings of the verb 'know' are deprived of an extension. Such a reaction would be unwise. Careful investigation will reveal analogous complexities and tensions for many or most of the concepts belonging to the manifest image: repeated solace in noncognitivism will almost certainly result in cognitive suicide. And it does not seem that there is *special* reason for noncognitivism in the case of 'know'.

So which view is correct? Our question does not by any means reduce to: 'Contextualism: for or against?' For recall that even if contextualism is true, it may not provide the key to our puzzles. My

---

[52] Consider Chomsky's (1980) remark 'In fact, it is not at all clear that the ordinary concept of "knowledge" is even coherent, nor would it be particularly important if it were shown not to be' (p. 82).

best guess, indeed, is that it is not the key. Put a gun to my head and I will opt for a treatment of the puzzles built around the materials of the 'Practical Environment' section above. But I am far from confident that this is the correct way to proceed. There is then the further question as to whether to embed those ideas within an invariantist semantical framework for 'know'[53]. Here, though more tentatively still, I would opt for invariantism over contextualism.

My own opinions should not matter much at this stage, however. I prefer to think of these pages as forming a helpful basis for the reader to conduct her own investigation of the puzzles at hand. To think it vital that I embrace some particular view would be to seriously misunderstand the nature of the philosophical enterprise.

A Concluding Parable

Let me close with a story.

Once upon a time there was a tribe that shared deeply conflicting tendencies. On the one hand, whenever they reflected on the many ways that people can and do make mistakes, they found skeptical thoughts altogether natural and compelling. Such moments of reflection seemed to provide great enlightenment. And during such moments, it seemed utterly manifest how little people know. On the other hand, the people in the tribe endowed the concept of knowledge with great normative significance. It provided the normative framework for the giving and requesting of information, and also for practical deliberation.

---

[53] It is easy enough to see how some of those materials might be integrated into a contextualist framework. For example, as Jonathan Schaffer pointed out in correspondence, one might happily add something like the following rule to Lewis's laundry list— The Rule of Praxis: possibilities which ought not to be ignored in any practical reasoning undertaken by the subject are relevant—and then make heavy appeal to that rule in the face of our puzzle. (Note though that the rule intuitively requires a context-invariant 'ought'.) A solution to the puzzles might, for example, blend an ascriber-sensitivity grounded in salience with a subject-sensitivity grounded in praxis. I do not wish to endorse a fusion of that kind here. Nor do I wish to rule it out.

Now the members of the tribe, like everyone else, had to speak and act. Given these exigencies, even the reflective ones regularly found themselves drawing lines between what is known and what isn't known, lines that corresponded hardly at all to the one they propounded in their skeptical moments. Even within this realm, there was instability: as interests and purposes shifted, so too did their sense of the line between what is known and what is not known. But rarely, if ever, did a near-global skepticism seem very compelling in the practical realm.

A dispute broke out among the tribespeople. One group called themselves the Theoreticians. They took the reflective moments very seriously. 'How could you not take those moments seriously?' they argued. 'Anyone who takes the time to think hard about it, secluded in their study, will find skepticism utterly natural!' And they were right: this tribe was indeed so constituted that, when so secluded, skepticism was an utterly natural thought. Another group formed that called themselves the Practicians. They were insistent on the normative significance of knowledge. 'It is a condition of deliberating and of asserting', they argued, 'that one treats certain propositions as known, others not. Isn't it quite obvious that we generally act and deliberate just as we ought to? Concede this normative point, and the view of the Theoreticians is unsustainable. Given the connections between knowledge and normativity, it makes no sense to say that we assert and act as we ought but know next to nothing.'

Debate raged. Theoreticians divided into global and near-global skeptics. Practicians discussed how the facts of knowledge were to be conceived given shifting practical environments in the life of a tribesperson. But the clash between the Practicians and the Theoreticians remained the most visible. And secretly, each felt very uneasy. The Practicians felt uneasy because, when secluded in their studies, they themselves felt the very natural compulsions that the Theoreticians had given voice to. In those moments they felt alienated from their own intellects, given the deliverances that their intellects were apt to press upon them. In those moments, they had to concentrate extremely hard on their favorite normative arguments, rehearsing them as a kind of mantra in order to stop the compulsions towards skepticism from overwhelming them. The Theoreticians felt uneasy too. They detected hidden claims to know in their own thoughts of understanding, insight, and enlightenment. And they too felt the need to talk and act and, just as the Practicians predicted, lapsed into nonskeptical thoughts and speeches when those exigencies took hold. When speaking about the Theoretical position itself, they found themselves with especially peculiar conflicting pressures. The need to speak induced tendencies to extend their sense of what is known to include their own speeches, but the content of the speeches reinforced their tendency to a skeptical point of view. Some of them lapsed into silence, as certain of their Ancient precursors had done.

The Practicians and Theoreticians searched for some common ground. 'You will at least agree,' contended the Theoreticians, 'that you don't know which is correct, the Practical or the Theoretical vantage point.' But the Practicians felt that this was already to prejudice matters in favor of the Theoretician. 'If the voice of the Practician is to be heard on the matter of what we know, it is also to be heard on the matter of what we know we know. The practical perspective encourages us to think that any tribesperson knows that any other tribesperson knows quite a lot. And if he knows this about any other tribesperson, surely he knows the same about himself.' The attempt to find reconciliation at the second level was a failure. Both the Practicians and Theoreticians remained uneasily attached to their respective positions.

Other groups sprang up. One group—a sort of epistemological cult—claimed not to find skeptical thoughts compelling, not even in quiet moments. 'You just haven't analyzed "knowledge" carefully enough,' they said. 'Once you do, your intellect will no longer be gripped by skepticism, not even in the study.' Neither the Practicians nor the Theoreticians believed them. Nor, in their heart of hearts, did the members of the group itself. The group disbanded, remembered as a historical curiosity. Another group, the Variantists, came along. 'You've all been speaking past one another,' they said. 'When you Theoreticians say "know" you are talking about one thing. When you Practicians say "know" you are talking about another.' This greatly disturbed both the Theoreticians and the Practicians. The one piece of common ground they had enjoyed was a tacit recognition that they had not be talking past one another.

Both attacked the Variantists, though for different reasons. The Theoreticians could not reconcile Variantism with their own sense of enlightenment vis-à-vis those other tribespeople caught up in the rough and tumble of life. The Practicians, meanwhile, could not reconcile Variantism with the normative lie of the land. But the Variantists remained. And everyone continued to feel uneasy. When in the study, the Practicians continued to feel the natural compulsions described by the Theoreticians. And when speaking and acting, the Theoreticians continued to feel the natural compulsions described by the Practicians. The Variantists continued to struggle to reconcile their Variantism with both these compulsions, and with their own natural compulsion to see everyone as talking about the same thing.

Debates continued. Conflicting tendencies remained. Each side offered its own explanation of how, despite these inner conflicts, buildings got built and books got written. But each group told a different story, narrated from an opinionated vantage point. (When reading *this* history of the tribe, Theoreticians complained that it had been written by a Practician, what with its talk of seeing that this, and recognizing that that.) Each group mused about what God would do when he came across a tribe with such conflicting tendencies. 'How would God interpret "know" in our mouths?' they wondered. 'When would God say "know" was used to express truths, when falsehoods?' Each quickly realized that no neutral perspective was possible on this question either. Its answer turned on the very questions they were debating. Debates raged on. The strands of the tribe's conflicting natures alternately took hold. Each camp remained uneasy.

Perhaps that tribe is very much like us.

REFERENCES

ARMSTRONG, DAVID (1973), *Belief, Truth and Knowledge* (Cambridge: Cambridge University Press).

AUDI, ROBERT (1988), *Belief, Justification and Knowledge* (Belmont, Calif.: Wadsworth).

——(1991), 'Justification, Deductive Closure and Reasons to Believe', *Dialogue*: 77–84.

AYER, A. J. (1956), *The Problem of Knowledge* (London: Macmillan).

BRUECKNER, ANTHONY (1985), 'Skepticism and Epistemic Closure', *Philosophical Topics*, 13: 89–117.

——(2000), 'Klein on Closure and Skepticism', *Philosophical Studies*, 98: 139–51.

CARROLL, LEWIS (1895), 'What the Tortoise Said to Achilles', *Mind*, 4: 278–80.

CHOMSKY, NOAM (1980). *Rules and Representations* (New York: Columbia University Press).

——(1993), *Language and Thought* (London: Moyer Bell).

——(2000), *New Horizons in the Study of Language and Mind* (Cambridge: Cambridge University Press).

COHEN, STEWART (1988), 'How to be a Fallibilist', *Philosophical Perspectives*, 2: 91–123.

——(1991), 'Skepticism, Relevance, and Relativity', in Brian McLaughlin (ed.), *Dretske and his Critics* (Cambridge: Blackwell).

——(1998), 'Contextualist Solutions to Epistemological Problems: Skepticism, Gettier, and the Lottery', *Australasian Journal of Philosophy*, 76: 289–306.

——(1999), 'Contextualism, Skepticism, and the Structure of Reasons', *Philosophical Perspectives*, 13: 57–89.

——(2000), 'Contextualism and Skepticism', *Philosophical Topics*, 10: 94–107.

——(2001), 'Contextualism Defended: Comments on Richard Feldman's "Skeptical Problems, Contextualist Solutions"', *Philosophical Studies*, 103: 87–98.

COHEN, STEWART (2002), 'Basic Knowledge and the Problem of Easy Knowledge', *Philosophy and Phenomenological Research*, 65: 309–29.

DEROSE, KEITH (1991), 'Epistemic Possibilities', *Philosophical Review*, 100: 581–605.

——(1992), 'Contextualism and Knowledge Attributions', *Philosophy and Phenomenological Research*, 52: 913–29.

——(1995), 'Solving the Skeptical Problem', *Philosophical Review*, 104: 1–52.

——(1996), 'Knowledge, Assertion and Lotteries', *Australasian Journal of Philosophy*, 74: 568–80.

——(forthcoming), 'Assertion, Knowledge and Context', *Philosophical Review*.

DRETSKE, FRED (1971), 'Conclusive Reasons', *Australasian Journal of Philosophy*, 49: 1–22.

——(2000a), 'Epistemic Operators', in Dretske, *Perception, Knowledge and Belief* (Cambridge: Cambridge University Press).

——(2000b), 'The Pragmatic Dimension of Knowledge', in Dretske, *Perception, Knowledge and Belief* (Cambridge: Cambridge University Press).

——(forthcoming), 'The Case Against Closure', in E. Sosa and M. Steup (eds.), *The Blackwell Companion to Epistemology*.

FELDMAN, RICHARD (1985), 'Reliability and Justification', *The Monist*, 68: 159–74.

——(1995), 'In Defense of Closure', *Philosophical Quarterly*, 45: 487–94.

——(1999), 'Contextualism and Skepticism', *Philosophical Perspectives*, 13: 91–114.

——(2001), 'Skeptical Problems, Contextualist Solutions', *Philosophical Studies*, 103: 61–85.

FINE, KIT (1975), 'Vagueness, Truth and Logic', *Synthese*, 30: 265–300.

FUMERTON, RICHARD (1987), 'Nozick's Epistemology', in S. Luper-Foy (ed.), *The Possibility of Knowledge* (Rowman & Allenheld).

GETTIER, E. (1963), 'Is True Justified Belief Knowledge?', *Analysis*, 23: 121–3.

GOLDMAN, ALVIN, (1976), 'Discrimination and Perceptual Knowledge', *Journal of Philosophy*, 73: 771–91.

——(1979), 'What is Justified Belief?', in G. Pappas (ed.), *Justification and Knowledge* (Dordrecht: Reidel).

——(1986), *Epistemology and Cognition* (Cambridge, Mass.: Harvard University Press).

GRAFF, DELIA (2000), 'Shifting Sands: An Interest-Relative Theory of Vagueness', *Philosophical Topics*, 28: 45–81.

GRICE, H. P. (1989*a*), 'Logic and Conversation', in Grice (1989*c*).

—— (1989*b*), 'Common Sense and Skepticism', in Grice (1989*c*).

—— (1989*c*), *Studies in the Way of Words* (Cambridge, Mass.: Harvard University Press).

HALES, STEPHEN (1995), 'Epistemic Closure Principles', *Southern Journal of Philosophy*, 33: 185–201.

HALL, NED (1994), 'Correcting the Guide to Objective Chance', *Mind*, 103: 505–18.

HAMBOURGER, ROBERT (1987), 'Justified Assertion and the Relativity of Knowledge', *Philosophical Studies*, 51: 241–69.

HANKINSON, R. J. (1995), *The Skeptics* (London: Routledge).

HARMAN, GILBERT (1968), 'Knowledge, Inference and Explanation', *American Philosophical Quarterly*, 5: 164–73.

—— (1973), *Thought* (Princeton: Princeton University Press).

—— (1986), *Change in View: Principles of Reasoning* (Cambridge, Mass.: MIT Press).

HAWTHORNE, JOHN (2000*a*), 'Reply to Cohen', *Philosophical Issues*, 10: 117–20.

—— (2000*b*), 'Implicit Belief and A Priori Knowledge', *Southern Journal of Philosophy*, 38, Spindel Conference suppl., 191–210.

—— (2002*a*), 'Lewis, the Lottery and the Preface', *Analysis*, 62: 242–51.

—— (2002*b*), 'Deeply Contingent A Priori Knowledge,' *Philosophy and Phenomenological Research*, 65: 247–70.

—— (forthcoming *a*), 'The Case for Closure', in E. Sosa and M. Steup (eds.), *The Blackwell Companion to Epistemology*.

—— (forthcoming *b*), 'Chance and Counterfactuals', *Philosophy and Phenomenological Research*.

HELLER, MARK (1999*a*), 'Relevant Alternatives and Closure', *Australasian Journal of Philosophy*, 77: 196–208.

—— (1999*b*), 'The Proper Role for Contextualism in an Anti-Luck Epistemology', *Philosophical Perspectives*, 13: 115–30.

HERBERGER, ELANA, *What Counts: Focus and Quantification* (Cambridge, Mass.: MIT Press).

HINTIKKA, J. (1962), *Knowledge and Belief* (Ithaca, NY: Cornell University Press).

HUME, DAVID (1968), *A Treatise of Human Nature*, ed. L. A. Selby-Bigge (Oxford: Clarendon Press).

JEFFREY, RICHARD (1983), *The Logic of Decision* (Chicago: Chicago University Press).

JOHNSON, E., HERSHEY, J., MESZAROS, J., and KUNREUTHER, H. (2000), 'Framing, Probability Distortions, and Insurance Decisions', in Kahneman and Tversky (2000).

KAHNEMAN, DANIEL, and TVERSKY, AMOS (1982a), 'Subjective Probability: A Judgment of Representativeness', in Kahneman *et al.* (1982).

—— —— (1982b), 'Judgment under Uncertainty: Heuristics and Biases', in Kahneman *et al.* (1982).

—— —— (2000), *Choices, Values and Frames* (Cambridge: Cambridge University Press).

—— SLOVIC, PAUL, and TVERSKY, AMOS (1982), *Judgment under Uncertainty: Heuristics and Biases* (Cambridge: Cambridge University Press).

KAMP, HANS (1975), 'Two Theories of Adjectives', in E. Keenan (ed.), *Formal Semantics of Natural Language* (Cambridge: Cambridge University Press).

—— (1981), 'The Paradox of the Heap', in U. Monnich (ed.), *Aspects of Philosophical Logic* (Dordrecht: Reidel).

KLEIN, E. (1980), 'A Semantics for Positive and Comparative Adjectives', *Linguistics and Philosophy*, 4: 1–45.

—— (1991), 'Comparatives', in A. Stechow and D. Wunderlich (eds.), *Semantik/Semantics: An International Handbook of Contemporary Research* (Berlin: De Gruyter).

KLEIN, PETER (1995), 'Skepticism and Closure: Why the Evil Genius Argument Fails', *Philosophical Topics*, 23: 213–36.

KRIPKE, SAUL (1977), 'Speaker's Reference and Semantic Reference', in P. French, T. Uehling, and H. Wettstein (eds.), *Midwest Studies in Philosophy*, 2 (Minneapolis: University of Minnesota Press).

—— (1980), *Naming and Necessity* (Cambridge, Mass.: Harvard University Press).

—— (1982), *Wittgenstein on Rules and Private Language* (Cambridge, Mass.: Harvard University Press).

—— (1997), 'A Puzzle about Belief', in Ludlow (ed.), *Readings in the Philosophy of Language* (Cambridge, Mass.: MIT; first pub. in A. Margalit (ed.), *Meaning and Use* (Dordrecht: Reidel 1979).

KYBURG, HENRY (1961), *Probability and the Logic of Rational Belief* (Middletown, Conn.: Wesleyan University Press).

—— (1970), 'Conjunctivitis', in M. Swain (ed.), *Induction, Acceptance, and Rational Belief* (Dordrecht: Reidel).

LAWLOR, K. (forthcoming), 'What the Contextualist Should Really Say to the Skeptic'.

LEPORE, ERNEST, and CAPPELEN, HERMAN (1997), 'On an Alleged Connection between Indirect Speech and Theory of Meaning', *Mind and Language*, 12: 278–96.

LEWIS, DAVID (1983), 'Scorekeeping in a Language Game', in Lewis, *Philosophical Papers*, vol. i (Oxford: Oxford University Press).

—— (1986a), 'Counterfactual Dependence and Time's Arrow', in Lewis, *Philosophical Papers*, vol. ii (Oxford: Oxford University Press).

—— (1986b), 'Causal Decision Theory', in Lewis, *Philosophical Papers*, vol. ii (Oxford: Oxford University Press).

—— (1994), 'Humean Supervenience Debugged', *Mind*, 103: 473–90.

—— (1996), 'Elusive Knowledge', *Australasian Journal of Philosophy*, 74: 549–67.

—— (1999), 'Putnam's Paradox', in Lewis, *Papers in Metaphysics and Epistemology* (Cambridge: Cambridge University Press).

LICHTENSTEIN, SARAH, FISCHHOFF, BARUCH, and PHILLIPS, LAWRENCE, D. (1982), 'Calibration of Probabilities: The State of the Art to 1980', in Kahneman *et al.* (1982).

LUPER-FOY, STEVEN (1984), 'The Epistemic Predicament: Knowledge, Nozickian Tracking, and Skepticism', *Australasian Journal of Philosophy*, 62: 26–49.

MAKINSON, D. H. (1965), 'The Paradox of the Preface', *Analysis*, 25: 205–7.

MALCOLM, NORMAN (1963), 'The Verification Argument', in Malcolm, *Knowledge and Certainty* (Englewood Cliffs, NJ: Prentice-Hall).

MANLEY, DAVID (unpub.), 'Knowledge and Psychological Explanation'.

MEYER, J. J. (2001), 'Epistemic Logic', in L. Goble (ed.), *The Blackwell Guide to Philosophical Logic* (Oxford: Blackwell).

NELKIN, DANA K. (2000), 'The Lottery Paradox, Knowledge, and Rationality', *Philosophical Review*, 109: 373–409.

NETA, RAM (2002), 'S Knows That P', *Nous*, 36: 663–81.

NICHOLS, S., STICH, S., and WEINBERG, J. (forthcoming), 'Metaskepticism: Meditations in Ethno-Epistemology', in S. Luper (ed.), *The Skeptics* (Burlington, Vt.: Ashgate).

NOZICK, ROBERT (1981), *Philosophical Explanations* (Oxford: Oxford University Press).

PALMER, F. R. (2001), *Mood and Modality* (Cambridge: Cambridge University Press).

PRYOR, JAMES (2000), 'The Skeptic and the Dogmatist', *Nous*, 34: 517–49.

QUINE, W. V. (1990), *Pursuit of Truth* (Cambridge, Mass.: Harvard University Press).

RADFORD, COLIN (1966), 'Knowledge – by Examples', *Analysis*, 27: 1–11.

—— (1967), 'Knowing But Not Believing', *Analysis*, 27: 139–40.

RUSIECKI, J., *Adjectives and Comparison in English: A Semantic Study* (New York: Longman).

RUSSELL, BERTRAND (1912), *The Problems of Philosophy* (Oxford: Oxford University Press).

SAINSBURY, R. M. (1997), 'Easy Possibilities', *Philosophy and Phenomenological Research*, 57: 907–19.

SCHAFFER, JONATHAN (forthcoming), 'Skepticism, Contextualism and Discrimination', *Philosophy and Phenomenological Research*.

—— (unpub.), 'From Contextualism to Contrastivism in Epistemology'.

SCHIFFER, STEPHEN (1996), 'Contextualist Solutions to Skepticism', *Proceedings of the Aristotelian Society*, 96: 317–33.

SLOTE, MICHAEL (1979), 'Assertion and Belief', in J. Dancy (ed.), *Papers on Language and Logic* (Keele: Keele University Library).

SLOVIC, PAUL, FISCHHOFF, BARUCH and LICHTENSTEIN, SARAH (1982), 'Fact Versus Fears: Understanding Perceived Risk', in Kahneman *et al.* (1982).

SOAMES, SCOTT (1999), *Understanding Truth* (Oxford: Oxford University Press).

—— (2002), *Beyond Rigidity* (Oxford: Oxford University Press).

SORENSEN, ROY (1988), 'Dogmatism, Junk Knowledge, and Conditionals', *Philosophical Quarterly*, 38: 433–54.

SOSA, ERNEST (2000), 'Skepticism and Contextualism', *Philosophical Issues*, 10: 1–18.

STALNAKER, ROBERT (1999), *Context and Content* (Oxford: Oxford University Press).

STANLEY, JASON (2000), 'Context and Logical Form', *Linguistics and Philosophy*, 23: 391–434.

—— (2002a), 'Nominal Restriction', in G. Peters and G. Preyer (eds.), *Logical Form and Language* (Oxford: Oxford University Press).

—— (2002b), 'Making it Articulated', *Mind and Language*, 17: 149–68.

—— (unpub.), 'On the Case for Contextualism'.

STINE, G. C. (1976), 'Skepticism, Relevant Alternatives, and Deductive Closure', *Philosophical Studies*, 29: 249–61.

STROUD, BARRY (1984), *The Significance of Philosophical Skepticism* (Oxford: Oxford University Press).

SWAIN, MARSHALL (1970), 'The Consistency of Rational Belief', in M. Swain (ed.), *Induction, Acceptance, and Rational Belief* (Dordrecht: Reidel).

TELLER, PAUL (1967), 'Possibility', *Philosophical Review*, 76: 143–68.

—— (1972), 'Epistemic Possibility', *Philosophia*, 2: 303–20.

—— (1975), 'All Kinds of Possibility', *Philosophical Review*, 84: 321–37.

UNGER, PETER (1975), *Ignorance: A Case for Skepticism* (Oxford: Oxford University Press).

—— (1984), *Philosophical Relativity*. (Oxford: Blackwell).

VAN FRAASSEN, BAS (1997), 'Belief and the Problem of Ulysses and the Sirens', *Philosophical Studies*, 77: 7–37.

VOGEL, JONATHAN (1987), 'Tracking, Closure, and Inductive Knowledge', in S. Luper-Foy (ed.), *The Possibility of Knowledge: Nozick and his Critics* (Totowa, NJ: Rowman & Littlefield).

—— (1990), 'Are there Counterexamples to the Closure Principle?', in M. Roth and G. Ross (eds.), *Doubting: Contemporary Perspectives on Skepticism* (Dordrecht: Kluwer).

—— (1993), 'Dismissing Skeptical Possibilities', *Philosophical Studies*, 70: 235–50.

—— (1999), 'The New Relevant Alternatives Theory', *Philosophical Perspectives*, 13: 155–80.

—— (2000), 'Reliabilism Leveled', *Journal of Philosophy*, 97: 602–23.

WILLIAMS, MICHAEL (1978), 'Inference, Justification and the Analysis of Knowledge', *Journal of Philosophy*, 75: 249–63.

WILLIAMSON, TIMOTHY (1994), *Vagueness* (London: Routledge).

—— (2000), *Knowledge and its Limits* (Oxford: Oxford University Press).

—— (2001), 'Comments on Michael Williams' "Contextualism, Externalism and Epistemic Standards" ', *Philosophical Studies*, 103: 25–33.

WITTGENSTEIN, LUDWIG (1969), *On Certainty* (Oxford: Blackwell).

WRIGHT, CRISPIN (1991), 'Skepticism and Dreaming: Imploding the Demon', *Mind*, 100: 87–116.

YOURGRAU, PALLE (1983), 'Knowledge and Relevant Alternatives', *Synthese*, 55: 175–90.

ZWICKY, A., and SADOCK, J. (1975), 'Ambiguity Tests and How to Fail Them', in J. Kimball (ed.), *Syntax and Semantics*, vol. iv (New York: Academic Press).

INDEX

Lightning Source UK Ltd.
Milton Keynes UK
18 December 2009
147689UK00001B/13/P